"This study reminded me that I must keep my eyes focused on Jesus PERIC instead of others. I now understand that He has a plan for me that was settle several points in the study I asked myself 'has Nancy been in my mind?' This 'new beginning' in my walk with Jesus." —**Lorrie Cabrera, Preschool Ministry Director**

"Every now and then we come into contact with someone who has experienced a direct word from God. This Bible Study reveals His words through the lives of Biblical characters and Nancy's own pilgrimage as He taught her how to walk with Him daily. It is a perfect guide for a woman on how to grow in the knowledge of Jesus Christ and to discover God in a very intimate fashion. You will grow when you do this study!" —**Dr. Dewey Davidson, Pastor**

"This study truly will open your heart to making 'The Next Step' with The Father. The frankness and transparency of this study called me to test my own level of commitment and transparency with God. It soon became apparent that the Lord's desire was to reveal Himself through this study and teach me what He was doing in *my* life through those difficult experiences. The Lord shared a priceless part of Himself through this study." —**Felecia Ligon, Owner, Brainfood Tutoring**

"My desire to participate in this study would be nothing less than a divine appointment, or encounter as Nancy likes to call it. Jesus wanted to meet with me through this study and He sure did make Himself ever present and known all through it. God used this study to speak words of fresh encouragement that came at the most perfect time." —**Tess Womack, Director of Bible Studies, Cartersville First Baptist Church, Georgia**

The Next Step...Ordained by Deity

Exposing God's Power in Your Spiritual Journey

Nancy Dempsey

WestBow
PRESS
A DIVISION OF THOMAS NELSON

WestBow Press books may be ordered through booksellers or by contacting:

WestBow Press
A Division of Thomas Nelson
1663 Liberty Drive
Bloomington, IN 47403
www.westbowpress.com
1-(866) 928-1240

Because of the dynamic nature of the Internet, any Web addresses or links contained in this book may have changed since publication and may no longer be valid. The views expressed in this work are solely those of the author and do not necessarily reflect the views of the publisher, and the publisher hereby disclaims any responsibility for them.

Any people depicted in stock imagery provided by Thinkstock are models, and such images are being used for illustrative purposes only.

Certain stock imagery © Thinkstock.

ISBN: 978-1-4497-0894-8 (sc)
ISBN: 978-1-4497-0893-1 (e)

Library of congress Control Number: 2010942198

Scripture taken from the HOLY BIBLE, NEW INTERNATIONAL VERSION®. Copyright © 1973, 1978, 1984 Biblica. Used by permission of Zondervan. All rights reserved.

Printed in the United States of America

WestBow Press rev. date: 1/13/2011

Dedication

To Ken, my beloved husband:

Your faith in me and steadfast support was instrumental in the accomplishment of God's call on my life to write *The Next Step*. You are a very special man. Your unfailing love for Jesus, your family, your church, and the lost world personifies the Lord's design for godly men. It's an honor to be your wife.

I love you dearly, Ken.

To the Single Ladies Class, my prayer warriors:

I will never forget your faithful support as I wrote *The Next Step*. Your prayers, cards, e-mails, hugs, and words of encouragement meant so much to me as I journeyed through each session. I will forever be grateful for your kindness and faith in me.

I love you, dear sisters in Christ.

To Amy Ellison, Tabitha Farr, and Priscilla Cheek, my editors:

I am so grateful for the great job you did as you came behind me making sure *The Next Step* was completed with excellence. Your skillful eyes and valuable insight have been priceless. I will forever be grateful for your support.

I love you co-laborers in Christ.

Contents

Introduction

"Since we live by the Spirit, let us keep in step with the Spirit" (Galatians 5:25).

You may be wondering about the title of this study. For me, the title describes exactly where I am now. I am taking "the next step" with God's Holy Spirit. I am living by the Spirit as I write. I am not a writer, but He is. I don't know where He is going to take me next, but for the present, He is taking me down memory lane and pointing out significant places that I'm to share with you. God has shown me that if I will lay open my life to others according to His timing and purpose, He will use it to bless them and bring glory to Himself. My desire is to walk in His perfect will.

I believe the Holy Spirit uses the Word not only to teach and direct but also to show us examples of ourselves in the lives of those in the Holy Writ. This is a different type of study. It will be a very personal journey as you examine your relationship with Jesus. Your homework will be to take time for examination, discovery, enlightenment, and revelation regarding the work of God in the lives of His people as well as your own life.

I want to begin with the process God used to position me at this keyboard and write what I have been sharing verbally with women for the past twenty years as a teacher and mentor. Before the Holy Spirit nudged me with the Word, He used three very significant people in my life to push me into considering such a difficult task. The first person was Ken, my handsome husband of thirty-three years. He has always encouraged and believed in me. On more than one occasion, he had suggested that I write a book about my life. My response was always, "I am not a writer; I am a teacher." I must admit I thought about it several times, yet I refused to go beyond my thoughts, telling myself I was incapable of writing a book.

The next person was Becky Garrison, a dear friend at my church who served as my prayer warrior while I led a mentoring ministry. I had begun to speak outside my church, and Becky was like Ken, always encouraging me and believing in me. She urged me to document my ministry in some type of publication. I told her I would consider it. As before, I thought about it several times but refused to go beyond my thoughts, telling myself I was incapable of such a task. Only this time, I thought, *What would I write about* my *ministry, and* who *would want to read it?*

The third person—and the one God really used to nudge me into serious consideration of such a task—was my pastor, Dewey Davidson. One night after visitation, Dewey asked me several probing questions regarding my relationship with Christ. I briefly shared a small portion of my past desperation and current state of deliverance and joy. He told me I needed to write it in the format of a Bible study and share it with women in our church who wanted to go deeper with Jesus. I told him I would pray about it. I thought about it very seriously for days. Again, Ken was my encourager, but again, I experienced doubt, fear, and feelings of inadequacy. All I knew to do was pray and wait.

Over the next couple of days, I thought, prayed, and listened for the Spirit to direct. Then the Word spoke, "Since we live by the Spirit, let us keep in step with the Spirit" (Galatians 5:25, NIV). The words jumped off the page of my Bible and straight into my heart. I never attempted to memorize it. It was and still is fresh in my mind. I knew then, as I do right now, that the Spirit had placed this verse deep within my heart for a special purpose. Over the next couple of days, He began to challenge me to discover His purpose for drawing me so strongly to the words "keep in step" in the verse in Galatians. The following paragraph describes the basis for writing this Bible study.

The Holy Spirit became a part of me when I took the "first step" of salvation. He began a new work in my life called sanctification. This called for another move on my part. I had to take the "next step" to obey Him and His Word. Within a couple of days, He revealed His purpose for captivating me with these three words: "keep in step." I was to write a Bible study based on my own spiritual journey as it relates to this verse. He gently nudged me to begin. To seal the deal, the following morning, I awakened with these words rolling over and over in my head, "Trust my Word." My only reply was a sincere, "Yes, Lord."

As I began to pull out my old journals, thoughts of fear and doubt flooded my entire being. The *One* who had called me immediately reminded me of His hand on my life. He replayed my deliverance from my past and reminded me of how He had brought me into a relationship full of hope. I am confident of this: Christ is in me. I am free to embrace His presence in my life and experience the delights that come from "staying in step" with Him. My role is to simply "trust and obey" Him moment by moment.

As I began to retrace my own journey, the Lord showed me a common thread in my life, a thread of crimson that had sewn my life back together time and time again. I've realized that life is made up of many seasons that are meshed together into a final life portrait. Some refer to this as the tapestry of their life. My portrait is a work in progress. It reminds me of a handmade quilt with every season represented by different colors of material sewn together with a beautiful crimson thread. This thread represents the blood of my Savior, who continues to rescue and restore me. Each stitch He sews changes me to be more like His image. One day, He will complete my portrait and I will be a beautiful display of His glory.

But in the meantime, I believe my life is becoming very much like the precious quilt my mother-in-law, Louise, made for Ken and me. It is a king-size quilt made from squares of material that were formerly clothes, mostly her dresses and pants she made herself. That quilt is on our bed as I write. Just recently, my daughter Andrea was looking at the quilt and recognized a piece of material that was from one of her Maw Maw's dresses. I enjoyed pointing out a couple of dresses that I remembered. As we talked about the quilt and her Maw Maw, the sweet memories brought tears and laughter. Everyone who knew Louise knew how much she loved her Lord, her family, and her church.

My desire is for every season of my life to have meaning and memories like Louise's and the precious gift of that quilt. I cannot do that in my own strength. I must trust and obey my Lord. As I began to look back over the years and many seasons of my life, I realized something very significant. Regardless of the season, stormy or joyful, each was sewn to the other with the crimson thread. I bowed my head as I caught a glimpse of His purpose for this undertaking and whispered, "Lord, I understand their struggles."

I meet so many women who are struggling with their spiritual journeys. They are enticed to walk on a path that looks like success when in reality it's a prison—a prison built on fear and insecurity. I know because I have been there. I also know that once the enemy gets you into his clutches, he will fight to keep you there. My life was wrecked with strongholds, all types of fears, self-consciousness, and insecurity for years. But over time, He brought me to a new path on my spiritual journey. This path required another "step" on my part. I took it, and God moved.

This study is based on the processes and truths my Lord has taken me through up to this point in my life. He is still using the same truths daily to keep me "in step" with Him. I still have days and seasons that include problems and failures on my part. Yes, there are times when I get out of step with the Spirit. However, He is always faithful to draw me to Himself and redirect my life. I am tremendously humbled that He would use my spiritual journey to help others. It is an honor and a privilege to share the "steps" I've taken that were ordained by Deity. My prayer is that God will touch every participant in an extraordinary way through this study.

Before you start, I ask you to empty yourself of any preconceived ideas and simply open your heart to experience God. My prayer is that you will clearly see our God through the journeys of this writer and those you study and through your own. My prayer for every participant is for her to learn how to live in the Spirit. Then, my sisters, you can have the assurance that each step you take in your own journey is ordained by God.

Let's begin right now allowing Jehovah-raah, the Lord our Shepherd, to ordain all steps!

Throughout the study, we will see God work in accordance with many of His names, which I have taken from Kay Arthur's book, *The Peace and Power of Knowing the Names of God*, and listed here.

Elohim: The Creator
El Elyon: The God Most High
El Roi: The God Who Sees
El Shaddai: The All-Sufficient One
Adonai: The Lord
Jehovah: The Self-Existent One
Jehovah-jireh: The Lord Will Provide
Jehovah-rapha: The Lord Who Heals
Jehovah-nissi: The Lord My Banner
Jehovah-mekoddishkem: The Lord Who Sanctifies You
Jehovah-shalom: The Lord Is Peace
Jehovah-sabaoth: The Lord of Hosts
Jehovah-raah: The Lord My Shepherd
Jehovah-tsidkenu: The Lord Our Righteousness
Jehovah-shammah: The Lord Is There

Gifts of Salvation

You will experience many journeys in this life, but your spiritual journey is by far the most important. Your spiritual journey begins with your invitation to receive the miraculous gift of salvation. Your acceptance of this gift is followed by another called sanctification. When your life on this earth is over, you are promised the gift of glorification. Before beginning session one, we will examine the miraculous way we receive this gift from Deity with a thorough explanation of salvation.

The *New King James Version Woman's Study Bible* makes the meaning of salvation very clear and easy to understand.

> Salvation can be described as "snatching" someone from serious danger. Just as you would "snatch" your child from before an oncoming automobile to save his life, the Lord Jesus saves or "snatches" every individual who trusts in Him from the pathway that leads to eternal death in Hell.

Based on this description, salvation is defined as God's "deliverance." Let's look at some verses of Scripture and see if the description fits. In Judges 3:9 of the Old Testament, God delivered Israel from its enemies by "raising up a *deliverer*, Othniel son of Kenaz, Caleb's younger brother, who saved them." In Romans 6:23 of the New Testament, God *delivered* sinners from eternity in Hell. This time, God chose His Son to be the Deliverer!

"For the wages of sin is death, but the gift of God is eternal life in Christ Jesus our Lord."

Now that we have seen what God does, we must look at what we must do to complete the deliverance.

Salvation—The First Step

As we walk through this life, the Spirit of God comes to every person in a very unique way, offering us salvation. Salvation is a person, Jesus Christ. He chooses the place, the day, the hour, even the very moment to communicate with us. He reveals the true state of our condition without Him. He also opens our minds to understand that we are in need of something we are incapable of gaining by our own efforts. Because He created us, He knows what will touch our inner being. It may be a message, a testimony, a verse of Scripture, or a song. He knows us better than we know ourselves. By the way, He has known us longer than we have known ourselves. We are told this in Jeremiah 1:5a, "Before I formed you in the womb I knew you."

He desires for us to know Him in a very personal relationship—like the perfect family. He also desires for us to become completely satisfied through our fellowship with Him. He is *with us* in this world, and he promises we will be *with Him* in His heaven … forever.

Here is how the *Woman's Study Bible* defines *justification* as an aspect of salvation:

> Justification is God's deliverance from sin's penalty. When a person accepts Christ into her life, she becomes totally free from the penalty of sin and spiritual death (Romans 3:23–25). The penalty for sins that have been committed in the past, or sins that will be committed in the future has been paid through the death of Jesus Christ on the cross.

When we respond to the Spirit's revelation of Jesus and accept Him as our Lord and Savior, we have taken what I call the "first step" of our spiritual journey in this life. When we accept Christ, the Holy Spirit immediately takes up residence in our life and begins the "next step."

Sanctification—The Next Step

The spiritual journey has begun. Sanctification is the work of the Holy Spirit in the life of the believer. It is an ongoing process to increase personal holiness. The *Woman's Study Bible* defines sanctification as, "God's progressive deliverance of a believer from sin's power" (Ephesians 5:26; 1 Thessalonians 5:23). The Holy Spirit has taken up residency in our life and brings with Him our spiritual gifts. These gifts are to be used to minister to others and to fulfill and satisfy the believer. The Spirit also brings the "Fruit of the Spirit," which is the character of God. He removes our character and replaces it with the miraculous transfusion of His attributes. This is a significant part of making us "holy" vessels.

Glorification—The Final Step

This is the final act of salvation, in which the believer is transformed into the likeness of Christ. Jesus completes this step when we are with Him in heaven. Glorification is God's ultimate deliverance of the believer from sin's presence. Glorification will not be actualized until the Lord returns for His children (1 Corinthians 15:51–57). While you are living on this earth, you will always be in the presence of sin. However, those who have trusted in Christ will one day be free from sin completely.[1]

Your personal response to God's action is also of utmost importance in salvation:

- You must know who Christ is, what He has done, and what He can do.
- You must have a conviction that this knowledge about Christ is true.
- You must act upon that knowledge and conviction, trusting in Christ daily.
- You must have a personal encounter with Christ, surrendering your life to the Lord. At this point, salvation or "deliverance" occurs. From that point through eternity, the power of Christ in you is greater than the power of sin over you (2 Timothy 1:12), and Christ, in turn, covers your sins by having paid the penalty for those sins through His death on the cross. You then are challenged to live for Him and grow in His grace.[2]

> According to the *Woman's Study Bible*, salvation requires not only God's initial action, but also your response. There are basically three aspects to God's salvation: justification, sanctification, and glorification.

Have you received the miraculous gift of salvation? If you have, then we can move on. If you aren't sure, I encourage you to stop and seriously pray, asking God to show you what you must know and do. If you have not confessed your sins, asking Jesus Christ to forgive you and save you, it will be impossible for Him to speak to you in this study. If you have accepted Christ, take a few moments to thank Him. If you have already received the gift of salvation but still have reservations, maybe you need to make Jesus "Lord" of your life. After being completely honest and open with Him as you confess your sins, you must give up control. This step is hard. When you make Jesus Lord of your life, you are willingly surrendering your will to Him. As your obedience allows His forgiveness to cover you with His peace, you will have a restored fellowship with Christ as a result. If you need to make Jesus Lord of your life, I encourage you to spend a few minutes in prayer about this serious step.

Session 1

Spiritual Marker #1
"The Encounter"

Each session begins with me sharing a significant marker in my spiritual journey. My prayer is that as I share my spiritual markers, you will begin to see how God is working in your life to accomplish His purposes through you. Today begins with my first step: salvation.

My Spiritual Journey—The First Step: Salvation

The Holy Spirit revealed Jesus to me, and I gave Him my heart at age ten. It was truly a miracle for me. To help you better understand this awesome miracle in my life, I want to share some details from my past and about my family with you.

My mother married three times and died at the age of sixty-two, divorced. She was lonely, fearful, and bitter. Shortly before she died of a stroke, I noticed a change in her sad life. She began to listen to different music—gospel instead of country and western, which had been her drinking and crying music. She also began to listen to preaching on the radio and would talk to me about it. I grieve when I think about all that she suffered and especially all that she missed in her relationship with Jesus. She never felt good enough or safe enough to be part of a church family. She continued to hand down the legacy that was handed to her by her father. What began as two people marrying their "first loves" ended with two lives and many generations ravaged by the poisoned tentacles of my father's alcoholism and my mother's dysfunctional past. Dysfunction breeds dysfunction until someone in the generational line decides to break that chain of bondage. My siblings and I decided a long time ago to do just that and safeguard the legacy we will leave our children.

I was born into a broken family with a long history of wounds and pain. My mother's name was Lila Floyd. She was the fifth of six children. Her father was only home long enough to make her life miserable. He was not a "churchgoer," as people from Alabama would say. I don't remember much about him, just that I didn't like being around him. There was something about him that was very pretentious, and his presence caused me to withdraw. My mother's mother worked at the local cotton mill and tried to make the best life for herself and her family that she could. Even though she was a hard worker and a devoted member of a local church, my grandmother, along with her six children, including my mother, felt the sting of poverty and abandonment. I didn't know my maternal grandmother well and always felt very uncomfortable around her. I would be left for long periods of time with her or my aunt Ruth. The hardness she seemed to wear like a cloak of protection was infectious. Gentleness and softness had been robbed from her during the years before I came along. She was never affectionate toward me. She didn't talk much either. When she did speak, her tone was always cold and commanding. She seemed to have more affection for her dog than she did anyone else. He was a German boxer, who was very dangerous and prone to bite strangers. I suppose she loved this dog for the protection he provided. When my grandmother focused her attention on me, it was to bathe me and then warn me not to get dirty. My grandmother polished my shoes, made me sit on the kitchen table, and told me not to move until my mother came. She required that my appearance and behavior be perfect.

As for me, I longed for the affection and attention of a loving mother. I must have been one of those kids who required close boundaries. I can still hear my mother saying, "Nancy is my 'strong-willed' child." I became fearful that my mother would die or that she would leave me and never come back. These fears consumed me for many years.

When my mother was sixteen years old, she attended a youth camp with her church friends, and there, she accepted Christ. Shortly afterward, she left the church and never attended any church on a regular basis. Only in my mother's latter years did she explain why she did not attend church. She told me the story of how the Ku Klux Klan had placed a cross in the front yard of their home and set it on fire as a warning to her father. He had been seen and was reported to be supporting a black house of prostitution. At that time, this conduct was unacceptable and would not be tolerated by certain men in some Southern cities, like my hometown of Anniston, Alabama. Instead of her church friends understanding and helping her, they ridiculed and ostracized her. She was a victim of the legacy her father had handed down to her.

My father was my mother's first and last "true love." My father, Fred Walker, had only one sibling, an older sister. His parents were the opposite of my mother's. They had a loving and prayerful home. They served Jesus in their local church. My father began to drink in his late teens in spite of the fervent prayers of his parents and counseling from his pastor. After marrying my mother, he continued to drink. Following the birth of my brother, his drinking lured him to places and people that eventually destroyed their marriage. After only twelve years of marriage, he and my mother divorced when I was only four years old. He suffered tremendous consequences from his chosen lifestyle, which should have scared him into complete and faithful sobriety, but he continued to drink and died at age forty-seven.

My mother remarried when I was five. Life seemed to take on a better look. I started school, and my family looked like everyone else's. I was much happier, and life was good in my eyes. There was no more drinking, fighting, or cursing and no more being left alone in a shabby apartment building all day long or being left with a babysitter who made me sit on the couch all day. Fears of abandonment and the death of my mother declined. I loved school, my teachers, and my friends.

A few years passed, and I was no longer the baby, but now the middle child with a brother five years older and a half sister nine years younger than me. My stepfather lost his job, and we all moved in with my mother's sister, Aunt Ruth, after whom I was named. Yes, my full name is Nancy Ruth. Aunt Ruth was a gifted vocalist and played the piano by ear. She loved to sing gospel songs and go to church. She was one of two aunts who loved me and talked to me about Jesus. We lived in a neighborhood full of kids my age. I loved playing outside, especially baseball and skating.

One significant summer, several of my friends and I decided to go to church. At this church, I received an invitation to attend a Sunday school party. I don't remember any of the girls at the party, only the Sunday school teacher who invited me. My next invitation was to vacation Bible school. It was during that week that I met Jesus. I want to describe my encounter just as I have always remembered it. The reason I call it an encounter is because that experience was exactly the definition of the word: a casual or unexpected meeting.

Vacation Bible school (VBS) was different from what it is today; more emphasis was placed on Scripture memorization. I can still remember the colored cards with as many as five verses on each card. Each day, the card was a different color and had new verses. We took the cards home and were charged with memorizing all the verses. The next day, we would quote the verses to our teacher. I loved doing that! I would work hard every night memorizing my verses. I can still remember asking my mother to let me quote my verses to her. She would respond with agitation instead of praise. In order to receive my mother's praise, I had to clean our house and take care of my sister. My worth was based on how I met others' needs. My need for praise was not met at home but at VBS that week. I really enjoyed being with all the kids my age, but I was the most excited to learn the verses perfectly and recite all of them to my teacher. I loved to see her smile at me. I reveled in her praises. I don't remember the prizes, just praises. Each day, we would go into the sanctuary and sing in the choir as we learned new songs. On the last day, as we practiced the songs we would be singing for VBS commencement, one of the teachers asked for volunteers to quote the verses we had memorized that week. I volunteered. After all were assigned, we began to sing again. As I began to say the verse assigned to me in my head, I was distracted by a piercing light that came straight through the stained-glass window on the left side of the sanctuary. At that moment, I understood the spiritual truths in the verses I had memorized and immediately knew I needed and wanted to ask Jesus Christ into my heart. I responded immediately and took my "first step." Salvation was mine. I talked with my pastor and prayed, asking Jesus to forgive me of my sins and come live inside my heart.

VBS commencement night was such a big thing for me. God knew I didn't have a Sunday dress, so He provided for me. Earlier that year, my favorite relative by far, my uncle Larry (Ruth's husband) had returned from a military assignment in Germany, bringing with him a beautiful dress. It was very formal with gold thread woven throughout the fabric. The buttons also had gold designs painted on them. Feeling like a princess, I wore that dress to the commencement that night. Even though my uncle Larry didn't come to the commencement, I knew he loved me and was thinking about me that special night. As far as I was concerned, he was the perfect man and a father figure. He treated me like his little girl, and I loved him with all my heart. Some of my happiest times as a child were when he was home from his army assignments.

It was the one and only time I wore that dress. I, along with many others, walked down the aisle of my first home church, Gurnee Avenue Baptist Church. We were so excited, yet we reverently stood before the church and made our public professions of faith in Jesus. Then each one of us was baptized and given a certificate. My mother, my grandfather, and my aunt on my biological father's side attended what I now realize was a major event in my life. I like to call it my "first spiritual marker."

⁓

Day 1
Our Spiritual Journey Begins

Encounters—One definition of encounter is an "unexpected meeting." Today, we will begin a full week of looking at the most miraculous, unexpected encounters ever recorded in history. To find them, we must go to the most important history book, the book of truth: the Word of God.

An unbeliever cannot understand the teaching or guiding power of the Holy Spirit. But to Christians who call upon the Holy Spirit to teach and guide them, He is their strength and help in times of need. I have already prayed for you, my sister, that you will be tremendously blessed.

This week will be spent gleaning personal truth and application from the book of Luke. Let's absorb all He has for us through two of the most miraculous encounters recorded in history. Just as I share my own thoughts and personal stories with you, God has chosen to share some of His thoughts and His Word with us. I want to encourage you to keep this in mind every time you open your Bible. We were on His mind before He created mankind. We are on His mind right now. We will be on His mind tomorrow. We are always on His mind!

Our goal for this session is to get a glimpse of the miraculous way God chose to unfold salvation among humanity. God's goals and plans for us are quite different from those of the workplace. During my career with AT&T, annual goal setting was a very important process. The purpose was to produce goals that achieved results in areas of priority (i.e., profit margins and customer base). Detailed plans and activities were developed to ensure goals were visible and being achieved. I am reminded of my years facilitating the laborious task. It was never easy. Often, tempers would flare, and the day would end with raw nerves. The strain of planning seemed to always bring out the worst in people, especially controllers driven by the need for significance among peers. Aren't you glad working with God is not like that? I am.

God's goal for mankind is to experience His deliverance through salvation. The next step is for us to become like His son, Jesus, through sanctification. The final step is glorification, in which we are made complete in the image of Christ. He is our Master Facilitator in an eternal goal-setting session. He keeps things moving in the process of sanctification until His goal of deliverance is accomplished in us. We are told in 1 Thessalonians 5:24 (NKJV), "He who has called you is faithful, who also will do it."

Before you begin, I encourage you to pray this prayer I have written and prayed for you.

> El-o'-him, my Creator, thank you for ordaining this moment in my life. Open my spiritual eyes that I may see the unseen and give me understanding of the remarkable way you chose to bring yourself into the lives of your creation: mankind. Thrill me with your presence as I walk through your Word. I ask this in the name of my Savior and Lord, Jesus Christ. Amen.

Our text for today is Luke 1:3 (NIV): "Therefore, since I myself have carefully investigated everything from the beginning, it seemed good to me to write an orderly account." The author is Luke, a physician and companion of the apostle Paul. He was referring to Jesus and the events that surrounded his life. Matthew Henry's *Concise Commentary* states that Luke wrote of the things Christians can surely believe, such as eyewitnesses and ministers of the Word who through Divine inspiration recorded these great events.[3]

> The theme and message of Luke's book is to give the true and complete story of Jesus' life. He wrote the fullest and most orderly story of His life. One of Luke's interests in writing this book was to show that Jesus loved all kinds of people. In the parables especially, he wrote down Christ's words about the poor and oppressed. The theme of joy is felt throughout the book, as Christ's coming brought joy, as well as hope and salvation to a sinful world.[4]

It is amazing how many people wish, dream, and hope for the magical thing or lucky number that will bring true satisfaction and significance. Luke found the *person* who could provide exactly what he needed. Jesus was the provider of the abundant life Luke needed and wanted. Just as Luke sought the eyewitnesses, we too want a letter of guarantee that Jesus can give us a life of satisfaction and significance. Did you know that a real letter exists? It reads: "I have come that you may have life, and have it more abundantly" (John 10:10, NIV). These are the words of Jesus, heard and written by his disciple John. Luke wanted to know the truth about life and the promises that had been made and repeated throughout generations about a better life to come. He found out that the real life had finally come. He was present. If we are going to see with our spiritual eyes the work of God in our lives over the next six weeks, we must address two topics before we are introduced to our partners in faith.

(1) Is truth in your life?

(2) Do you sense His presence?

Let's begin with truth. Look up these verses in the New International Version of the Bible and fill in the blanks. Ask the Holy Spirit to reveal the meaning of each verse to you.

- John 14:6: "Jesus answered, 'I am the way, the _____, and the _____. No one comes to the Father except through _____.'"

- John 8:31–32: "To the Jews who had believed him, Jesus said, 'If you _____ to my teaching, you are really my disciples. Then _____will know the truth, and the _____ will set you _____.'"

- John 17:17: "Jesus said, 'Sanctify them by the truth: your _____is truth.'"

Now try to fill in the blanks from memory. If you need to, look back at the verses for the answers:

- Who is the truth? _____

- Who is set free by truth? _____

- Who sets us free? _____

- Who is life? _____

- The _____ is truth.

Now, let's look at a couple of verses that address "life in Christ." Look up these verses and fill in the blanks. Ask the Holy Spirit to reveal the meaning of each verse to you.

- John 20:31: "But these are _____ that you may _____ that Jesus is the Christ, the Son of God, and that by believing you may have _____ in his name."

- 1 John 5:13: "I write these things to _____ who believe in the name of the Son of God so that you may _____that you have eternal life."

- Romans 6:23: "For the wages of sin is _____, but the gift of God is _____ _____ in Christ Jesus our Lord."

Now try to fill in the blanks from memory. If you need to, look back at the verses for the answers:

- Why were the Scriptures written? _____
  _____

- Eternal life is the _____ of God.

- To whom were the Scriptures written? _____
  _____

- Write John 1:1–3, 14.

  _____

  _____

  _____

What do these verses say to you?

_____

_____

_____

Have you given Jesus your life and received His gift of eternal life? If you are not sure, ask yourself this question: "Do I know for sure that if I were to die tonight I would go to heaven?" If you cannot answer that question positively, then I would encourage you to take a step of faith with Jesus and give him your life. I have written a prayer for you to use to take the most important step of your life.

> Dear Jesus, I am a sinner, and I am asking for your forgiveness. I believe that you died for me and that your precious blood is the only thing that will cleanse me from all my sin. By faith, I now receive you, Jesus, as my Lord and my Savior. I trust You, alone, for the salvation of my soul. Help me Lord to do your will each day for the rest of my life. In the holy and powerful name of Jesus, I pray. Amen

Reflect for a few moments on what you have done. Look back at the verses we have meditated on today. Now offer Jesus a prayer of thanksgiving for the *gift of eternal life* you have received today. Write your prayer on the space below.

_____

_____

If you have given your life to Christ before starting this study, then reflect on your salvation experience and the verses we have meditated on today. Offer Jesus a prayer of thanksgiving for the *gift of eternal life*. Write your prayer on the space below.

_____

_____

Dear one, if you trusted Christ for salvation today, I rejoice with you! Welcome to the family of God. Now, go immediately and tell someone!

See you tomorrow at the altar of incense with Zechariah!

Day 2
Fear Has No Respect For Man

Yesterday, we began by looking at the opening comments from Luke. Luke was serious about standing for the truth. Ladies, we must be serious about standing for the truth, especially in our world today. Before we can go a step further, it is very important for you to do an exercise that will play a very important part in how this week's homework speaks to you. Take a few minutes and reflect on your own salvation experience. Now, write it out completely. Write every detail you can remember. Even if you think some part of it is insignificant, write it anyway. As vividly as possible, describe your thoughts and impressions. Take your time. If you sit quietly and let your experience roll through your mind, I promise you the Holy Spirit will expand and highlight more than you can imagine. He will show you significant and meaningful snapshots of your experience. Be sure to begin with the date, place, and event. Try to recall your family situation and your age. Take the time to include your personal biography prior to that life-changing day. Feel free to use my experience as an example. I know this will take some time, but it will be worth it! Once you have written your salvation experience on a separate sheet of paper, make a copy. Place one copy at the end of today's homework and another at the beginning of day 5.

Your salvation experience is a miracle! Nothing can compare. It is a miracle that a holy God would forgive us, deliver us from eternal death, and give us eternal life. And to top it off, He would come and live in us to prove the power of His name! Jesus is our *Immanuel*, which means "God is with us." Yes, wherever we are, He is there, also. He is our *Jehovah-shammah, the Lord Is There*.

> "Whom have I in heaven but you? And earth has nothing I desire besides you. My flesh and my heart may fail, but God is the strength of my heart and my portion forever" Psalm 73:25–26.

Throughout my life, He has always been there. At that miraculous moment of my salvation, He was there. When I responded in obedience to His call, He became my *Immanuel* (Matthew 1:23). This is what He did for you too. This miraculous encounter is for *all*.

> "For God so loved the world that He gave His one and only Son, that whoever believes in Him shall not perish but have eternal life" (John 3:16).

Take a moment to read my journal entry about a miraculous *encounter* I experienced.

> Ken and I are in Jacksonville, Florida, as I write today. After my quiet time, I love to walk with my iPod blasting praise music. This morning was not like most. I was enjoying the music and beauty of the ocean when I was interrupted with an encounter I have never experienced before. In a flash, two lifeguards passed in front of me and dived into the ocean to rescue a young man in distress. A helicopter flew overhead with the blasting of a panicked voice attempting to give directions from a loudspeaker. Everyone on the beach stopped in their tracks and turned their attention to the three men in the ocean. Even with my iPod blasting, I heard the blaring voice of panic. I stopped and joined the others, and immediately saw a young man struggling. Then he was gone, under the water. I prayed and then began to wonder if his mother or

friends were there. It was extremely quiet on that beach for a few minutes. The two lifeguards were swimming with all their strength, trying to move against the undertow and crashing waves. The most frightening thing for everyone was the rapidly escaping *time*. "Hurry, before it is too late, Lord; don't let him drown" was my immediate prayer. Another blast from the helicopter and the lifeguards quickly changed their course of search with an abrupt turn to the left. The waves worsened, pulling and pushing the lifeguards madly. I began to plead with the Father to rescue all of them. Then I saw three heads surface following the crash of several huge waves. Slowly, they moved toward the shore. The scene was beautiful. The young man in distress was in the middle. His arms were over the shoulders of the two lifeguards while they held him tightly around his waist. As they approached the shallow waters, I could not contain myself. I began to clap. I was saying "thank you" to *three men who saved his life…two lifeguards and Jesus.* The young man was fine after a few minutes on shore. I assumed he was alone since I never saw a mother figure or friends. I continued on my walk as the news team took pictures and interviewed the young man and his rescuers.

Usually, when I see young men on surfboards, they are having a great time riding the waves. I wondered what caused this young man to weaken and be overtaken by the sea. Was he momentarily distracted by something and then simultaneously hit by a huge wave? It reminded me that there are times in our lives when we get pulled into something that is over our heads, beyond our strength, and has the potential to destroy us. Yet, there are others around us who seem to ride the waves of life without any problems. I am sure this particular young man never thought he was in danger. He probably never doubted his ability. I have no doubt who rescued that young man.

> It was Jesus – Jehovah-shammah: The Lord is There.

We can't always trust ourselves, but we can always trust God and His Word. Sometimes, we are overwhelmed with a *good* distraction that will take our focus off Christ's best for us and hinder our ability to stay in step with Him. This is why we must allow the instructions found in Galatians 5:25 to "keep in step with the spirit" to become our moment-by-moment purpose. In our scripture for today, we will see huge distractions that come from "doubting the Word of God."

Now we are prepared, yes prepared, to see miraculous encounters from God's Word. Put on your spiritual glasses and open your Bible to the book of Luke. Luke was probably writing the books of Luke and Acts in Rome during Paul's imprisonment there. As the apostle Paul's companion, Luke was very aware of the lies that were circulating among the people and different religious groups. Some of these lies were birthed from jealousy and were used to draw and hold a crowd for self-seeking fame-aholics. Luke wanted those who read his book to know the certainty of the things they had been taught.

Read Luke 1:5–25, and let this amazing story soak in. When Luke wrote this, the angel's message had been fulfilled. Luke put to words the fulfillment of the prophecy given to Isaiah.

> A voice of one calling: "In the desert prepare the way for the LORD; make straight in the wilderness a highway for our God. Every valley shall be raised up, every mountain and hill made low; the rough ground shall become level, the rugged places a plain.

And the glory of the LORD will be revealed, and all mankind together will see it. For the mouth of the LORD has spoken. (Isaiah 40:3–5)

In the text for today, we see a beautiful picture of how God unfolded Old Testament prophecy through an unexpected encounter. Now read the validation of this prophecy in Matthew 3:1–3:

In those days John the Baptist came, preaching in the Desert of Judea and saying, "Repent, for the kingdom of heaven is near." This is he who was spoken of through the prophet Isaiah: "A voice of one calling in the desert, prepare the way for the Lord, make straight paths for him."

What an encounter to stand in the presence of God's messenger! Can you imagine? As we look at the conversation between Zechariah and Gabriel, it is important that we discover the *motivation* behind Zechariah's response to Gabriel.

- Zechariah's response in Luke 1:18: "How can ___ ___ _____ of this? I am an _____ man and my wife is _____ _____ in years."

- Gabriel's response in verse 19: "I am Gabriel. I stand in the _____ of God, and I have been sent to _____ to you and to tell you this good news."

- Gabriel's response in verse 20: "And now you will be _____ and not be able to speak until the day this happens, because you did not _____ my words, which will come _____ at their proper time."

Zechariah was the only person in the temple. The assembled worshipers were praying outside. Zechariah was at the altar of incense located in front of the curtain that is before the ark of the testimony where God told Moses he would meet with him (Exodus 30:1–6). Zechariah knew the history and order of things ordained by God. He knew the purpose of that moment was to meet with God. The angel startled Zechariah, and he was gripped with fear. The angel immediately consoled him by telling him not to be afraid, his prayer had been heard and his wife would bear him a son.

The word *fear* is preceded by "gripped with." The definition of *grip* is a tight hold, manner or power of holding, or mastery or command. One of the definitions in *Strong's Concordance* for fear as used in this verse is "what is feared" or "what is caused by the intimidation of adversaries."[5]

> He is Jehovah-shalom:
> The Lord of Peace.

Could Zechariah have been intimidated or hurt into doubting the goodness of God? Maybe Elizabeth's barrenness had brought ridicule and shame. Did her pain add fuel to Zechariah's own disappointment in not having a son? Was their home marked with failure? Based on the definitions of *gripped* and *fear*, we can see where Zechariah could have been "mastered by fear and doubt."

You can be sure that Satan wants you to be so "mastered by fear" that over time your strength is zapped and your courage wanes so that when the undertow and crashing waves of life unexpectedly hit you, you are helplessly pulled under. Satan also wants you to be so mastered by fear that your life is a constant cycle of doubt and unbelief. When God speaks to you, you can't hear Him because of the clamor of your own doubting and unbelieving words. You doubt that He would do for you what you believe He would do for others. I have experienced both places: I have been "mastered by fear" as well as suffered with "doubt and unbelief." How about you? Are you mastered by fear? Do you cycle back and forth between doubting God and believing Him? What *fear* has mastered you? What *particular thing* do you believe He will do for others that He won't do for you?

- Has God ever *muzzled* you? If He has, why?

_____

_____

Stop right now and pray. Talk to Him about your answers to these questions. Allow *Him* to work in your heart. He loves you and wants to bring peace to these areas of your life. Jesus said, "Peace I leave with you; my peace I give you; I do not give to you as the world gives. Do not let your hearts be troubled and do not be afraid" (John 14:27).

As I thought about Zechariah's response, I realized how much I am like him. It's so easy for me to judge him as I look at his doubting questions. But aren't we like that too? Many times, God has spoken encouragement and direction to me through His Word, a sermon, or even a friend, and I would respond with doubt and questioning.

Do you agree that it was best to silence Zechariah? The last thing poor Elizabeth needed was a negative husband spewing words of doubt in the days she would carry and deliver their son, John the Baptist. Zechariah needed this miraculous encounter with God's messenger more than He realized at the time. The fear and doubt would become joy and hope. The couple would hold *him*—the *fulfillment* of the message from God. What a plan and purpose for Zechariah and Elizabeth! God did not make Zechariah and Elizabeth guess or try to figure out His plan for their lives. They did have to wait, but when the time had come, God spoke. He has not changed. You and I may have hopes and dreams that differ from our Old Testament couple, but when they are unmet, we are wounded and can easily fall prey to the power of negativity. My own unmet dreams, failures, hurts, and disappointments took a toll on my life over the years. I found how God felt about my messed-up life in Jeremiah 29:11.

Turn to Jeremiah 29:11, and fill in the blanks:

- "'For I know the _____ I have for _____,' declares the LORD, 'plans to _____ you and not to _____ you, plans to give you _____ and a _____.'"

Look at this verse now, with the expanded meanings for the words *hope* and *future*.

"'For I know the plans I have for you,' declares the LORD, 'plans to prosper you and not to harm you, plans to give you <u>what is best for you</u> and <u>you will be contented</u>.'"(Emphasis added)

Write this verse again, replacing all the "you" places with references to yourself.

Jeremiah 29:11:

_____

_____

_____

This has been a great day with our Old Testament couple, Zechariah and Elizabeth. I challenge you to memorize Jeremiah 29:11.

◌

Day 3
Guilt Can Crush Our Confidence

Yesterday, we saw how fear and doubt can move into the most precious place of our lives: our fellowship with God. I wonder if Zechariah regretted his question and comment to Gabriel. Read his words again: "How can I be sure of this? I am an old man and my wife is well along in years." What did you hear? I heard overwhelming feelings that shout, "God can't do this in my life, much less my marriage!" In retrospect, I believe that I have, like Zechariah, allowed the glare of fear and the clamor from my own thoughts to completely block the beauty of an encounter with Him. Hindsight is always 20/20, but it will not bring back an opportunity of a lifetime. In situations like this, it usually brings regret. I'm sure you have experienced seasons that seemed to have more hindsight revelations. Haven't you had enough of those? I have! I want my spiritual eyes to be 20/20 all the time.

Let's move on and "see" what God has for us today. God could have retracted all that Gabriel said, but He didn't. Neither did Zechariah's response change God's mind or plans. It simply exposed Zechariah's heart. It appears that Zechariah did not believe God would do for him what He had done for Abraham and Sarah.

I have also allowed unhealthy thoughts and emotions to affect my fellowship with God. The following is a cycle I would experience when I would react just like Zechariah. An opportunity would come for me to believe God for the impossible, but in my heart, I would wimp out. After a season of waiting and not seeing, I would begin whining. Then I would moan and say I was trusting God, but in reality, I had already begun to judge Him. Matthew 7:1 tells us not to judge, or we too will be judged. Because I had judged God, the Holy Spirit had to expose my sin. Instead of doing what God tells me in 1 John 1:9—"If we confess our sins, He is faithful to forgive us our sins and purify us from all unrighteousness"—I would hesitate and withdraw from God.

This is just what Adam and Eve did; they ran from God's voice because they knew they had disobeyed. This part of the cycle got me in more trouble than I could handle. My hesitation would quickly move to stubborn rebellion, which ignited anger, and the end result was shame from my ugly behavior. By this time, my sins had become so big in my own eyes that I believed God wouldn't want to forgive me, much less purify me from all my unrighteousness. Guilt would overtake my emotions and cause havoc in my life and marriage. In the past, I have beaten myself unmercifully with the hammer of guilt. I believe "self-condemnation" is included in the meaning of the following verse: "Therefore, there is no condemnation for those who are in Christ Jesus," (Romans 8:1). What a cycle! Have you been there? Are you there now? *God knows us.* "O LORD, you have searched me and you know me" (Psalms 139:1).

Read 1 Chronicles 28:9b, and fill in the blanks.

- "The Lord _____ every heart and _____ the motive behind the _____."

Let's take another look at Luke 1:18. Fill in the blanks.

- "Zechariah asked the angel, 'How can I be _____ of this? I am an _____ man and my wife is well along in years.'"

Let's look at *Webster's* definitions of the words you placed in the blanks:

- *Sure* means reliable, certain, without doubt, bound to happen or do.

- *Old* means having lived or existed for a long time, time long past.

I wonder if Zechariah was in a cycle of guilt when Gabriel appeared. He wasn't an ordinary Jew. He was from the tribe of Levi, the priests. He couldn't run away from his priestly duties. He had to serve in the temple and pray for the sins of the people. I wonder how many times he thought about the son or daughter for whom he and Elizabeth had prayed. Children were considered a blessing from God. Barrenness was believed to be an indicator of God's displeasure. This must have been even worse for a priest and his wife.

> "Hope deferred makes the heart sick, but a longing fulfilled is a tree of life" (Proverbs 13:12).

As the years passed, how did he deal with the scorn and shame that barrenness brought? I wonder if on this particular day, when Zechariah was alone in the temple, his own shattered dreams overshadowed his calling. Did he struggle to ask one more time for that which was hopeless in his own eyes? Maybe these were the thoughts that preceded his words to Gabriel: "This is impossible because Elizabeth and I are beyond the child-producing season of our lives. It would take a true miracle of God."

Have you prayed and asked God for something and He seems to be saying no? If yes, describe the situation and your feelings.

_____

_____

_____

Read Luke 1:26–38 slowly, and meditate on it for a few minutes. As soon as you read verse 26, you were taken back to yesterday's lesson. What was spoken is becoming visible. It is in the sixth month of Elizabeth's pregnancy that God speaks again. Let's look for parallels in the encounters of Zechariah and Mary. Reread Luke 1:10–20, 26–37. I've listed seven parallels you will use in the next exercise.

Look for significant comparisons with Zechariah and Mary's encounters with God's messenger. Use the following table to answer these questions.

- Which one should have been the quickest to believe God's messenger and why?

  _____

- God's timing was _____.

- Zechariah's fear came when he _____; Mary's when she _____.

- What did the "yes of God" mean for Zechariah and Mary? _____ _____.

- _____ will be great in the sight of God.

- Jesus' _____ will never end.

- Mary's answer required no confirming _____.

13

- Why was Zechariah unable to speak (verse 20)? _____
_____

- What were the last six words Gabriel spoke to Mary (verse 37)? " _____
_____ _____ _____
_____."

Parallels	Zechariah's Encounter	Mary's Encounter	Comparison
Preparation	Zechariah is preparing to burn incense to the Lord.	Mary is preparing to be married to Joseph.	Both in time of preparation
God's Timing	Gabriel appeared to Zechariah.	Gabriel went to Mary.	Unexpected encounter
God's call is frightening.	When Zechariah saw Gabriel, he was startled and gripped with fear.	When Mary heard Gabriel's greeting, she was troubled and wondered what it meant.	Zechariah was surprised with fearful emotions. Mary was surprised with troubled thoughts.
The "Yes" of God	Gabriel said "Do not be afraid, Zechariah; your prayer has been heard. Your wife will bear a son, and you are to give him the name John."	Gabriel said "Do not be afraid, Mary. You have found favor with God. You will be with child and give birth to a son, and you are to give him the name Jesus."	Gabriel told Zechariah "yes" his prayer had been answered and his wife Elizabeth would bear him a son. Gabriel told Mary "yes" she was highly favored and her God would bless her with a son.
Miraculous Blessings	John will be a delight and joy; many will rejoice because of his birth; he will be great in the sight of the Lord; he will never drink wine or any fermented drink; he will be filled with the Holy Spirit from birth; he will bring many of the people of Israel back to the Lord; he will go on before the Lord in the spirit and power of Elijah, making ready a people prepared for the Lord.	Jesus will be great and will be called the Son of the Most High. The Lord God will give him the throne of his father David, and he will reign over the house of Jacob forever; his kingdom will never end.	John, miraculous son of Elizabeth John, son of a priest (Zechariah) John the Baptist made ready a people prepared for the Lord. Jesus, miraculous son of Mary Jesus, son of the Most High God Jesus, the King of Kings, will rule over the house of Jacob forever; his kingdom will never end.
Acceptance of God's Word	Zechariah asked the angel, "How can I be sure of this? I am an old man and my wife is well along in years."	"I am the Lord's servant," Mary answered. "May it be to me as you have said."	Zechariah heard everything the angel said, but his unbelief spoke. Mary's reply required no sign for the confirming of her faith.
Word Fulfilled	Verse 24—After this Elizabeth became pregnant.	Verses 39–43—Immediately, Mary visits Elizabeth and her pregnancy is also confirmed.	Verse 37—For nothing is impossible with God.

Day 4 will be another day of adventure as we look at the unfolding of Mary's encounter with the Holy Spirit!

⌐∫⌐

Day 4
The Impossible Becomes Possible

I hope you are beginning to grasp the miraculous things God has done, can still do, and will do when we least expect it. He is amazing, isn't He? Today, we are going to look at Mary's encounter with the Holy Spirit. Read Luke 1:28–35. Notice Gabriel's words, "The Holy Spirit will come upon you, and the power of the Most High will overshadow you." Look at the meanings of "come" and "overshadow" from Strong's Concordance. Let their meanings sink into your mind for a few minutes.

Come—to supervene, i.e., arrive (from "there" to "here"), occur, attach. Figuratively, it means to influence, come up, come on, or come there.

Overshadow—to cast a shade upon, i.e., (by analogy) to envelope in a haze of brilliancy. Figuratively, it means to invest with supernatural influence.

> Additional information: Overshadow—From a vaporous cloud that casts a shadow the word is transferred to a shining cloud surrounding and enveloping persons with brightness. Used of the Holy Spirit exerting creative energy upon the womb of the virgin Mary and impregnating it. A use of the word which seems to have been drawn from the familiar Old Testament idea of a cloud as symbolizing the immediate presence and power of God—Luke 1:35.

Additional information from the *Holman Bible Dictionary*: "Overshadow—To cast a shadow over; to envelop."

> "Luke 1:35 describes the mystery of the virginal conception in terms of Mary's being "overshadowed" by the power of God. Luke's picture does not involve sexual intercourse of a god and human woman, as was common in pagan myth. The Spirit is Creator, not consort (or spouse) Gen. 1:2; Ps 33:6; and especially where the Spirit's role is life-giver (Job 33:4, Ps. 104:30).

The verse begins to take on a different picture now, doesn't it? I love to rewrite a verse and use different words taken from the original definition. This does not change the meaning, but it can enhance your spiritual vision and understanding. Before you read mine, try it on your own. Take your time. You may want to use another concordance, commentary, or dictionary. It will be well worth your time."

_____

_____

_____

This is how I chose to put the verse together from the definitions from Strong and Holman.

> "The Holy Spirit will leave heaven and arrive in your presence, and the power of the Most High will wrap you in a haze of brilliancy. The Holy Spirit will exert creative energy producing resurrection life and this miraculous conception will occur."

In the book of Matthew, we see a different word regarding Mary's encounter with the Holy Spirit.

> This is how the birth of Jesus Christ came about: His mother Mary was pledged to be married to Joseph, but before they came together, she was found to be with child *through* the Holy Spirit. (Matthew 1:18)

Here is a look at the verse with the last sentence changed to include the word "through."

> The Holy Spirit will leave heaven and arrive in your presence, and the power of the Most High will wrap you in a haze of brilliancy. *Through* the exerting creative power of the Holy Spirit, resurrection life will be produced and this miraculous conception will occur.

Let's do a quick meaning search for the word *through* using *Webster's Dictionary*.

Through means from end to end, by way of, to places in, throughout.

The power of the Holy Spirit has no limits. He hovered over the waters of the earth in Genesis 1:2, awaiting God's spoken commands to begin creation. In Genesis 1:3, God said, "Let there be light," and there was light; light was created by the power of the Holy Spirit. Just imagine with me for a moment while Gabriel is talking to Mary, God is waiting for Mary's response. As soon as she said, "Behold the handmaiden of the Lord. Let it be according to your word," God released His will *through* the power of the Holy Spirit.

While Gabriel is talking to Mary, our elderly couple is experiencing the visible evidence of God's words being spoken to Mary at that very moment. "Even Elizabeth your relative is going to have a child in her old age, and she who was said to be barren is in her sixth month" (Luke 1:36). Isn't God's timing amazing? He *interrupted* a fearful and unbelieving Jewish priest to tell him his prayer had been heard and

> He interrupted me at ten years old as I thought about a memory verse.

his wife would miraculously give birth to his son. He *interrupted* a young Jewish girl's wedding plans to tell her she had been chosen to miraculously give birth to the Son of God. What did he interrupt when His Words came to you?

_____

_____

_____

"For nothing is impossible with God!"—These were the last words Gabriel spoke to Mary. Why didn't he say them to Zechariah, who was so fearful and doubting? Zechariah had stated the reason for his doubting with these words, "How shall I know this? For I am an old man, and my wife is well advanced in years?" It would truly be a miracle for Zechariah and Elizabeth to conceive.

Read Genesis 15:1–7 about the promise of a son. At this stage, conception was still possible for Abraham, who fathered Ishmael (chapter 16).

Complete verse 6: "Abram _____ the Lord, and He (the LORD) credited it to him (Abraham) as _____."

Read Genesis 17:1–21 about the promise of a son. At this stage, conception appeared humanly impossible because of their ages.

Complete verse 17: "Abraham fell facedown; he _____ and said to himself, "Will a son be born to a man a _____ years old? Will Sarah bear a child at the age of _____?"

Read Genesis 18:1–3, 9–15 about the promise of a miracle. At this stage, conception would require a miracle.

Complete Genesis 18:14: "And the Lord said, 'Is _____ too hard for the LORD? I will return to you at the _____ time next year and Sarah _____ _____ a son.'"

Read Genesis 21:1–7 about a promise fulfilled. "And the LORD visited Sarah as He had said, and the LORD did for Sarah as He had spoken." Complete Genesis 21:2: "Sarah became _____ and bore a son to Abraham in his old age, at the ____ _____ God had _____ him."

Nothing is impossible with God! Zechariah knew this story inside and out. It had been passed down from generation to generation. He knew God had performed and could perform a miracle. But just as Abraham did in Genesis 17, Zechariah fell into unbelief. Just as God did the impossible in the lives of Abraham and Sarah, Zechariah and Elizabeth, and Mary, He can do in ours. Ask yourself this question, "Do I believe God still does the impossible?" If you are a Christian, He already has. When you accepted Jesus as your Lord and Savior, the impossible became possible and the miraculous gift of salvation was given to you! Ephesians 2:8 states, "For it is by grace you have been saved, through faith, and that not of yourselves; it is the gift of God, not of works, so that no one can boast." Salvation is beautifully represented in the conception of Jesus. His Word comes upon us, into us, and through us by the power of His Spirit and gives us Himself. It is a miraculous encounter with the Most High God!

I loved this time spent looking at the miraculous conception of Jesus, and I pray you did too!

❧

Day 5
The Invisible Made Visible

God is not a God of partiality—regardless of who you are or what you have done, He will still offer Himself to you as Savior. Salvation is the greatest miracle of all. It is the invisible power of God Almighty that creates Himself in us. As we close this session, I pray that you have seen personal parallels that validated the truth of His Word in your life.

Have you been wondering why session 1 is entitled "Spiritual Marker #1—The Encounter"? A "spiritual marker" identifies a time of decision when you clearly knew that God guided you. This week, we have looked at Zechariah's and Mary's encounters with God through His messenger, Gabriel. The encounters marked their lives spiritually, emotionally, and physically. When you experienced your first encounter with God through salvation, you too were marked in the same way. To draw this week to a close, we'll focus our time today on examining more details around "Spiritual Marker #1—The Encounter."

Day 1: Our Spiritual Journey Begins

In John 14:6, we are told that "Jesus is the way, the truth, and the life." Whether you encountered Him as your Savior before this study or on day 2, by now, you should have written about your personal encounter. Did you remember to place a copy with today's lesson? After all we have learned and taken in this week, I challenge you to reread your personal experience and note any changes or additions you may want to make.

Day 2: Fear Has No Respect for Man

Almost immediately after my baptism, I began to experience fear concerning my salvation experience. Every time I disobeyed my mother, she would angrily say these damaging words, "You can't be saved, Nancy, or you wouldn't misbehave like that." You can imagine the pressure those words put on a ten-year-old girl. Because my mother got so angry with me, I believed God was angry with me too. My inability to be perfect in my mother's eyes formed a belief in my mind that God expected perfection as well. This mind-set took years to change. You can imagine the questioning that took place in my young mind. Remember the story of the young man who was rescued by the lifeguards? His comments to the reporter indicated he hadn't seen the waves, nor had he noticed the heavy undertow. He was taken by surprise! I was taken by surprise by my mother's hurtful words. Condemnation crashed over me like huge waves as she judged the validity of my salvation by my misbehavior and imperfection. I was crushed and believed she must be right. This lie was like the mighty undertow. I began to fear my new friend, Jesus.

Have you been wounded by a similar situation? If yes, write a brief description.

_____

_____

_____

We looked at the factors that caused Zechariah to be mastered by fear and unbelief. Even though Zechariah prayed for a son, he had stopped believing God would provide. Have you ever asked God for something He alone could provide, only to give up on it later? Or is there something you really desire that only God can provide, but you haven't asked him? Don't be muzzled by fear. Ask Him now!

_____

_____

_____

Day 3: Guilt Can Crush Our Conscience

On this day, I shared my personal cycle of guilt and the unmerciful beating I would give myself with the hammer of guilt. Just imagine the added pain in Zechariah's and Elizabeth's lives from those around them. Times have not changed. There are those who judge us, taunt us with their blessings, and stifle our hope with faithless lives. The words of man can encourage or kill, but the words of God hold miraculous power. They hold the power of life. What He speaks becomes a reality.

When I was ten years old, God chose to do a miracle in my life; he saved me and gave me Himself forever. He used His Holy Scriptures to open my eyes to my need.

Fill in the blanks with your personal information:

- When I was _____, He chose to do a miracle in my life; he saved me and gave me Himself forever. He used _____.

God told Zechariah his prayer had been answered. God told Mary she was highly favored. Each was blessed with a son. The Lord has also shown us great favor by blessing us with the privilege of being His daughters.

What is the greatest "yes" (answered prayer or unsolicited blessing) God has ever given you outside of your salvation?

_____

_____

_____

Day 4: The Impossible Becomes Possible

Don't you love day 4? What is impossible for man is possible with the Most High God! We are told in Genesis 1 that He chose the formless and empty and spoke creation into existence. The word *said* used in the creation text "And God said" is the Hebrew word *amar,* which means "to say, speak, tell, command, answer." When God spoke creation into existence (Genesis 1:3), it was the first occurrence of the word.[6] Let's look further at the power of God's words.

Then God said, "Let us make man in our image, in our likeness, and let them rule over the fish of the sea and the birds of the air, over all the creatures that move along the ground" (Genesis 1:26). The word *make* used in this verse is the Hebrew word *asah,* which means "to create, do, and make from nothing."[7]

> **"In awe I see the visible man made by the invisible hands of God – Elohim: The Creator" (author).**

The Invisible Becomes Visible

We are told in Genesis 2:7 that God formed the man from the dust of the ground and breathed into his nostrils the breath of life, and the man became a living being. The word *dust* is from the Hebrew word *aphar*, which means "dust (as powdered or gray) hence clay, earth, mud."[8] God used "aphar" to bring forth His invisible image. *The invisible is made visible.* I can picture an unknown form being compressed and molded until man was complete physically. I can hear the breath of God and see the chest move as man takes his first deep breath. Picture the work of the invisible Holy Spirit coming upon Mary and entering her womb. Just as God breathed life into man, the invisible Holy Spirit breathed His life into her egg creating Jesus, the Son of Man. Jesus was fully God in the temple of man.

When we accept Christ, the invisible presence and power of the Holy Spirit comes upon us and becomes part of us in order that He may be visible through us.

Zechariah and Mary were like Abraham and Sarah; they could not *see* how God could possibly give them a son. Just like Abraham and Sarah, they *saw* at the appointed time. The impossible became possible, fulfilling the Word of God.

Has God opened your eyes this week? Are you seeing things you haven't seen before about yourself?

What has He made visible to you this week?

_____

_____

_____

God wants us to know Him. We are told in Jeremiah 24:7: "I will give them a heart to know me." As we know Him, we will trust Him and recognize His voice as He reveals His purpose for our lives.

It has been a great week! Let's close today in prayer.

> Father,
>
> You are the invisible God who makes yourself visible to your children. Give us eyes to see you, ears to hear you, and hearts to know you. May we know you as Paul penned in Philippians 3:10 (Amplified Bible), "My determined purpose is that I may progressively become more deeply and intimately acquainted with Him, perceiving and recognizing and understanding the wonders of His person." Thank you for ordaining our step of faith and giving us your Son.
>
> I pray this in the name above all names, Jesus Christ, the Son of God.

✍

Session 2

Spiritual Marker #2
"The Wandering"

In session 1, we looked at salvation, the first step in our spiritual journey. Sessions 2 through 6 focus on our sanctification journey. For the remainder of this study, we will look at the progressive steps along that path. The spiritual markers for each week represent different steps in our journeys that have been *ordained by Deity*.

Let me give you a picture of how easily we can take a similar process used in the workplace or even our homes to illustrate the way the Lord works in our lives to accomplish sanctification. Before we begin, let's quickly review the meaning of sanctification.

Sanctification is God's progressive deliverance of a believer from sin's power.[9]

Let's consider the process of a person's first job. She is excited and eager to begin. The first thing a person usually experiences is an orientation followed by training. Upon completion of initial training, the new employee may be assigned to work alongside another employee for a period

> **"Sanctification is the miraculous transformation of becoming less of who we have become, as we become more of who God made us to be"** (author).

of time. This is usually referred to as "on-the-job training." After all training is complete, the new employee is ready to begin performing her assigned duties. Expertise and skill do not come automatically. It takes time and effort to become proficient and meet the standards for satisfactory performance in the new job.

In my work environment with AT&T, regardless of length of employment, you were subject to monthly performance reviews. A supervisor would spend about thirty minutes observing you perform your job and then give you feedback. Positive reinforcement for doing a good job was always enjoyable and inspiring for me as an employee. The least enjoyable review was when an area of performance needed to be corrected. Sometimes, it simply required a review of procedures and training. If it was an area affecting customer service, such as addressing a customer in a discourteous manner, then corrective training was immediately given to the employee. If the poor performance continued, the next step was disciplinary action. The employee would be suspended from work for a day or more, possibly without pay. If the behavior persisted, the final step was termination. As a supervisor, I really disliked having to administer those last two steps.

Have you ever compared our Sanctifier, the Holy Spirit, with your boss? I did that for years without realizing it! Sometimes, we compare Him with a controlling parent, spouse, or friend. I've been guilty of that too. As we begin the journey of sanctification, a new boss comes into our life. Our new boss is the third person that makes up the Godhead, also called the Trinity—the Father, Son, and *Holy Spirit*. When we repent of our sins and accept Christ as our Savior, we are told in Jeremiah

31:34b that "the Lord will forgive our wickedness and will remember our sins no more." Our new boss, the Holy Spirit, will teach, correct, guide, and comfort us as long as we live on this Earth. We will stumble and fall from sin's power, but we can be confident that He is our helper who will never leave or forsake us. He will pick us up and put us back on the right path when we sin. He is *Jehovah-shalom: the God of Peace* referenced in 1 Thessalonians 5:23, who works in us to deliver us from sin's power and ultimately deliver us from sin's presence. The Holy Spirit is our spiritual boss. His job is to watch over us and help us deal with sin. We can either ignore Him or embrace Him. If we ignore Him and give in to sin's power, He will deal with us through conviction, which is a very clear and specific knowledge of our sin. Why? Because He loves us!

This reminds me of the new employee whose performance doesn't meet the standard. She has to be retrained. When we accept Christ, the perfect boss comes into our life to apply training that never falls short. Regardless of the number of performance reviews or the amount of retraining and discipline, we are never terminated. We never lose our position as His children. He constantly examines our motives, and He delights in blessing our obedience.

My Spiritual Journey—Second Step: Sanctification

> May God himself, the God of peace, sanctify you through and through. May your whole spirit, soul and body be kept blameless at the coming of our Lord Jesus Christ. The one who calls you is faithful and He will do it. (1 Thessalonians 5:23–24)

I didn't know about sanctification when I accepted Christ. No one explained to me the transforming work of the Holy Spirit. I had wandered for sixteen years trying to succeed in my own strength. Things began to change when I was twenty-six and married Ken Dempsey. I know, without a doubt, that Ken is the man God created just for me. I am eager to share how God brought us together, but for now, I must begin with the first steps of my sanctification at age ten.

> He is Jehovah-mekoddishkem, The Lord Who Sanctifies You.

Immediately after I accepted Christ, my life began to change. I attended church alone and became very involved in Sunday school and other groups. I can still picture the pews and the place I liked to sit. Easter morning of my sixth-grade year, I got dressed up in my new dress and shoes and walked to church—alone. This would be the last time I attended a service at my home church. Shortly afterward, my circumstances at home began to change. My mother became sick. Since I was the oldest daughter, the role of homemaker defaulted to me. I was definitely not trained for it, but nevertheless, it was mine. The normal homemaking chores and caring for my younger sister were easy compared to caring for my mother. She was very disturbed and would withdraw to her bed to lie in a fetal position. She isolated herself from her family. The silence was the worst part. My stepdad was also silent. I knew my mom and stepdad loved me, but I never heard them say to me, "I love you, Nancy." There was no affection from either of them. There were no hugs or smiles, and this fueled my insecurity. I tried to do everything I could to make things better. I worked endlessly, trying to keep the house in order while balancing my schoolwork and caring for my younger sister, thinking it would help calm the unpredictable changes in my mother's mental health.

Darkness began to take hold, and my "first step" of salvation began to fade. My carefree days as a child were over. Life began to change as over the years my days seemed to bring more struggles and disappointments. As I moved into my teenage years, I resented the responsibilities at home and longed for the motherly nurturing I remembered as a small child. I never forgot my "first step." I would replay the days in VBS and the experience of Jesus coming into my heart over and over again. I would think about God and all of my questions that had gone unanswered. I deeply missed my church and all the people who had nurtured me with a different kind of love. As the days and years passed, I became lonelier and lonelier.

My teenage years were marked for disaster. Insecurity and the need for love consumed me. I was dead set on remaining pure, but the enemy had set me up for failure. The summer before my fifteenth birthday, I attended a party and played a game that involved kissing. I don't remember the guy, but I do remember the kiss! I left there different. I felt older and pretty. I had been kissed by several guys, and I had enjoyed every kiss. The affection I desperately longed for was satisfied momentarily that night. For the first time since I was a child, I was on the receiving end, and I loved it. Soon afterward, I was invited to another summer party. At this party, I met what most people refer to as their "first love." He was my age and very popular among the girls. His kiss was different, and by September, we were a couple. I was so excited and felt like a princess. Little did I know, over the next two years, I would experience yet another season of deep loneliness. The enemy aimed and struck, deeply wounding me at the very place I was the most desperate: my need for love. Not only did he wound me, he also pushed me into a pit of shame. The relationship I thought was perfect was really a prison.

Although this is difficult to write, I know you may be exactly where I was. I was so desperate for love that for two years, I tolerated emotional and physical abuse. In the early months of our relationship, things remained pure and sweet. As my boyfriend's popularity soared among the girls, I felt the wounds of their envy and the wounds of his straying eyes. I became jealous and more insecure while he became arrogant and more controlling. I stood firm in my desire to remain pure, but he weakened my resolve by threatening to end the relationship. One day, he pushed too far, and my strong rejection of him sexually was met with a reply that demolished my self-control. He said, "If you really love me, you will. I love you and want us to be together forever, but if you don't do this, I'll leave you for good."

I understand now that he didn't love me. He loved himself. My consent opened the door for verbal and physical abuse. He also continued to use threats and intimidation to coerce me into continuing our sexual relationship. This continued through my sophomore year. I was miserable and helpless. To make matters worse, my mother would not leave her bed except when absolutely necessary. My parents were oblivious to the events in my life. I fulfilled my role at home and in my relationship with my boyfriend. I needed a way out of the relationship, and it came. That summer, he broke up with me. He had found someone else, and I was set free from his grip. I was free from him, but I was still bound by shame. I had to be strong for my mother, so I again looked for love and found it … in all the wrong places. I attended church very little after my traumatic "first love" experience. When I did go, as soon as I walked in the door, I felt overwhelmed by condemnation and shame.

Still driven by the need for love, the summer before my senior year, I met the man who is the biological father of my two sons, David and Paul. We dated for a brief six months and then married. The next eight years were very difficult, and the marriage ended in divorce. Just prior to the divorce, I had been promoted to a management position on my job. At that point, I felt confident that I could support my children and myself. I didn't need or want another man in my life. My focus was now my career. Although I made a huge change in my lifestyle, I was still the same person inside. I received occasional recognition for my job performance, but my private life was in shambles. I needed help, but I didn't cry out to God. I hid my insecurities behind a mask of arrogance and control, not realizing these were the very things other people had used to cause my early wounds. It is so true that "hurt people hurt people." No area of my life was untouched. As a mother, I was not loving or patient. I was strong and confident on the job and weak and insecure at home. Loneliness began to call my name. I had answered that call too many times and didn't want to go there again. Being weak, I knew I could easily be persuaded to do the wrong things. I could correct an employee's behavior, but I could not correct my own! I wanted to run away from myself. I tried to pray but felt too condemned. God knew my situation and had a plan that would change my life forever. His plan included Ken Dempsey.

I had met Ken the summer prior to my junior year in high school. His older brother Bruce and his wife, Janice, lived in an apartment located upstairs over our house. Ken and I talked a couple of times but never seriously. At the end of my junior year, Ken joined the air force. We wrote to each other faithfully, but when he came home from basic training, I hurt him. He was very serious about me, but I didn't feel the same. I had not been honest with him in my letters, and breaking the news of my true feelings caused our relationship to end abruptly. Again, "hurt people hurt people."

God used my job to bring Ken into my life a second time. I met his younger brother's wife, Becky, after she transferred to my office from another city. After a short conversation with her, I discovered that Ken was her brother-in-law. Soon afterward, I dreamed about Ken, so I called him. He had never married, and he wanted to see me. That night, he came to my house after work, and a new relationship began. I saw him every day until we married four months later on April 24, 1975. I was amazed that he would want me. I could see him wanting to be with my two sons but not me. He fell in love with us, and we fell in love with him. Even before we married, he prayed with the boys every night and took us with him to church on Sunday. He has not changed in his love for me or for our children or our grandchildren. Church is still very important to our entire family. God found me in my desperation and provided for my needs. This miraculous step in my spiritual journey was truly ordained by Deity!

Day 1
Running Away on a Dead End Road

Session 1 concluded with a prayer expressing a desire to know our Lord more intimately. In Jeremiah 24:7, we are told that God will give us a heart to know him. Let's begin by embracing that truth and understanding our role in the relationship. Jesus tells us how to interact with Him in Matthew 7:7–8 (NKJV).

> Ask, and it will be given to you; seek, and you will find; knock, and it will be opened to you. For everyone who asks receives, and he who seeks finds, and to him who knocks it will be opened.

I challenge you to ask, seek, and knock throughout each session. As you work through your daily assignments, ask the Holy Spirit to give you answers to your questions, help you find the direction you need, and open the areas of your mind and heart with truth. You will be asking for good things from Him, and He will answer. Jesus goes on to tell us in Matthew 7:9–11 (NKJV) that God loves his children and responds to them as their Father.

> What man is there among you who, if his son asks for bread, will give him a stone? Or if he asks for a fish, will he give him a serpent? If you then, being evil, know how to give good gifts to your children, how much more will your Father who is in heaven give good things to those who ask Him.

As we study our characters for this week, keep in mind that we are looking for the visible work of our invisible God. In this session, we will see how God made himself known to Moses and Hagar. Both were significant people in the plans and purposes of God. Today, we begin with Moses—the man God chose to deliver His people, the Israelites, from slavery in Egypt. Exodus 1:1 tells us the children of Israel had come to Egypt. Before we meet our character, Moses, it is important that we find out why the Israelites had come to Egypt.

Read Genesis 42:1–7 and answer the questions.

- Where had they come from? _____

- Why did they go to Egypt? _____

- Who is Joseph in this text? _____

We are told in Exodus 1 that the generation of Joseph and his brothers had died, but their descendants had remained fruitful and increased in strength and numbers. A new king took over Egypt and saw their potential. He set taskmasters over them to afflict them with hard labor. The Israelites continued to multiply, and the king of Egypt perceived them as a threat. He attempted to stifle their fruitfulness by ordering the Hebrew midwives to kill all male babies as soon as they were born. The midwives did not obey the king because their fear of him was surpassed by their fear of God. The Israelites continued to multiply and grow in strength. The king's fear of their potential also grew into a final command to eliminate them. He issued a decree to kill all male children by drowning them in the Nile River (Exodus 1:22).

God's chosen people, the Israelites, who had been established in the land of Canaan, ended up in much worse condition than they were in during the physical famine. They were being forced to watch the death of their own nation as each male child was murdered. Their only hope was for their God to come on the scene. They needed a deliverer desperately. God saw their bondage and heard their cries. God sent their deliverer, *Moses*, from the tribe of Levi.

In Exodus 2:1–10, we are told how Moses came on the scene. God used the same river to bring deliverance as Pharaoh did to bring death. Moses' birth and placement in the palace was the intentional providence of *El-Elyon, the God Most High,* the Redeemer of Israel (Psalm 78:35).

Our next look at Moses is outside the walls of the palace. Exodus 2:11–14 describes how Moses experienced the invisible hand of God. In Acts 7:22–29, we see how Moses discovered the truth of his own nationality. Moses, having been raised within the king's palace, was "educated in all the wisdom of the Egyptians, and was powerful in speech and actions." He would have read about Joseph, the Hebrew, who was second to Pharaoh in power over Egypt. He would have known the history of the Israelites and how a famine in Canaan had forced them to come to Egypt, resulting in the reunion of Joseph with his father, Jacob, and his brothers. Moses had probably read the last words Joseph spoke to his brothers, "I am about to die. But God will surely come to your aid and take you up out of this land to the land he promised on oath to Abraham, Isaac, and Jacob" (Genesis 50:24). If he knew all this, then he knew who he was.

We also learn in Acts 7:23 that "when Moses was forty years old, he decided to visit his fellow Israelites."[10] That visit was a turning point in Moses' life. He defended his own people because he assumed his brethren would recognize him as God's deliverer for them.

> Moses boldly owned the cause of God's people. It is plain from Hebrews 11 that this was done in faith, with the full purpose of leaving the honors, wealth, and pleasures of his rank among the Egyptians. By the grace of God he was a partaker of faith in Christ, which overcomes the world. He was willing, not only to risk all, but to suffer for his sake; being assured that Israel were the people of God.[11]

Read Hebrews 11:24–25 (NIV) and fill in the blanks.

- "By _____ Moses, when he had grown up, refused to be known as the _____ of Pharaoh's daughter. He _____ to be mistreated along with the people of God rather than to enjoy the pleasures of _____ for a short time."

In Exodus 2:13–14, we see God use the words of Moses' own people to push him out of the palace for good.

- What were their words? _____

- What was Moses' reaction? _____

- What were Moses' thoughts? _____

That event brought Moses to a dead-end road as a prince of Egypt. He would soon become a priest for his people. The providence of God in Moses' life was moving forward. God's providence is spread across humanity as He unfolds his purposes for His people. Listen to the words God spoke to Jeremiah: "Before I formed you in the womb I knew you, before you were born I set you apart; I appointed you as a prophet to the nations" (Jeremiah 1:5). God's purpose for Jeremiah was to be a prophet to all the nations. Let's look at the truths from these verses and apply them to ourselves.

"Before I formed you in the womb"—*Webster's* defines before as "in front, ahead, in advance; in the past; previously."

Fill in the blanks from Psalm 139:16.

"Your eyes saw my _____ body. All the days _____ for me were _____ in your book *before* _____ of them came to be."

"I set you apart"—The word *sanctification* comes from the word *sanctify*, which means to reserve for sacred use; to make holy, to set apart or separate unto God.

Who sets us apart? *Jehovah-mekoddishkem, the Lord Who Sanctifies You.*

"I appointed you"—The last part of Jeremiah 1:5 refers to the appointment of Jeremiah to the *position* of prophet to all the nations.

God positions you to use your gifts according to His purpose for your life. Just as God's thoughts of creation became a reality, so do His thoughts of us before we are formed in our mother's womb. Before God heard the cries of Israel, he was thinking of redemption for them and planned the call of Moses. You and I are in the very thoughts of God. Stop and think about that for a moment. Through salvation's gift, we are being sanctified—set apart for His sacred use. He has given us spiritual gifts to minister to the lost, needy, hurting, and desperate.

> When you accept Christ, you are given spiritual gifts to use in ministry to others.

Before we move on, it is important that you do the following exercises:

- On a separate sheet of paper, briefly list events in your life from early childhood to the present that you believe were the providence of God.

Example: Event—Attended VBS / Received Christ as Savior

- Also on a separate sheet of paper, list your spiritual gifts (if known).

- If you are presently using your spiritual gifts in the church, list where God has appointed you: _____

- There are many online resources available to learn more about your spiritual gifts.

Recently, I ran across this awesome quote by Matthew Henry. "Duty is ours—events are God's."[12] Let's meditate on this profound truth a moment. What did those strong words say to you? I am reminded of how often I've tried to orchestrate events in my life and then expected God to make them fit my desires. I had things backward. God will bring us His plans. Our duty is to follow them.

As we close today, meditate on this beautiful truth:

You were the invisible thoughts of God, made visible by His hands. You are set apart by His Spirit, appointed to fulfill His plans.

See you tomorrow at the well of Midian!

Day 2
Running in to God

Yesterday, we looked at the early events of Moses' life and saw the protecting hand of God. Moses was chosen by God to bring about the deliverance of His people from their harsh and cruel bondage in Egypt. Their deliverer would be one of their own, from the tribe of Levi. This tribe would later be designated by God to be set apart and serve as priests to the nation of Israel. The day ended with abrupt changes in Moses' life. Reread Exodus 2:13–15, and then answer the following questions.

- Who tried to kill Moses? _____

- What course of action did Moses take? _____

- Where did Moses end up? _____

Moses, a prince of Egypt, ran away from the consequences of his actions right into the providence of God. Moses, the murderer, is now positioned at the well of Midian. Scripture does not include the details of Moses' journey from Egypt to Midian, but you and I can imagine some of his thoughts. What do you think Moses might have been thinking?

I think Moses was forced, probably for the first time, to deal with guilt and self-condemnation. Imagine him dealing with thirst and exhaustion as he approached the well. Moses, the prince, left power and position and wandered into the unknown as a hopeless and confused alien. The possibility of Moses becoming the next Pharaoh of Egypt was gone. Moses had one goal: to survive. God had a different plan for Moses, one that had been settled before Moses was born. Moses would be more than a prince. He would be a priest of the Most High God. I like Matthew Henry's description of Moses.

"Many who, by their birth, are obscure and poor, by surprising events of Providence, are raised high in the world to make men know that God rules."[13]

Moses wandered a great distance in the desert and ended up at the well of Midian. Awaiting Moses was a test of his "temper." Would he react the same way *this* time?

Read Exodus 2:16–22, and fill in the blanks.

- This time, Moses came to the defense of _____.

- This time, Moses drew _____ for them and their _____.

- This time, Moses was rewarded with an invitation to _____.

God is so amazing! He is always in control. He knew Moses better than Moses knew himself. He knew Moses was ready for a "do-over." He orchestrated the event and the timing for Moses. Moses was given an opportunity to do what was right, and he did it.

Isn't it a good feeling to get it right? Aren't you glad we get "do-overs?" I believe every "do-over" I have been given is a blessing from God. God blessed Moses with a "do-over." It came in the way of a "temper test." God knew this was the best place to start with Moses. He knew Moses was ready to do things differently. He loved Moses when he was a murderer just as much as he did when Moses was a hero. God generously blessed Moses with a new family, a wife, and to top it off, a son. God did all this before Moses knew Him personally … as His God.

Without failures and mistakes, there would be no need for "do-overs." God made us with tempers. Without the Holy Spirit's guidance, our tempers can get us in more trouble than we can handle. God will use consequences to transform our tempers into usable strength. Then He will provide a "do-over" in the places we have failed because of our tempers. I like to call it the "temper test." We either pass or fail. As believers, we get to study and learn through the Word of God, the guidance of the Holy Spirit, and the counsel of others. We can avoid the "temper test" by applying the truths we learn.

According to *Webster's*, *temper*, as a verb, means to make less intense, to make hard, as steel. As a noun, the meaning changes to a state of mind, self-control, rage.

- Based on these definitions, which would accurately describe Moses' temper fit in Egypt?

  _____

I've had "temper fits" when I didn't get my way or when someone hurt me. The results were damaging, and some were irreversible, like those from Moses'. God used circumstances to "temper" (the verb) Moses. He used the *consequences* to bridle his "temper" (the noun) and increase his patience. God desires for us to be a people who are "temperate," which, according to the *American Heritage Dictionary*, means "exercising moderation and self-restraint."

Let's look at two verses we need to remember when we experience a "temper test."

Fill in the blanks in these verses:

- Proverbs 29:11: "A _____ gives full vent to his _____, but a _____ man keeps himself under _____."

- James 1:19–20: "My dear brothers, take note of this: Everyone should be quick to _____, slow to _____ and slow to become _____, for man's anger does not bring about the _____ life that God desires."

Here are a few sensitive questions for you to consider and answer.

- Have you had a "temper fit" that brought severe consequences?

- If yes, what ignited your temper?

  _____

- What were the consequences?

  _____

- If God gave you a "do-over," what was it, and what were the results?

  _____

  _____

- How do you feel about that incident today?

_____

My temper fits have brought seasons of drought along with an unquenchable thirst for love and acceptance. My past forced me to wander until I came upon the well of God's provision. I am so glad my Lord brought me to His well of love and acceptance. He also knew I needed the love and acceptance Ken would provide long before I even knew or loved him. Moses needed the same things we all need: *love and acceptance*. God demonstrated his love and acceptance to Moses throughout his entire life. He protected Moses as a baby, as a prince, and as a murderer wandering through the desert all the way to that well. God's provision of blessings began at that well for Moses. He also knew Moses needed the love and acceptance Zipporah would provide long before he ever knew or loved her.

The American Heritage Dictionary defines well when used as a noun as "a deep hole in the earth to obtain water or oil; a spring; fountains; a source to be drawn upon. God's "well" provided a fresh start and a new chapter in Moses' life.

> He is Jehoval-jireh: The Lord Who Provides.

Meditate on the words of Isaiah 43:19.

> "See, I am doing a new thing! Now it springs up; do you not perceive it? I am making a way in the desert and streams in the wasteland."

- Reflect on the definition of *well*. What does Isaiah 43:19 say to you?

_____

- Have you wandered upon a "well of God's provision" for your life? If you have, briefly write the reason for your wandering and the provision God gave you at His well.

_____

If you have not experienced His "well of provision," spend a few minutes asking the Lord to fulfill His Word in your life. Pour out your heart to Him, and give Him your temper or inability to trust Him. Thank Him for hearing your prayer. He intimately knows you and loves you more than you can comprehend. Allow Him to love and guide you, just as He did Moses. If you have experienced the refreshing "well of His provision," spend a few minutes in praise and thanksgiving for His goodness and tender mercy. Boldly acknowledge Him as your *Jehovah-jireh, the Lord Who Provides.*

See you tomorrow at the tent of Abraham and Sarah!

℘

Day 3
Running Ahead of God

Today, we will look at our second character for this week's study: Hagar, the Egyptian maidservant of Abraham's wife, Sarah. To better understand the story of Hagar, we need to look briefly into the lives of her masters, Abraham and Sarah. The story opens with Abraham and Sarah on a journey. They weren't *wandering* according to *Webster's* definition, which is "to roam idly about." They were moving according to the instructions of the Lord. Let's look closer at the Lord's instructions.

Fill in the blanks in Genesis 12:1.

- "The Lord had said to Abram, 'Leave your _____, your _____ and your father's household and go to the _____ I will _____you.'"

Abraham and Sarah's birth names were Abram and Sarai. God changed their names in Genesis 17:5 and 15.

Fill in the blanks in these verses.

- Verse 5: "No longer will you be called _____; your name will be Abraham, for I have made you a _____ of many _____."

- Verse 15: "As for Sarai your wife, you are no longer to call her _____; her name will be Sarah."

On day 5 of session 1, we looked closely at the events of God's promise unfolding in the lives of Abraham and Sarah. God said they would have a son, and they did. What was impossible for man was possible with God. Our character in this session comes on the scene before the promised son, Isaac, is conceived. The same providential hand of God that drew Hagar into the tents of Sarai and Abram drew Moses from the Nile into the Egyptian palace.

Read Genesis 16:1–6, and then answer the following questions:

- Who did Sarai blame for her not having children?

  _____

- What was Sarai's plan to have a child?

  _____

  _____

- When Hagar knew she was pregnant, she _____ Sarai.

- Whom did Sarai blame for the wrong she was suffering?

  _____

- How did Abraham handle Sarai's complaint?

  _____

- Why did Hagar run away?

  _____

Hagar became Abram's concubine. Even though this was acceptable and legal in the ancient Near East to ensure a male heir, it still violated the Creator's plan for marriage.[14] God's plan for marriage is very clear in Genesis 2:24: "For this reason a man will leave his father and mother and be united to his wife, and they will become one flesh." Hagar's "position" as Sarai's personal maidservant reflected honor, obedience, and trustworthiness. However, this "position" stripped her of all personal rights, making her totally subject to Sarai's every wish.

As Abram's child grew within Hagar, things began to change. Her position as Sarai's maidservant no longer made her feel good. Maybe she began to focus more on herself, her relationship with Abram, and their child. You can image the looks, thoughts, and emotions that arose between these two women. There is no rage like jealous rage. The bigger Hagar grew with child, the worse things got around the tents of Abram. Finally, Hagar went too far, and Sarai went to Abram. He gave her permission to do as she pleased with Hagar. We are told in (Genesis 16:6, NKJV) that Sarai dealt harshly with her, and Hagar fled from her presence.

Let's examine the treatment of Hagar.

The word _mistreated_ is used in the New International Version and _harshly_ is used in the New King James Version to describe how Sarai dealt with Hagar. _Webster's_ defines _harsh_ as "unpleasant, especially to the sense of hearing; extremely severe or exacting; stern." _Webster's_ defines _mistreat_ as "to abuse."

Nothing has hurt me more deeply than harsh words. I have even experienced harsh words along with a slap across the face. When I put the two definitions together, I visualize Sarai saying very hurtful words to Hagar and attacking her physically. Think about this scene. Let your imagination work for a moment and put into words the visual you get of Sarai's treatment of Hagar:

_____

_____

Harshly spoken words can deeply wound us.

Fill in the blanks.

- James 3:8: "No man can _____ the tongue. It is a restless _____, full of deadly _____."

Kind words spoken can help our anxiousness.

Fill in the blanks:

- Proverbs 12:25: "An anxious heart _____ a man down, but a kind word _____ him up."

Words from the Lord give direction and understanding.

Fill in the blanks:

- Psalms 119:130: "The unfolding of your _____ gives light; it gives _____ to the simple."

Hagar ran away from the terrible encounter with Sarai and ended up in the desert. Read Genesis 16:7–12, and then answer the following questions:

- Who finds Hagar? _____

- What two questions does he ask her?

1. _____

2. _____

I don't think Hagar would have intentionally run into the desert. Anger and hurt often blind us and prevent us from seeing the right path. But God knew what was going on in Hagar's life. If you are like me, sometimes in the midst of difficult circumstances, I lose sight of the fact that God knows all that pertains to me. Did you wonder why the angel asks her the two questions written in verse 8? Matthew Henry's commentary gives us great insight.

> Hagar was out of her place, and out of the way of her duty, and going further astray, when the Angel found her. It is a great mercy to be stopped in a sinful path, either by conscience or by providence. She had privileges in Abram's tent. It was good for her to live with a religious family, which was to her advantage. If she went back to Egypt, she would return to idol gods, and into danger in the wilderness through which she must travel.[15]

He gave direction rather than condemning her for running away.

Fill in the blanks in verse 9.

- "Then the angel of the Lord told her, 'Go _____ to your mistress and _____ to her.'"

The angel of the Lord encouraged her with a promise of a future.

Fill in the blanks in verse 10.

- "The angel added, 'I will so _____ your descendants that they will be too numerous to count.'"

The angel of the Lord acknowledged her child and her misery.

Fill in the blanks in verse 11.

- "The angel of the Lord also said to her, 'You are now with child and you will have a _____. You shall name him Ishmael, for the Lord has _____ of your misery.'"

If you didn't notice, let me point out the two words, "I will," spoken by the angel of the Lord. This declaration of the angel of the Lord shows this Angel was the eternal Word and Son of God.[16] Imagine an Egyptian servant being visited by the Lord.

Have you ever run away from some hurt and gotten off the right path? If you have, dear friend, give your hurt to Jesus. He knows where you have been and where you are headed. Close in prayer, giving Him everything and returning to your place with Him.

Write out your prayer:

_____

_____

_____

Tomorrow, Hagar will introduce us to the Lord Who Sees—El Roi!

Day 4
Rescued by God

Let's reflect a moment on the wounding of Hagar. I imagine blinding tears that caused her to stumble as she ran down the road that led to Shur. She is emotionally drained and physically exhausted. She slows down and turns off the road to drink from a nearby spring. Before she can quench her thirst, she meets the Living Water and He quenches the rage within her heart. Hagar's encounter with the Angel of the Lord should make us aware of God's concern for us. Dear sisters, take comfort in knowing that He is not a God of partiality. He *does hear* our cries of misery, and he *does see* our situation. He *does come* to our rescue with words of consolation and direction.

Our last look at Hagar's situation was encouraging. All of us have run away from *something* or *someone*. Maybe it was in our past, or maybe it is happening today. Whichever, all of us know to some degree what Hagar felt like in that desert. It's devastating physically and emotionally. Until I allowed El Roi to rescue me from my past and calm my present, I too ran away from people and situations. Like Hagar, I would run away from Godly people and places. I ran right into the hands of the wrong people, getting myself into situations that added to my low self-esteem and bottomless pit of pain. The last person Hagar wanted to see or talk to was Sarai. Before we move on, we must address the fact that Hagar's wounds were more than likely prompted by her actions toward Sarai. As always, a review of the text will provide the truth.

Read Genesis 16:3–6. Fill in the blanks in verses 4 and 5.

- "When she _____ she was pregnant, she began to _____ her mistress."

- Then Sarai said to Abram, "You are responsible for the _____ I am _____. I put my servant in your arms, and now that she _____ she is pregnant, she _____ me. May the LORD _____ between you and me."

Sarai was provoked by Hagar. To despise someone means to treat him or her with contempt or scorn. The word *despise* used in this verse takes on a stronger meaning in the transliteration of the Hebrew word *kaw-lal*.[17] It means to be trifling or to curse. God heard every word spoken. He knew every thought. He saw deep into both of their hearts and knew their motives. Jesus appeared in the form of an angel to Hagar. He didn't condemn her. He corrected Hagar and then gave her directions that would reconcile the situation between her and Sarai.[18]

This is how Jesus works in our lives and our relationships. He always shows up when we are ready to listen to him. As we willingly receive His words, our eyes behold truth—the truth of who He is and what He requires of us.

Read verse 15, and fill in the blanks.

- "So Hagar bore Abram a _____, and _____ gave the name _____ to the son she had borne."

It is obvious that Hagar obeyed the Lord and went back to her position in the tents of Abram. Sometimes people and situations invade our lives, and we become victims of abuse. The enemy will use our victimization to mislead us into doing or believing things that can push us into a crisis. The truth is this: unless God intervenes, we are doomed. Moses' unbridled temper pushed him further than he intended to go. The same thing happened to Hagar. Being a maidservant to Sarai was nothing compared to being a surrogate mother. Hagar may have appeared willing, but on the inside, she was devastated. Then with the passing of time, she discovered she was pregnant, and her hurt and anger exploded on Sarai.

Here is a snapshot from my past that in some ways is parallel with Hagar's. I was tired and in need of a "refreshing encounter" from the Lord.

> Several years ago, I was called upon to take care of my dear aunt Sissie (my father's sister). She had experienced three serious health problems in a short period of time. Since she lived in another town, I had to be away from home for long periods of time. My third stay with her was the most difficult and began taking a toll on me physically, emotionally, and spiritually. I began to embrace self-pity. This harmful emotion greatly affected my relationship with my Lord. I pulled away instead of clinging to the One who could refresh and strengthen me for the task at hand. Adding to this trying time, my aunt spent a month in the hospital with an extremely contagious infection. The stress intensified, and I wanted to run away. During this time, as I resentfully sat with my aunt, Jehovah-jireh, the Lord Who Provides, began to move. As I sat in the hospital, I overheard my aunt's friend talking about a woman who had just been admitted to the intensive care unit of the hospital. The woman she spoke of was a woman I knew from high school. Immediately, I went to the ICU and asked if I could see her. Amazingly, I was allowed to visit with her for five minutes. During those five minutes, God began His refreshing. I visited her every day until she went home. My time with this woman was definitely ordained by God. As she recovered physically, I recovered spiritually. She left the hospital and was taken back to a local nursing home. She had cerebral palsy, which restricted her to a wheelchair. She required full-time assistance. During my stay with my aunt, I visited her often. In that season of both of our lives, God used two weak vessels to strengthen and refresh each other. My friend's love for God and His Word poured on me like a spring of cool water. I've continued to visit her and cherish our special friendship. She calls me her "Timothy," and I call her my "Paul." God's purpose was to redirect my focus back to Him. Like He did with Hagar, He rescued me from myself. Jesus gently corrected me, gave me direction, and refreshed me so I could continue to care for my dear aunt. This was God's call on my life for that season, and I am grateful.

Please take few minutes to answer the following questions.

- Do you feel trapped, overwhelmed by guilt, or victimized by the hands of another? Do you need God to rescue you? Do you want Him to do something today?

If you answered "yes" to any of the questions, I want to encourage you to give it to Jesus right now. I strongly encourage you to do the following: find a private, quiet place where you can get alone with Jesus and read Psalm 46:10. Let's focus on the first line: "Be *still* and *know* that I am God." Meditate on the meaning of the words *still* and *know*. *Still* means "to relax, sink down, be quiet," while *know* means "to know, to learn to know, to perceive, to see, know by experience, to be instructed."[19] Acknowledge Him as your *El Roi, your God who sees* you inside and out. Acknowledge Him as your

Jehovah-jireh, your Lord who provides. Pour out your heart, telling Him your needs. Agree to do whatever He directs you to do. Thank Him for hearing your prayer.

Let's close our session today by being still a few more minutes before our God, expressing our gratitude and praising Him for who He is. You may want to sing to Him. He loves to hear us sing "Jesus Loves Me."

See you tomorrow for one more look at Hagar!

꿀

Day 5
No Longer Wandering

Have you enjoyed studying the lives of Moses and Hagar? When the Holy Spirit first brought their names to my mind as the characters for this week, I wondered what He was going to show us from the lives of such different people. I hope you have been blessed this week as much as I have.

This session has been about sanctification, the second step of our spiritual journey. Proverbs 5:21 tells us that "a man's ways are in full view of the Lord, and he examines all his paths." As long as we live on this earth as God's children, we will be moved along the spiritual path of sanctification. In 1 Thessalonians 5:23–24, we are told that "God himself, the God of peace, sanctifies us through and through making our whole spirit, soul, and body blameless at the coming of Jesus. The one who calls you is faithful and he will do it."

The second spiritual marker is entitled "The Wandering" because that is exactly what I did from the time I accepted Christ until I got involved in church. The definition of *wander* is to move about aimlessly or with no destination or purpose; to roam; or to stray from a given place, path, group, or subject. My personal definition of "involved" is faithful attendance and participation in the local church by ministering to the body of Christ and reaching out to the lost. According to 1 Thessalonians 5:23–24, we can be sure that God takes care of the sanctification process. The process did not become visible to me until I stopped wandering and became regularly involved in church.

How did I know God was working in me? Beginning with my salvation, I had always thought about Him. I talked to Him, asking questions and sharing my heart. I didn't realize I was praying until years later. People who knew the Bible and loved Jesus were like magnets that drew me to them. I never doubted my salvation experience. But I did doubt that Jesus would allow me to be as close to Him as others seemed to be. I attended several different churches for short periods of time before I married. I would go with friends and, on special occasions, with my Aunt Sissie.

From the time of my salvation until I married Ken, often the steps I took placed me on paths that brought relational dead ends, trouble, and heartache. My life was severely scarred from wounds I received during that time. Many times, I was like Moses and Hagar, running away from the consequences of my own actions or the wounds from someone else. At the time, I didn't realize it, but God was using all the paths I took and all the problems I experienced to put my feet on a level path with Him.

Day 1: Running Away on a Dead-End Road

Moses was brought to a place in his life that challenged who he really was. Could he remain in the palace of Pharaoh and defend the harsh treatment of his people, the Israelites? Even though Moses committed murder, God used it to end Moses' position as a prince of Egypt. This dead-end road forced Moses to take a different direction.

In your spiritual life, have you been going in a direction that seems to take you in circles or has become a dead end? Sometimes we follow our own voices or the voice of someone else. The Lord wants us to follow His voice. Jesus used the term *sheep* metaphorically to represent "those who belong to the Lord."[20] Fill in the blanks in John 10:27–28.

- "My sheep listen to my _____; I _____ them, and they follow me. I give them _____ life, and they shall never _____; no one can snatch them out of my _____."

Moses entered the palace as a baby drawn from the waters of the Nile River. He left the palace a fugitive and wandered in the desert until the providential hand of God drew him to a well. Have you been moved to a new place physically or spiritually and you don't understand why? If so, think about where you are now. Just as Moses saw the purpose of his move, you can be sure you will too.

Day 2: Running into God

On day 2, we focused on the circumstances that removed Moses from the palace and took him far away to the well of God's provision. God knew that Moses had a quick temper. He also knew what it would take to unleash the deep rage within him. The consequences of Moses' "temper fit" took him farther than he ever imagined. Moses found a new beginning at the well of Midian. The first two things he did there were very important. They were the very things God would call Moses to do for the rest of his life.

Read Exodus 2:15–21, and answer the following questions.

- What was Moses doing when shepherds attempted to drive away the daughters of Reuel from the well?

  _____

- What two actions did Moses take?

  _____

- What did Reuel do for Moses?

  _____

Moses was given more than just a "do-over." He was introduced to priesthood. The actions of Reuel, the priest of Midian, demonstrated the love and acceptance of God. Even though he was told Moses was an Egyptian, He graciously invited him into his home. Moses was provided the same things we are to live the abundant life. God provides us with the "living water," meaning the Holy Spirit and others to help us stay on God's path for our lives. God first provided Moses with water at the well of Midian. Then He used Reuel to provide him with food, a home, a job, and a wife. To top off the blessing basket, God gave Moses a son. Instead of God giving Moses what he deserved, He showered him with love and acceptance. It is a beautiful picture of God's mercy.

I suspect that while Moses wandered in the desert, he made peace with the God of his people. When the daughters of Reuel saw Moses, they assumed he was an Egyptian because of his clothes, but his actions revealed who he had become. Moses was a changed man—changed by the providential hand of his God.

God will always provide a well of provision for us. Jesus, the Living Water, will quench our thirsty soul. The body of Christ, the church, is like a home that provides loving acceptance and spiritual food for spiritual strength.

Read Exodus 3:1–10, and answer the following questions:

- Who spoke to Moses?

  _____

- What was the Lord concerned about?

  _____

- What was the Lord going to do?

  _____

- Who was God sending to bring them out of Egypt?

  _____

And the end of the story, Moses obeyed God, and the Israelites were delivered. As they began their journey with God, Moses and the Israelites sang to the Lord a song of praise and thanksgiving for His mighty deliverance from the Egyptians. We must not forget that we, too, have been delivered from the penalty of sin, and we, too, are on a journey with God. So, let's sing a song of praise and thanksgiving to our Lord using a verse from the song Moses and the Israelites sang. Make up your own notes and have a great time of worship!

> "In your unfailing love you will lead the people you have redeemed. In your strength you will guide them to your holy dwelling" (Exodus 15:13).

Day 3: Running ahead of God

Sometimes life takes us into the lives of people we think are wonderful only to find out later that they are not who we thought they were. Hagar had been with Sarai for a while, and as far as we know, Sarai trusted her. When Sarai placed Hagar in Abram's tent, the results were devastating, and unbelief was exposed. Sarai lost hope in God and chose to believe she could not have children. Her actions were the result of disappointment. Abram did not argue with Sarai but chose to simply agree. Hagar was not given a choice. "Unbelief worked, God's almighty power was forgotten."[21]

The three had been set up for a fight. The day came for the fuse to be ignited. Hagar may have felt overwhelmed with the burden of responsibility that had been placed upon her. She may have already begun to experience morning sickness. Everyone may have been congratulating Sarai and Abram, leaving Hagar feeling even worse. Wasn't she the real mother?

Have you ever been in a triangle that took a huge toll on everyone involved? If God brought a situation to your mind as you read this, I encourage you to pray about it and trust God to help you do the right thing. The following verses are instructions that will help in situations like this.

Fill in the blanks.

- 2 Timothy 2:24: "The Lord's _____ must not _____; instead, he must be kind to everyone, able to teach, not resentful."

- Colossians 3:13: "Bear with each other and _____ whatever _____ you may have against one another."

- Ephesians 4:32: "Be _____ and _____ to one another, _____ each other, just as in Christ _____ forgave _____.

41

- Matthew 6:14: "For if _____ forgive men when _____ sin against you, your heavenly Father will also _____ you."

Make sure all wounds in any relationships have been addressed and settled. If those you need to talk with are deceased, you can still settle the past in the right way. Choose a time and place you can be alone. Sit before the Lord and acknowledge your actions and the actions of others. Agree with the Lord about the sin, and ask Him to heal the wounds and provide the peace. When you have finished, write your activities and thoughts in your journal. It will make a huge difference in the days ahead. Remember: *Jehovah-shalom, the Lord of Peace*, is with you.

Day 4: Rescued by God

Let's begin with a recap of Hagar's instructions. She is told to go back to the tents of Abram and submit to Sarai. Before she departs the place of holy ground, she acknowledges that she has seen the God of Abram and He has seen her. It is at that moment she gives Him the name El Roi, meaning "the God Who Sees." It's apparent that Hagar shared her encounter with the angel of the Lord with Abram since Scripture tells us in Genesis 16:15 that "Hagar bore Abram a son, and Abram gave the name Ishmael to the son she had borne." Before we move forward to the final episode of Hagar's life within the tents of Abram, we must look at a very important change God makes in the lives of Abram and Sarai.

Read Genesis 17:1–16, and record your thoughts to this question:

- Why did God change Abram's and Sarai's names?

_____

Matthew Henry offers great insight into this act of God. "The covenant was to be accomplished in due time. The promised Seed was Christ and Christians in Him. And all who are of faith are blessed with faithful Abram, being partakers of the same covenant blessings. In token of this covenant, his name was changed from Abram, "a high father," to Abraham, "the father of a multitude.""[22]

I can't move on until I focus on the beauty of verses 15 and 16. Imagine the state Abraham was in by the time God Almighty concluded verse 14. At the close of those dynamic verses of "I will," I can imagine the ninety-nine-year-old Abraham full of emotion, yet deep inside overwhelmed with questions—especially about the long-awaited child for him and Sarai. Then his thoughts are interrupted as God begins with "as for Sarai your wife" and changes her name to Sarah followed by "I will bless her" and "will surely give you" a son by her. He closes with this beautiful blessing for Sarah as He defines her name: "I will bless her so that she will be the mother of nations; kings of peoples will come from her."

Now, let's move on and examine the final wounds between these two strong women that changed the life course of Hagar and her son. Read Genesis 21:1–21, and answer the following questions:

- What did Sarah see that upset her with Ishmael?

_____

- What did God tell Abraham to do?

_____

- Where was Hagar when she encountered the angel of God?

  _____

- What did he tell Hagar to do?

  _____

- Who opened Hagar's eyes, and what did she see?

  _____

This encounter was worse than the first one. This time, the wounding targeted Isaac. Hagar wounded Sarah twice; she wounded her personally the first time, and then she wounded Sarah's son. Hagar's wounding of others backfired on her more severely this time. _Wounded_ people _wound_ people. Instead of taking our wounds to God, we often continue in a cycle of wounding and being wounded. We seem to focus on the pain rather than a remedy. I really like the way Matthew Henry describes this cycle:

God is always willing to provide a remedy for our wandering and our wounds. If you are trapped in a cycle of wandering and wounding, pray right now for El Roi, the God Who Sees, to open your eyes to see and receive His provision.

> "Many who have reason to be comforted, go mourning from day to day, because they do not see the reason they have for comfort. There is a well of water near them in the covenant of grace, but they are not aware of it, till the same God that opened their eyes to see their wound, opens them to see their remedy" (Henry, 39).

I have enjoyed this week and hope you have too. Get ready for a journey through the lives of Joseph and Abigail!

Father,

You are the invisible God, who provides encouragement and direction to your wandering children. Help us embrace Your sanctifying power that lives within us and transforms us as Paul penned in 2 Corinthians 5:17, "Therefore, if anyone is in Christ, he is a new creation; the old has gone, the new has come!"

I pray this in the name above all names, Jesus Christ, the Son of God.

Session 3

Spiritual Marker #3
"The Preparation"

In session 2, we began looking at the meaning of sanctification, God's progressive deliverance of a believer from sin's power. Our daily assignments provided an in-depth look into the lives of Moses and Hagar. We learned that regardless of the reason for our "wandering" or where it takes us, God wants to come and rescue us. We must be willing to face the truth of our situation and confess our mistakes. We must believe that God will forgive us, refresh us, and restore us for His purposes. We saw Him do this in the lives of Moses and Hagar. He has done this for me many times, and He will do it for you. His "well of provision" never dries up.

God is committed to delivering us from sin's power through sanctification. My early years were filled with guilt from continual stumbles into sin. I felt defeated because I thought *I* was totally responsible for cleaning up my act. I did not know that the *Holy Spirit*, who lived inside me, would clean up my act *for me*. He would wash me with forgiveness from head to toe every time I fell into the dark and dirty trenches of life. He would never refuse His forgiveness as long as I came to Him seeking it. Even though my past was like a wall keeping me from getting closer to Him, I knew deep inside that He was pursuing me.

Ephesians 5:26 explains the process used by the Holy Spirit to clean the dark and dirty places in our lives. This verse explains the purpose of cleansing, which is to make us holy. The more you and I choose to trust and obey His Word, the more the Holy Spirit empowers us to live holy lives. You could simply say that as He washes us over and over again with the truth of His Word, we become cleaner and cleaner. We will be perfectly clean, sparkling white and radiantly beautiful in holiness when we meet Jesus face-to-face.

I love the comparison in Ephesians 5:8 that describes us as children who were once *darkness* but who are now *light* in the Lord. Therefore, we are to "walk as children of light."[23] The Greek word for *darkness* in this verse is *skotos* meaning both moral and spiritual darkness. The Greek word for *light* is *phos*, meaning to shine or to make manifest, especially by rays. Man, naturally, is incapable of receiving spiritual light in as much as he lacks the capacity for spiritual things (1 Corinthians 2:14). For this reason, believers are called "sons of light" (Luke 16:8), not merely because they have received a revelation from God, but because in the New Birth (salvation), they have received the spiritual capacity for it.[24]

We *are* light. We have the capacity to see and comprehend spiritual truths. We also have the capacity to help others see spiritually. The book of John tells us that John the Baptist was sent from God to bear witness of the Light and that all, through Him, might believe. That Light was the Word, the Son of God, Jesus. He is the true Light, who gives light to every person (John 1:6–9).

"The Son is able to create His own image in anyone and everyone."[25]

As we allow the Holy Spirit to control our lives, we can expect changes in our position within the body of Christ. We will begin to move from *spectator to participant*. I've learned over the years that He will prepare us for ministry within the body of Christ. Sometimes, a strong desire to do something in our church fills our minds to the degree that we are compelled to talk with our pastor or a wise friend. This is how God moved me into starting a mentoring ministry in my church. Other times, He brought assignments to me through close relationships in my home and church. My pastor strongly encouraged me to write this study. Over the years, I have learned that He assigns us the very thing that will take us strides in the classroom of sanctification. I've also learned that He will either prepare you prior to a new assignment or during it. Either way, He will do a new work in your life, and he will prepare you accordingly.

My Spiritual Journey—Third Step: Sanctification's Preparation

My new life with Ken was wonderful. In the early months of our marriage, I would daydream of Ken and think about how lucky I was. The same question always interrupted those moments, "How in the world did I get Ken Dempsey?" I would answer myself every time with the same sad conclusion, "Surely, it was luck, because if he really knew me, he wouldn't have married me." I worked so hard to be perfect in front of him. Before long, I began to look forward to times when I was alone and could just be the real Nancy. Have you ever been there? You know that eventually the real you will come forth. Jealousy will expose us every time. I will never forget our first fight. It is still painful when I think about it because we were both wounded deeply. That particular fight abruptly ended our honeymoon season and cast us into the most difficult season of adjustments we would ever encounter. I now know had we not been in church at the time, we could have destroyed each other and greatly hurt two precious little boys.

Throughout our marriage, difficulties have taken their toll, but we have never allowed them to stifle our love for each other or our love for our Lord. There have also been times of difficulties within our church that have taken a toll on the unity among our church family. In those times, our commitment to Christ and to each other sustained us through the troubled waters. When we accept Christ, we become His bride. We are told in Isaiah 54:5 that *our Maker is our husband*. "The LORD Almighty is His name."

When Christ came to earth in human form, He left His Father. When He began His earthly ministry and ultimately died on the cross, He left His mother. This was for the purpose of cleaving to the object of His love—His people. As He is received into the hearts of sinners, they become one flesh. The whole focus and course of a life is changed both by marriage and a personal experience with Jesus Christ. Marriage and becoming a child of God demand death to self and accountability to God and to others. In marriage, two hearts are grafted together, making each dependent on the other for life. Through the infilling of the Holy Spirit and His control in the life of both partners, this picture of marriage and the parallel relationship of Christ and His Bride come into focus. The Holy Spirit fills and fulfills both.[26]

When I accepted Jesus, I didn't know the full depth of my Savior's sacrifice and love for me, much less the marriage He and I would share. When I married as a teenager, I continued to struggle with spiritual questions and stumbled into places of sin. When Ken came into my life, Christ began to use him and the church to guide and teach me spiritual truths, especially who I was in Christ. Even while growing spiritually, I still made poor choices and bad habits beckoned my flesh to obey. Ken's strong resolve often pushed me when I was ready to give up. The "old Nancy" demanded my cooperation while the gentle voice of the Holy Spirit gave me continuous warnings as I slipped and fell again and again. Gradually, I began to resist more of the slippery places and walk more on paths of truth.

On July 25, 1977, Andrea Raye Dempsey claimed the hearts of her parents and two brothers. She brought into our home and our hearts a glow that was desperately needed. During the season of my life when I had David and Paul, I was excited but didn't fully understand that children were a gift from God. When I think back to those days, I'm overwhelmed with gratitude for the grace He showered on my life. There are still times when I think about our three children, and I am overwhelmed that God would trust Ken and me with such wonderful gifts from Him. I agree wholeheartedly with the words of James, the half brother of our Lord, "Every good and perfect gift is from above, coming down from the Father …" (James 1:17).

With the increase in our household, a hectic schedule was soon to follow. Ken and I served in many areas within the church, and our children participated in everything offered for them. I also worked a full-time job as a manager with AT&T. The more I served in the church, the more I disliked my job with AT&T. I didn't understand the battle going on between my spirit and my flesh. I soon became so troubled that I began to doubt my salvation experience. Before long, it all seemed to close in on me. My doubts soon birthed questioning of the "abundant life" Jesus told us about in John 10:10 (NASB): "The thief comes only to steal and kill and to destroy; I came that they may have life, and have it abundantly."

The Greek word for *abundantly* is *perissos*, meaning "what is superior and advantageous." I was so tired of "doing and being" everything I thought others, including Jesus, expected of me. Regardless of my best efforts, I always seemed to let someone down or sadly disappoint myself. To make my life even more miserable, I usually fell apart from the condemnation I felt sure was from God. After years of struggling with my walk with the Lord, I finally accepted the truth that something was either missing or seriously wrong with my relationship with Jesus. Others around me seemed to be experiencing wonderful adventures in their relationship with Jesus. As for me, I felt like it was a second job. Little did I know that through a large countywide revival, God would begin to renew me. Here He began moving me into a new season with Him and into a new place in ministry. On the third night of the revival, the Holy Spirit touched my aching heart and led me to the altar. I knew I was saved, but I knew something wasn't right and I needed Him to help me. As I cried out to Him, my faithful Jesus came to this prodigal daughter. At the time, I didn't know what He was doing, but I knew what I had to do. That night, I made Jesus the *Lord of my life* and humbly submitted my life to *His leadership*.

Immediately, my life began to change, and I embraced it with excitement and energy. My gray and gloomy days began to transform into a rainbow of hope. The first thing I noticed was a stronger desire to attend church and learn. My first assignment to serve was easy—I sang in the choir. I loved it! Soon afterward, He added to my places of service within the church. I began caring for the babies on Sundays. As a mother of three, I felt qualified and took on the care of these children with ease. About a year later, Ken accepted the position of director of children, and I was reassigned as the new Sunday school teacher for fourth-grade girls and boys. I really enjoyed working with this age group, especially since my lesson preparation required more study time. I prepared well, and we learned together. Often, I would leave knowing they had taught me more than I had taught them. It was during this assignment that God sent me to a type of boot camp where He did an "extreme makeover" in my life.

The minister of students asked me to attend youth camp as a counselor for the girls. I knew this was over my head, but if God wanted me to go, then I had to go! I was one of two counselors with my co-laborer, Tracey, who was young enough to be my daughter and spiritually mature enough to be my pastor's wife. God was there and showered blessings over the entire group from Meadowbrook Baptist Church. I will never forget it. That was the week in which I began to fully understand what it meant to make Him Lord. This trip did something new and different in my life. My quiet times with Him changed from being one-sided. I began to talk to Him differently and pour out my heart. As I read the Bible, I sensed Him revealing deeper truths. As I counseled the girls, He gave me scriptures that met their needs. Miraculous insight always came to my mind as I ministered to girls with deep hurts and problems. I could have stayed there forever! On the last day, I cried most of the way home.

The day after we returned home, Tracey called to tell me she had talked with her mom about our times together during the week and what a blessing I had been to her. I was astonished that she felt that way. She had been the one to bless me. She told me her mom wanted to meet me and asked if I could come over the next morning. I agreed and was inspired as soon as I met Tracey's mom, a strong Christian teacher and speaker named Benji Clark. God used Benji in a mighty way to bring me encouragement and stir my faith. I only met her one time. She prayed with me and gave me verses from Isaiah 60:1–4 and Isaiah 61:1–3, saying that God had impressed her to give them to me, and I was to mark them because they were my "call" verses. You will find these verses written for you in session 4. I didn't understand but accepted her words and the verses without question. That day and those words became permanent images in my mind. Take a moment to look up those precious verses in Isaiah and I am sure that you will be as blessed as I was the first time I read them. He knew what I wanted and what I needed. He knew the best way, the best time, and the best place to proclaim His call on my life. Years later, I realized the significance of my meeting with her. What she told me has, in fact, become my ministry. A dear pastor and friend, Mark Maulding, gave me these affirming words of truth, "If God said it, He will do it." Benji Clark was the vessel used to speak His call into my life. It was Jesus who set the course of my life that day!

An *encounter* with Jesus is never forgotten because of the eternal *mark* it leaves on your life.

Day 1
Unbridled Jealousy Breeds Rage

We concluded session 2 with a prayer asking God to help us embrace His sanctifying work in our lives. I've come to realize that the more I seek to know Him, the more I want to obey Him. The song "Trust and Obey" is one of my favorite songs. God used the first verse of this moving old hymn to draw me gently back to Him. I will share more details in a later session, but for now, I must tell you that over the years, each verse of that old hymn has been fleshed out in my life by the mighty hand of Jesus.

"Trust and Obey"

> When we walk with the Lord in the light of His word, what a glory He sheds on our way! While we do His good will, He abides with us still, and with all who will trust and obey. Chorus: Trust and obey, for there's no other way to be happy in Jesus, but to trust and obey.[27]

As we go forward on our path of sanctification, keep in mind that we will continually move from one season of preparation to another. This process has a divine purpose. In 2 Corinthians 3:18 (NLT), we are told that "the Lord—who is the Spirit—makes us more and more like him as we are changed into his glorious image." The *New King James Version Woman's Study Bible* gives us great insight for this verse:

> The image of God is His reflection in us. What a magnificent concept—God's creation of mankind in His image—patterned after Him, mirroring a family resemblance of Him. This does not pertain to the physical nature but rather to the spiritual and moral nature.

How are we like God?

- We are capable of communicating, and in so doing, we can bless or curse (James 3:9).

- We are creative, and creativity gives us joy and satisfaction (Proverbs 31:13–22).

- We experience emotions and feelings; we long for relationship and fellowship (Psalm 16:11).

- We discern between right and wrong (Isaiah 6:5).

- We act and are responsible for our actions (John 3:18).

- We long to pursue Him. Mary sat at Jesus' feet, listening to Him. Jesus let her know that sitting at His feet was important (Luke 10:42).

The characters we will study this week are Joseph, the son of Jacob, and Abigail, the wife of Nabal.

As we study portions of their journey, our goal is to see the purpose of God's preparation in their lives. We'll see how God blessed their resolve to "trust and obey" Him, regardless of their circumstances.

Today, we begin with Joseph, another man God chose to bring peace and deliverance to the children of Israel. The saga of Joseph's life opens in Genesis 37:2. As we travel through the pages of Genesis examining the uncanny circumstances in Joseph's life, our intent is to draw deep insight and direction for personal application. Our text opens with the identification of Joseph's home, the land of Canaan. He is a young man of seventeen, tending the flocks of his father with his brothers. What appears to be normal is not normal at all.

> Dorothy Patterson states that "even though the original intimate relationship between God and humanity was severed by the Fall (Genesis 3:5-7), God has pursued His children down through the ages, sending His Son that we might be reconciled to Him and become His daughters and sons, His heirs (Romans 8:14-17). His image can be reflected in us. Through Christ the image is brought back into focus so that His glory shines from the reflection" (pg. 866).

Read Genesis 37:1–11, and answer the following questions.

- What is the first thing we learn about Joseph that made his brothers angry enough to hate him?

  _____

  _____

- What did Joseph do to inflame his brothers even more?

  _____

  _____

- What effect did Joseph's dream have on his brothers and father?

  _____

  _____

Joseph and Benjamin were the youngest sons of Jacob from his marriage to Rachael. Their ten half brothers were the sons of Leah, Zilpah, and Bilhah. Can't you imagine the jealousy and resentment that gripped the older brothers, as Jacob glaringly showed partiality to Joseph with the *richly ornamented robe*, while they wore the simple garb of working shepherds? In the next scene, we see *sibling rivalry* ignite into rage and revenge as the brothers plot to kill Joseph. Joseph and his brothers could never have imagined the final outcome created by their expulsion of Joseph into the hands of slave traders.

Read Genesis 37:12–36, and fill in the blanks in the following verses.

- Verses 19–20: "'Here comes that _____!' they said to each other. 'Come now, let's kill him and throw him into one of these cisterns and _____ that a ferocious animal devoured him. Then we'll see what becomes of his _____.'"

- Verses 21–22: "When _____ heard this, he tried to _____ him from their hands. 'Let's not take his life,' he said. 'Don't shed any _____. Throw him into this cistern here in the desert, but don't lay a _____ on him.' Reuben said this to rescue him from _____ and take him back to his _____.'"

- Verses 23–24: "So when Joseph came to his brothers, they _____ him of his robe—the _____ _____ robe he was wearing and they took him and _____ him into the cistern."

- Verses 26–27: "_____ said to his brothers, 'What will we _____ if we kill our brother and cover up his blood? Come, let's _____ him to the Ishmaelites and not lay our _____ on him; after all, he is our brother, our own flesh and blood.' His brothers agreed."

- Verse 36: "Meanwhile, the Midianites _____ Joseph in Egypt to Potiphar, one of Pharaoh's officials, the captain of the guard."

Partiality had birthed jealousy and resentment. Over time, hatred filled their hearts and rage accomplished evil revenge. No longer would the "dreamer" boast of his future rule over them. The favored one's "richly ornamented robe" had now become a bloody garment of deceit. Instead of them bowing down to Joseph, he would be the one to bow as a slave servant to an unknown master in Egypt. Little did they suspect they would see Joseph again, much less bow to him.

Before we look at Joseph in the house of Potiphar, let's draw some application from the root of his sudden removal from the family. Moving to Egypt was probably the last thing Joseph wanted to do, especially since he was the recipient of his father's partiality. If you are the favored one, life is good. But if you aren't, the glare of favoritism can lead to jealousy. Jealousy that is embraced will bring forth hate, resentment, revenge, and ultimately rage that can lead to irreversible actions.

Read Genesis 37:4, 10–11, 18, and fill in the blanks.

- Verse 4: "When his brothers _____ that their father loved him more than any of them, they _____ him and could not speak a _____ word to him."

- Verses 10–11: "When he told his father as well as his brothers, his father rebuked him and said, 'What is this _____ you had? Will your mother and I and your brothers actually come and _____ down to the ground before _____?' His brothers were _____ of him, but his father kept the matter in mind."

- Verses 17b–18: "So Joseph went after his brothers and found them near Dothan. But they saw him in the distance, and before he reached them, they _____ to _____ him."

In these verses, we clearly see the birth and growth of *hate* in the hearts of Joseph's brothers. There are three stages of hate that reveal the process and nature of their actions toward Joseph.

First Stage: In Genesis 37:4, we are told Joseph's brothers hated him. The Hebrew word for *hate* is *sana*, which means *hateful*, to hate personally.

Second Stage: In Genesis 37:4 and 11, we are told that Joseph's brothers *hated him all the more and were jealous* of him. The strong sense of the word typifies the emotion of jealousy.

Third Stage: In Genesis 37:18, we are told Joseph's brothers *plotted to kill* him. The word covers emotions ranging from bitter disdain to outright hatred.[28]

As we looked at the injustice to Joseph, I suspect some of you were like me, mentally wandering off to a time and place in your past that held a similar episode. Some of you may have experienced the same emotions as Joseph's brothers. You may have been the recipient of hatefulness, jealously, or rage that brought a severe injustice.

For most of my life, I was very jealous of my brother, Jimmy. I was convinced that my mother loved him more than she did me. There was something between them that was very special. She was always protective over him, and I couldn't understand why. It seemed that he never did anything wrong. It was quite the contrary with me. I never did anything right. I was the strong-willed child. My brother was every mother's dream, and I was every mother's nightmare. Often, I would lash out at my mother with these words: "You don't love me like you love Jimmy. He's your favorite!" I wanted to be her favorite. I'm not proud of this, but I held on to that jealousy for years. One day, my mother told me the reason for their closeness. My father did not want children when Jimmy was born. His selfishness and addiction to alcohol was bad, but his jealousy of my mother's love for Jimmy sent him over the edge. You can imagine the hurt and injustice they both suffered. To make their injuries worse, when Jimmy was five years old, I was born. Immediately, my father began showing partiality to me, *his favorite*. His actions produced wounds of jealousy, resentment, and bitterness, and they played a huge part in the death of their marriage.

Today's session will end with a personal look at jealousy. The root of jealousy is pride or self-centeredness. Human jealousy is often translated in Scripture as "envy."[29]

> "Man's jealously of man imprisons, but God's jealousy for man restores" (author).

Answer the following questions. What behaviors are listed along with jealousy in Romans 13:13?

_____

_____

- What action words are associated with jealousy in 2 Corinthians 12:20?

  _____

  _____

- According to Galatians 5:19–21, what are the results of living in the sinful nature?

  _____

  _____

- Has someone's jealousy wounded you? If it has, briefly write down the root of their jealousy and how you were wounded.

  _____

  _____

- Has your jealousy wounded someone? If it has, briefly write down the root of your jealousy and how you wounded this person.

  _____

  _____

Close in prayer asking God to heal the wounds you have received or have inflicted because of jealousy. Ask Him to show you any areas of pride and self-centeredness in your life. Ask Him to cleanse your heart of these attitudes and actions and fill you with more of Himself.

See you tomorrow at the house of Potiphar and his naughty wife!

Day 2
Godly Jealously Brings Restoration

We have a lot to cover today, but it will be worth our time. Our purpose is to see how God *prepared* Joseph to be used in the lives of others, especially his own family. In order to cover all the text, I will briefly summarize the events in Joseph's life. I want to encourage you to allow the same unseen hand of God that ordered Joseph's life to touch your heart during today's study. We can be sure He has a plan for our life. He may or may not take us down a path like Joseph's, but we can know for sure He will fulfill it.

Joseph has been brought to Egypt where God begins the next step of his *preparation*. He is bought and moved into the house of Potiphar, which adds an amazing twist in the story. Read Genesis 39, and fill in the missing blanks in verses 2–4.

"The LORD was _____ Joseph and he _____, and he lived in the house of his Egyptian master. When his master _____ that the Lord was _____ him and that the LORD _____ him success in everything he did, Joseph found _____ in his eyes and became his attendant."

The *American Heritage Dictionary* defines the word *with* as "a companion of; accompanying; next to."[30] One of the names given to our Savior is Immanuel, which means "God is with us."

The invisible Lord was with Joseph and recognized by Potiphar.

This time, Joseph is faced with another type of rage. When the spoiled wife of Potiphar attempts to seduce Joseph, he responds with conviction that he could not do such a wicked thing against his master, Potiphar, nor his God. She demanded his submission, but Joseph refused, leaving her angry, full of rage, and set on revenge. She lies to her husband, calling Joseph a slave who had attempted to sexually assault her. In verse 19, we are told that Potiphar burned with anger and put Joseph in prison.

Again, we see the imprisoning of another from jealousy.

Read Genesis 39:20–23, and answer the following questions.

- Who was *with* Joseph, and what did he do for him?

  _____

- How did the warden treat Joseph?

  _____

In chapters 40 and 41, we see the anger of Pharaoh condemn his cupbearer and his baker to prison. Immediately, the prison warden assigned them to Joseph's care. Sometime later, the cupbearer and baker have disturbing dreams and tell Joseph. Joseph's interpretation revealed a good message for the cupbearer and a bad message for the baker.

Read Genesis 40:14–15, and answer the following questions.

- What did Joseph ask the cupbearer to do when all went well with him?

  _____

- What reason did Joseph give for asking this favor?

  _____

Joseph's interpretation came to pass. The cupbearer was restored to his original position, but the baker was hanged. Complete verse 23 to see the outcome of Joseph's request of the cupbearer.

- "The chief _____, however, did not _____ Joseph; he _____ him."

We ended chapter 40 with Joseph being forgotten and begin chapter 41 with two full years having passed. Joseph is still in prison awaiting God's deliverance. Just because God chose not to record anything during those years doesn't mean He wasn't working in Joseph's life.

I have encountered long seasons of waiting and wondering what God was *preparing for me*. I'm finally realizing that each new season includes a new *preparation in me*. The length of time is perfectly calculated by the Father. Sometimes, I get quite impatient, and then I realize that "waiting" is often part of His plan to grow patience in me. I think Joseph grew in patience during those years. Have you had a season of growing in patience? If you have, take a few minutes to thank God for it.

In chapter 41, Pharaoh has two dreams that are very disturbing to him. He sought people to interpret the meaning of the dreams, but no one could. In verse 9, we are told that the chief cupbearer was reminded of his *shortcoming*, which always means *fault*. He had failed to keep his word to Joseph. The word *fault* means "crime or sin in the sense of missing the mark or the path; sin against a man or God."[31] Sometimes, we fail to show gratitude to those who have helped us in stressful times. The Lord knows our heart better than we do. When we miss the mark such as the cupbearer did, He is faithful to expose the selfishness that often hides behind forgetfulness. I choose to believe that our *Jehovah-Shammah, the Lord Is There*, reminded the cupbearer.

Read chapter 41, and answer the following questions.

- Where was Joseph when Pharaoh sent for him?

  _____

- What was Joseph's response when Pharaoh asked if he could interpret dreams?

  _____

- What was Pharaoh's response to Joseph's interpretation of his dreams?

  _____

- What did Pharaoh put Joseph in complete charge of?

  _____

- Joseph experienced a lot of pain and prison time. I believe He pondered the purpose of those days and chose to trust God and patiently wait on His deliverance. I also believe Joseph knew the Lord was there with him.

In verse 57 of chapter 41, we are told that "all the countries came to Egypt to buy grain from Joseph, because the famine was severe in all the world." Joseph's family was forced to come to Egypt for corn. Jacob sent ten of his sons to buy the grain and kept Benjamin, the youngest, with him for fear something bad might happen to him as it did with Joseph.

> When the tired, hungry band of shepherds was brought before the luxuriously dressed Egyptian official wearing the Pharaoh's signet ring and the gold chain of office, they did not recognize the arrogant young boy they had nearly murdered. But Joseph instantly knew them and initiated a series of tests and ordeals that reads like an account of psychological torture.[32]

Joseph had learned over time that God loved him and would provide for and protect him, but he wasn't sure of the hearts of his brothers. His last encounter left him suspicious and deeply wounded by their actions. "Joseph was hard upon his brethren, not from a spirit of revenge, but to bring them to repentance. Not seeing Benjamin, he suspected that they had made away with him, and he gave them occasion to speak of their father and brother."[33]

Joseph knew his brothers needed to come clean. He had experienced the separation and loneliness that jealousy had imposed. He knew imprisonment from false accusations and selfishness. He also knew his brothers were bound in a prison of lies and could only be redeemed through repentance and confession of their sins upon him and their father Jacob.

Exodus 20:5–6 describes the *jealousy* of God. "You shall not bow down to them or worship them; for I, the LORD your God am a jealous God, punishing the children for the sin of the fathers to the third and fourth generation of those who hate me, but showing love to a thousand generations of those who love me and keep my commandments." God's *jealousy* "refers directly to the attributes of God's justice and holiness, as He is the sole object of human worship and does not tolerate man's sin. In its most positive sense, the word means 'to be filled with righteous zeal or jealousy.' God is not tainted with the negative connotation of the verb."[34] God is *for* us. He is jealous for us to remain in close relationship with Him. He is full of devotion to us. Joseph was full of Godly jealousy for his family and devotion to his God.

Read Genesis 47:1–11, and answer the following questions.

- What did Joseph request from Pharaoh for his family?

  _____

- What did Pharaoh tell Joseph to do regarding his personal livestock?

  _____

- Who blessed Pharaoh?

  _____

The story concludes with God's restoration of Jacob's family. As we end today's lesson, I want to challenge you to seek God concerning any relationships that need to be restored in your life. I've found that when a relationship becomes the least bit uncomfortable, it is often from a root of jealousy. If not dealt with, it can quickly become a prison of anger and bitterness. Freedom is available when we choose to replace "our jealousy of" with a "Godly jealousy for." If we have been hurt by someone else's jealousy of us, we must choose to forgive that person. It begins with a prayer of openness to

God, verbalizing our hurt and our choice to forgive and bless those who have hurt us. God honors our sincere devotion to Him and promises to be *with us* as we seek restoration.

See you tomorrow at the tent of Abigail!

Day 3
An Oath Scarred by Distrust

Today, we will turn our focus to Abigail, the wife of Nabal. The Hebrew name Abigail means "my father rejoices." After studying the text, I am not surprised by the meaning of her name. We will learn from this great lady what causes our heavenly Father to rejoice in us.

Our text for today and tomorrow will be one chapter, 1 Samuel 25. Before we dive into our time together with Abigail, we must cover some background information that sets the stage for her entrance into 1 Samuel. I have provided chapter summaries similar to yesterday's homework. They will help familiarize you with the events that have taken place and bring us to Abigail's home. There are three characters we will examine: David, the son of Jesse; Abigail; and her husband, Nabal.

Fill in the blanks in 1 Samuel 25:1.

- "Now Samuel died, and all Israel assembled and mourned for him; and they buried him at his home in Ramah. Then _____ moved down into the Desert of Maon."

Why did David move? We can find the answer in the following chapters. To make this a quick investigation, I've listed the actions of God and the reactions of Saul and David.

- In 1 Samuel 15, we learn that God rejected Saul as king because he turned away from him and failed to obey his instructions.

- In 1 Samuel 16, we learn that God chose David to be the new king and the Spirit of the Lord departed from Saul.

- In 1 Samuel 17 and 18, we learn that David's popularity with the people ignited anger and jealousy in Saul toward David that soon turned into hate.

- In 1 Samuel 19–23, we learn that Saul decided to kill David. His pursuit of rage caused David to be constantly running and hiding from Saul.

What really caused David to move? Circle your answer: Saul's disobedience or Saul's jealousy.

Before Abigail comes on the scene, we must look at a critical scene between David and Saul. Read 1 Samuel 24, and answer the following questions.

- What did David's men encourage him to do?

  _____

- What did David do to Saul instead of killing him, and how did it affect him?

  _____

- What did David say to his men after Saul left the cave?

  _____

- When David went out of the cave and called out to Saul, what posture did he immediately take before Saul?

  _____

- Why did David refuse to lift his hand against Saul?

  _____

- What was the oath Saul requested of David?

  _____

As you can see, David's life had been upside down and inside out ever since he left the shepherding fields. He made an oath not to cut off Saul's descendants or wipe out his name from his father's family. I hope you noticed that Saul did not make the same oath to David. And now Samuel, whom he loved and trusted, was dead. No wonder David moved down into the Desert of Maon.

As you read 1 Samuel 25:1–31, allow yourself to visualize each scene.

The focus for today will be on Abigail and how God ordered her steps right into His plans. The text describes her as intelligent and beautiful. She also scored high marks in the areas of patience, humility, and devotion to God. She was amazingly courageous considering she was married to Nabal. Even though Nabal was rich, he was not charitable. "He had no honour or honesty; he was churlish, cross, and ill-humored; evil in his doings, hard and oppressive; a man that cared not what fraud and violence he used in getting and saving."[35]

Your initial thoughts may have been like mine, "How did such a wonderful woman get stuck with such an awful man?" Abigail probably entered this union through no choice of her own because parents arranged most marriages in her day. I have a compassionate heart for women who, as I have, made poor choices in marriage and suffer the consequences. I always advise women considering marriage to pray, seek godly counsel, and don't rush. Allow yourself enough time to get to know the person and observe how he reacts and deals with people and circumstances. Be sure you have true peace before making a lifetime commitment.

It is possible that Abigail and Nabal were childless since none were mentioned. What we do know is that she tolerated him and had a good relationship with the servants. She and the servants were probably accustomed to mending the damage from Nabal's insults. She was very discerning and knew how to handle her husband while protecting him and others from his crude blunders. Nabal's biggest blunder would be his last.

Answer the following questions about Nabal's last blunder.

> "By a present Abigail atoned for Nabal's denial of David's request. Her behavior was very submissive. Yielding pacifies great offenses" (Henry, 285).

- What did Nabal refuse to do for David?

  _____

- What was David's response?

  _____

- What did Abigail do to protect both men?

  _____

58

Hunger and fear can take a toll on people. David and his men had experienced both over a lengthy period. They were tired physically and emotionally. Insults and harsh words can easily set anyone off under these circumstances.

God's timing was perfect as we see in verses 22–24.

Briefly answer each question.

- How had David approached Saul?

  _____

- How did Abigail approach David?

  _____

- What do you think David felt at that moment?

  _____

- What important truths does Abigail present to David?

  _____

David needed to be reminded of the offenses he had experienced at the hand of Saul. Just as he had bowed to Saul out of respect for his position as king, Abigail had bowed before him out of respect for his position as God's anointed shepherd-king who would replace Saul. Her words of wisdom and truth also exposed the condition of David's heart. Even though he had made an oath to protect Saul, he was scarred by Saul's distrust of him. When someone distrusts us without cause, it is very wounding to both parties. David left Saul a wounded young man and then encountered Nabal. This was like pouring gasoline on an open fire.

Wounded people wound people.

It's interesting to me the words Abigail chose for her closing comments. Our session will end today around those verses. Fill in the blanks in verses 30 and 31.

- "When the Lord has done for my master every good thing he _____ concerning him and has _____ him leader over Israel, my master will not have on his conscience the staggering burden of needless _____ or of having _____ himself. And when the _____ has brought my master success, _____ your servant."

The Hebrew word for remember is *zakar*, which means "more than to recall; it means to retain in thought so as to tell someone who can take action."[36] This is what Joseph was asking in Genesis 40:14: "But when all goes well with you, *remember me* and show me kindness; *mention me* to Pharaoh and get me out of this prison." Abigail wanted basically the same thing, except her prison was her marriage. Abigail trusted God to take care of her. She refused to allow her unstable marriage to hinder her devotion to God. I'm sure you will never forget Abigail after your encounters with her today and tomorrow. She is one of my favorite women in the Bible.

God can do miracles in unstable lives and relationships. Spend a few minutes bowing in prayer before the Lord "remembering" a friend, relative, or co-worker. If you need someone to "remember" you, let

God be that person and pour out your needs to Him. He does not forget! He will take action! Close by "remembering" God's blessings on your life, and write a short prayer of gratitude.

Our session tomorrow will begin with David's reply to Abigail. Get ready, my sisters, for the perfect ending to this story!

Day 4
An Oath Saved by Devotion

We ended our session yesterday with Abigail's request for David to "remember her." It is so important to "remember" the requests of others and get back with them. Abigail wanted David to apply action to her request. Let's examine his reply.

Read 1 Samuel 25:32–35, and answer the following questions:

• Who did David praise and why? _____
_____

• Who did David bless and why? _____
_____

David accepted Abigail's provisions and granted her request. He made another promise not to harm the cruel man or his household. This time, it was not a king but a fool, Nabal the Calebite. Isn't it like God to test the condition of our hearts? David was tempted in the cave to kill Saul, but he was stopped by the conviction of his heart. The words of Nabal hardened David's heart even more. His threats and plans were far more dangerous than the words of Nabal. This time, he was convicted by the words of Abigail. Her mission was successful, but can't you imagine the dread she experienced as she returned home to another day within her own prison? I can imagine her praying, "El Roi … thank you for protecting your anointed one from spilling innocent blood. I know you also see my circumstances and will deliver me."

Read the remainder of our text, and fill in the blanks in the following verses:

• Verse 37: "Then in the morning, when Nabal was _____, his wife told him all these things, and his _____ failed him and he became like a _____."

• Verse 38: "About ten days later, the _____ struck Nabal and he died."

• Verse 39: "When David _____ that Nabal was dead, he said, 'Praise be to the LORD, who has upheld my cause against Nabal for treating me with _____. He has kept his servant from doing _____ and has brought Nabal's _____ down on his own head.'"

Regardless of her circumstances, Abigail remained devoted to God and respectful to Nabal and David. Regardless of David's threats and plans, God demonstrated His faithfulness to avenge wrongs done to David by striking Nabal dead. Devotion and faithfulness trumps evil every time! As women, we can definitely learn from Abigail. In our times of trouble and hurts, it is so easy to speak before thinking and talking to God about our situation.

As I read verse 39, the word *heard* captured my attention, and I immediately searched back through the scriptures for a person to identify as the messenger of Nabal's death. My search ended as it began; the messenger was not recorded. Curiosity sent me in another direction that I want to share with you. This will be fun and food for thought.

Answer the questions.

- Could the messenger in verse 39 have been the same person talking to Abigail in verses 14–17?

- If he is, how is he identified?

  _____

- Could this servant have been one of the _____ David mentions in verse 7?

This would have been just like David to add protection to a herd of sheep and their shepherds, especially during a time of shearing. After his encounter with Saul, the time spent with them was probably refreshing. I can imagine the stories told and advice given by the shepherd-king David. Can you imagine two men of kindred spirits under the stars, sharing and listening to each other's hearts? David may have found a new friend who had also talked with God under the stars. Could David have heard about Nabal's death from this new friend? It is possible, but you and I aren't told. What we do know is that God brings people into our lives, regardless of where we are, to be instruments of His preparation and plans for our lives.

Our final look at Abigail begins with the last sentence in verse 39 and continues through 42. After David acknowledged God's work in the situation with Nabal, he "remembered" Abigail and sent word to her. I would like to think that God chose this same messenger to take the news of Nabal to David and David's proposal to Abigail. I hope he was a groomsman in the wedding, don't you? I love this part and the beauty of God's hand leading and guiding to bring redemption. Read the remaining verses, and answer the following questions:

- How do you think Abigail felt when she heard the words, "David has sent us to you to take you to become his bride"?

  _____

- Why do you think Abigail bowed down with her face to the ground and said, "Here is your maidservant, ready to serve you and wash the feet of my master's servant"?

  _____

  _____

- Why do you think she took five maids with her?

  _____

  _____

Abigail took those who had been the closest to her. We can imagine the misery she endured. Just as God surrounded David with devoted men to help him fight the attacks of Saul, I believe He did the same for Abigail in her marriage to Nabal through five devoted maids. I also believe they were bridesmaids in her wedding to David, don't you? Abigail's story should inspire and infuse us with courage. The following comments by F. B. Meyer beautifully describe our devoted and courageous lady.

> Never let the evil disposition of one mate hinder the devotion and grace of the other.
> Never let the difficulties of your home lead you to abdicate your throne. Do not step

down to the level of your circumstances, but lift them to your own high calling in Christ.[37]

Abigail's devotion to her God fueled Godly jealousy in her heart for His anointed. God used her to soften the wounded heart of David. David was used to prove that El Roi, the God Who Sees, "remembered" Abigail's request.

Verbally abusive people are everywhere. They are in the schools, workplaces, homes, subdivisions, churches, clubs, recreational events—more places than we can count. They are everywhere, and we either tolerate or deal with them. Abigail is a perfect example of how to deal with this type of person. In her situation, she lived with him and remained loyal and respectful while being open and honest. She prayed and kept her focus on God and lived upright before Him, Nabal, and others. We must do the same things Abigail did and rest in the knowledge that El Roi sees our circumstances and remembers our requests.

See you tomorrow for a final look at Joseph and Abigail!

Day 5
Preparation's Deliverance

When you began this session, you may have wondered why I chose Joseph and Abigail. I didn't; God did. I remember wondering, "What parallels could possibly be drawn from their lives?" As I prepared, it didn't take long for me to see many parallels. Humanly jealousy is bad, but godly jealousy is good. The evil of one man often imprisons another, but devotion to God sustains and strengthens the victimized. God's mighty hand brings down the evil and lifts up the righteous.

The third step becomes an ongoing journey of walking with Jesus into new places and different seasons of our life. He knows exactly where we need to go and what we need to learn in preparation for the next assignment. I am so glad we are prepared before we are assigned! Joseph was prepared for more than just becoming the governor of Egypt. He was prepared and then positioned in Egypt "to preserve for his family a remnant on earth and to save their lives by a great deliverance" (Genesis 45:7).

Abigail was prepared for more than becoming the bride of David. She was prepared and positioned to persuade David "not to have on his conscience the staggering burden of needless bloodshed or of having avenged himself" (1 Samuel 25:31).

> "In order for God's people to do works of service, we must be prepared to use our gifts from God" (author).

In the introduction of this session, I shared my journey following my marriage to Ken up to God's "call" on my life. The countywide revival I mentioned was a definite marker in my life. When I reached the age of thirty, things began to move in another direction for me spiritually. God began preparing me for His service within the body of Christ. Preparation is not always comfortable or fun. Often, it is just the opposite. The first thing I noticed was how unequipped I was in the areas in which He placed me. I was very uncomfortable and nervous. As soon as I would become comfortable and begin to enjoy my new assignment, He would move me to a new place, and it started over again. When Benji Clark read my "call verses," I was blown away. I was not filled with awe and excitement, but overwhelmed with questions. Surely, He knows that I could never do what these verses say or become an oak of righteousness. I was in a state of shock and doubt. But regardless of my feelings and thoughts, He began to prepare me. The lessons got longer and the tests harder. Application no longer encouraged but painfully exposed. It was not fun or comfortable.

Preparation—The *American Heritage Dictionary* defines *preparation* as "the act or process of preparing; readiness; preliminary measures; a substance, as medicine for a particular purpose."[38]

There are times when God's preparation is like taking bitter medicine. Often, I would try to avoid it, but when I did take it, I would get better. Looking back, I see that each "measure" He took in my life was for a particular purpose. Every believer has been given one or more spiritual gifts "to prepare God's people for works of service" (Ephesians 4:12). I received the gift of teaching when I received God's gift of salvation, but when He moved me into the position of teacher at my church, I was not ready or prepared to teach. Thank God for excellent teaching materials and helpers. I will never forget a young high school girl who helped me get adjusted to my class. God used her to show me my shallowness in Biblical knowledge without embarrassment. The lesson was on the stoning of Stephen, the first Christian martyr. I read the condensed story that had been written for their fourth-grade level of understanding. Somehow, I left out verses 55 and 56, which described Stephen looking up to heaven and seeing Jesus standing at the right hand of God and then verbalizing what he saw to all present. The young girl added that part of the lesson tactfully as I finished. Her comments were something like this, "When Jesus arose from the dead and went to heaven, He sat down next to his Father who is God. When we are mistreated, Jesus stands up and takes notice just like He did when Stephen was being stoned." That was a large dose of humbling medicine that will always be remembered with a grateful heart.

Day 1: Unbridled Jealousy Breeds Rage

Years of pampering and partiality toward Joseph resulted in dangerous levels of jealousy among his brothers. Joseph intensified their jealousy by flaunting the "robe" and bragging about dreams of his destiny as a "ruler." Even though his dreams came true, Joseph had to be prepared to handle his position according to God's purpose. Jealousy is an act of sin. An example would be when we experience jealousy that easily becomes an act of hostility toward someone we think is a rival. Let's see that according to Scripture.

> **"Forgiveness heals the wounds from sin, removes the fear from guilt and brings love's restoration" (author).**

Fill in the blanks in Proverbs 27:4. "Anger is _____ and fury is _____, but who can stand before _____?"

That is why it is so important for us to know the truth from God's Word and act on it. Our jealousy must be transformed from "sinful jealousy of" to "godly jealousy for."

Day 2: Godly Jealousy Brings Restoration

Joseph was prepared and positioned to demonstrate the actions of God at the appointed time. He wasn't the only one being prepared. Time may dull the ears of our conscience, but it doesn't remove the guilt of sin. Joseph's brothers would never be able to forget their deeds of rage. The weight of guilt would grow heavier until they finally bowed in repentance.

Fill in the blanks in Genesis 45:3.

- "Joseph said to his brothers, 'I am Joseph! Is my father still alive?' But his brothers were not able to _____ him because they were _____ at his presence."

Fill in the blanks in Genesis 45:15. "And he _____ all his brothers and _____ over them. Afterwards his brothers _____ with him."

"Jealousy, unlike envy and covetousness, can have a positive connotation. God's protection of His people from their enemies is the fruit of this holy jealousy."[39]

Read Ezekiel 39:25–28, and list the blessings described for those He brings out of captivity.

_____

_____

Day 3: An Oath Scarred by Distrust

What is an oath? The *American Heritage Dictionary* defines the word *oath* as "a formal promise to fulfill a pledge, often calling upon God as witness."[40]

- Have you ever made an oath? If so, what was it pertaining to?

  _____

- Have you ever broken a promise to someone? If so, how did you feel?

  _____

- Has anyone ever broken a promise to you? If so, how did you feel?

  _____

Can you imagine the hurt and disappointment Abigail experienced in her marriage to Nabal? Both made an oath to God when they married, but Nabal did not keep his part. I can imagine the scenes where he lashed out with ugly comments and threats, scarring her heart. Abigail knew Nabal could not be trusted, so she chose to trust God and let him take care of her. God's intervention was a blessing for more than just David and Abigail. The innocent were spared, and God's purpose went forth.

Fill in the blanks in Proverbs 19:21.

"Many are the _____ in a man's heart, but it is the Lord's _____ that prevails."

Often our wounds are reopened, and our broken heart becomes scarred. Unless we run to God, our hearts harden and our minds become consumed with suspicion. We become overly sensitive and begin to look for the worst in others rather than the best. Even the slightest rejection can set us off and results in wounding the innocent. We must be like Abigail and choose to trust God, allowing His peace to calm us and His Spirit to direct us.

Day 4: An Oath Saved by Devotion

David was devoted to God and knew that God would avenge him on his enemies. Abigail's humility and strong devotion to God marked the life of David. She was a gift to him during a very difficult season. God, who knows all things, knew how David would respond. It was a place of preparation and renewal for him.

There are times when we are so wounded that we need someone to remind us that God will take care of our enemies. We hear the Holy Spirit whisper, "Let go of your anger, and let me take care of that," but we just can't get it off our minds. That is when we need a person like Abigail to help us. If you are in need of an Abigail, ask God to send her to you. He delights in helping us through his people.

We know more about David than we do Abigail, but we can imagine that she must have dreamed of being free from her prison of marriage to Nabal. I think she dreamed of being rescued by her Prince Charming, who would carry her off to live happily ever after. I believe she talked to God about her dreams as well as her disappointments. We can do that too! If you haven't, start this very moment.

David's gratitude and strong devotion to God also marked the life of Abigail. He was a gift to Abigail during a very difficult season. God, who knows all things, knew Abigail would accept David's proposal of marriage. It was a place of preparation and renewal for her. Her name, Abigail, means "my father rejoices"—and He did. Ladies, you can be sure our Father rejoices in us when we embrace His preparation!

We will journey with Job and Esther in our next session!

Father,

Thank you for showing us how much you love us and are concerned with every season of our lives. Thank you for revealing the weaknesses and strengths of those who have gone before us. It is so encouraging to know that we aren't the only ones who fall short. Knowing that we can walk in Godly jealousy for others and be steadfast in devotion to you is so amazing. We choose to believe your Word that tells us "we can do all things through Christ who strengthens us" (Philippians 4:12, NKJV). I pray this in the name above all names, Jesus Christ, the Son of God.

Session 4

Spiritual Marker #4
"The Testing"

In session 3, we continued our look at God's progressive deliverance from sin's power. As I shared my journey, I hope you were able to see the beginning steps of a specific plan for my life. During that season of my life, I didn't understand the ways of God. There were many times I was very uncomfortable and even unhappy in the places God ordained for me. A glance into our past can be helpful, especially when what we thought was bad was really good. It can make us grateful for those days. Looking back can be painful, but it is well worth it.

Our focus in today's session is on the "testing" we encounter on our spiritual journey. The testing of the Holy Spirit reminds me of one of my college professors. On the first day of class, he provided the usual course syllabus. His lectures and visual aids added tremendous insight and delightfully captured my attention. Open-book tests were not on the syllabus, but everyone liked them—especially since they came immediately following an interesting lecture. The open-book tests were short and easy, making it possible for everyone to make a good grade. The scheduled tests were much harder. The questions revealed the depth of my understanding and retention. I can remember the professor well but only small snapshots of the material. I am so grateful my retention of that material isn't required for me to succeed now!

Isn't that similar to what we experience when the Holy Spirit attempts to teach us selected material in the Bible? He chooses the course and draws us to participate. Just as the professor used other things to enhance learning, the Holy Spirit will use people, circumstances, songs, and more to help us learn spiritual truths. Often, He will give us an open-book test that is intended to prepare us for future tests in our lives. If we fail, He will review and test us until we pass. Relief flooded my heart when I learned that God would give me "do-over" tests in areas of failure in my Christian walk until I got it right. As children of God, we can overcome sin's power through the persistent teaching and power of the Holy Spirit.

We are told in Romans 8:13–14 that "if you live according to the sinful nature, you will die; but if by the Spirit you put to death the misdeeds of the body, you will live, because those who are led by the Spirit of God are sons of God." A close examination of the word misdeeds in this verse reveals the definition of "wicked acts."[41] We are given strong words of application in Romans 12:2, "Do not conform any longer to the pattern of this world, but be transformed by the renewing of your mind. Then you will be able to test and approve what God's will is—His good, pleasing and perfect will." As we resist the conforming power of the world, the Holy Spirit renews our mind. How does He do such a miraculous work? He uses the light of Truth to dispel the darkness of sin in our life. As we obey Him, we will see this process firsthand.

We must understand that sin weakens and causes us to fail, but truth frees and strengthens us to succeed. Spiritual tests help us see where we are lacking or how much we have overcome through the help of the Holy Spirit. When we pass a spiritual test, we demonstrate our willingness to participate in our own sanctification.

Romans 12:2, from the New Living Translation gives us a clear picture of this process: "Don't copy the behavior and customs of this world, but let God transform you into a new person by changing the way you think. Then you will learn to know God's will for you, which is good and pleasing and perfect." We will be tested throughout our lives for our good. I've often thought that maybe the road of sanctification wouldn't have been so bumpy if I had known about the work of the Holy Spirit earlier in my life. He is always preparing us, dear sisters. He also teaches us how to prepare ourselves. Our final preparation will not be inward but outward. Meditate on the words of Revelation 19:7–8 that describe the adornment of the bride of Christ.

> "Though I dwell in darkness, the Lord is a light for me...He will bring me out to the light and I will seek His righteousness" (Micah 7:8-9, NASB).

> Let us rejoice and be glad and give Him glory! For the wedding of the Lamb has come, and his bride has made herself ready. Fine linen, bright and clean, was given her to wear. [Fine linen stands for the righteous acts of the saint.]

In this verse, we see that the bride has dressed herself in the robe of Christ's righteousness. She is ready for the wedding feast of the Lamb where she will partake of the fullness of His presence. This is another picture of *Jehovah-tsidkenu, the Lord Our Righteousness*.

My Spiritual Journey—Fourth Step: Sanctification's Tests

In closing session 3, I shared this statement about our spiritual journey: an *encounter* with Jesus is never forgotten because of the eternal *mark* it leaves on your life. Today, we begin with this same statement because of the second encounter that marked my spiritual path. Looking back enables us to see how God ordains His purpose and plans for us. In my case, He chose a godly woman, Benji Clark, to direct me to specific scriptures that would define the ministry He had created me to do within the body of Christ. Here are the verses I marked in my Bible on June 12, 1984.

> Arise, shine, for your light has come, and the glory of the LORD rises upon you. See, darkness covers the earth and thick darkness is over the peoples, but the LORD rises upon you and his glory appears over you. Nations will come to your light, and kings to the brightness of your dawn. Lift up your eyes and look about you: All assemble and come to you; your sons come from afar, and your daughters are carried on the arm. (Isaiah 60:1–4)

> The Spirit of the Sovereign LORD is on me, because the LORD has anointed me to preach good news to the poor. He has sent me to bind up the brokenhearted, to proclaim freedom for the captives and release from darkness for the prisoners, to proclaim the year of the LORD's favor and the day of vengeance of our God, to comfort all who mourn, and provide for those who grieve in Zion—to bestow on them a crown of beauty instead of ashes, the oil of gladness instead of mourning, and a garment of praise instead of a spirit of despair. They will be called oaks of righteousness, a planting of the LORD for the display of his splendor. (Isaiah 61:1–3)

The day before I wrote the first word of this study, God drew my attention to an oak tree leaf lying on the walking path in a park near my home. I picked it up, and the last part of verse 3 immediately came to my mind. I knew it was a sweet reminder of Isaiah 61:3. The plan of our Savior is for us to become strong women of righteousness, who have been restored and used to display His glory. Benji Clark was an "oak of righteousness." The Lord used her to initiate His call on my life to minister to women. Little did I know the hope that swelled in my heart that day would result in the path of ministry I am walking on today. If you had told me I would be writing a Bible study, I would have laughed and vowed that would never happen! But here I sit with a cup of coffee, years of journals, many Bible versions, commentaries, dictionaries, and my *Strong's Concordance*. I am excited to begin the daily lessons on our characters Job and Esther. I can't wait to see what God has for us to perceive about and learn from their stories that seem to be so different from each other. Personally, I would skip the next saga of my journey and move on with Job and Esther, but I must be obedient.

After my meeting with Benji Clark, my life began to change rapidly. The following week, I began teaching the senior high girls in my church, and within a couple of months, I was director of the youth department. I spent a very intense year with my girls and loved every minute. We grew together as God taught us through His Word and the work of His Spirit. He did amazing things in our lives. Young girls who were on the brink of destruction were rescued and set on a new course with Jesus. He did it all, not me. That which was impossible was made possible through Him. I was simply a willing, desperate vessel amazed that He would use me. My cry for more was filled with satisfaction and joy. My first taste of the abundant life was so fulfilling.

A year later, Ken and I sensed God calling us to move our family to another church. It was so hard to leave, but the peace that came with the decision assured us we were doing the right thing. I immediately began to serve in the youth department, again teaching senior high girls. At the end of our first year at this church, my life was shattered by the unexpected death of my mother. I was strong during the funeral and even for a couple of weeks afterward, but then I began to fall apart. I couldn't stand the dark thoughts of anger toward God that seemed to overwhelm me. With each passing day, I turned to my flesh for comfort and soon convinced myself that we needed to move to Atlanta, Georgia. There, Ken and I could move up the ladder of success and have a better life for our family. My flesh had won. Feeling anger toward God and pity for myself positioned me on a journey down the path of self-promotion. I deceived myself into believing I could run away from sorrow. We were not even settled into our new jobs and new home when I realized I was still running from my sorrow. My anger grew at God, and I began to lash out at Ken and my children. My heart continued to lead me astray. I felt trapped in a whirlwind of dark emotions. My dear sister, we cannot trust our own hearts. We are told in Jeremiah 17:9: "The heart is deceitful above all things and beyond cure."

The next five years were the most miserable years of my life. I continued to feed the sickness of self-promotion while attending church and going through all the motions of being a good wife, mother, and church member. During those years, I took drastic steps in an attempt to obtain personal significance. I enrolled in a local college and spent three years focusing on my education. My family suffered and probably would have fallen apart had it not been for Ken. I even accepted a promotion while ignoring a red flag and inner voice that shouted, "Stop! Don't go there!"

While I juggled all the self-centered demands of my own flesh, Jesus got my attention. One night, while driving to class, I began to hum a song. At first, I didn't know what I was humming. As I kept humming, a few of the words came to my mind. I was amazed when I finally realized the song was an old hymn, but I couldn't remember the title. I kept humming and then began to sing, "Trust and obey, for there's no other way, to be happy in Jesus, but to trust and obey."[42]

Before I ever accepted Jesus as my savior, He drew me to think about Him in what is still my favorite hymn, "Holy, Holy, Holy." This time, Jesus was calling me to trust and obey Him; otherwise, I could never be happy and at peace with Him. Deep within my soul, I knew something was about to happen in my life. I drove on to school and tried to dismiss the song but couldn't. As I drove home that night, for the first time in a long time, I began to talk to Jesus honestly. All my questions either started with "why" or "if." After all my questions, I arrogantly demanded that He appear in the seat next to me so I would know He was real. I went too far and grieved the Holy Spirit living in me.

The Word reveals and heals our deepest problems. Meditate on the following scriptures, which describe the behavior that can come from deep sorrow that is not dealt with or is allowed to fester and grow into a stronghold of flesh.

> Do not let any unwholesome talk come out of your mouths, but only what is helpful for building others up according to their needs, that it may benefit those who listen. And do not grieve the Holy Spirit of God, with whom you were sealed for the day of redemption. Get rid of all bitterness, rage and anger, brawling and slander, along with every form of malice. (Ephesians 4:29–31)

As soon as the word *seat* left my lips, a deafening silence consumed the inside of the car, and an evil darkness seemed to crawl up my back and over my shoulders. I have never been as scared in my life. I immediately let down all the windows and began to sing "Jesus Loves Me" at the top of my lungs all the way home. Soon afterward, I shared my experience with Ken. After listening intently, he calmly told me God had answered my challenge to appear. He had shown me what it was like for the hedge of His protection to be removed from around me. Ken reminded me that God loves me and knows exactly what to do to get my attention. He had been merciful and patient with me for a long season, but it was time for things to change. The following verse in Psalm 80:12 reminds me of that unforgettable night:

> "Why have you broken down its walls so that all who pass by pick its grapes?"

The Holy Spirit had wooed me through the wonderful words of "Trust and Obey." When I failed to heed His gentle song of direction, He used the doubts and fears that held me captive to draw me back to Him. My rage was replaced with repentance as I ran back to Him like a little child singing "Jesus Loves Me."

My wounded heart slowly began to heal. He was pursuing me, and I knew that I had to trust and obey Him. Within a couple of months, He had orchestrated an intense time of Christian counseling with my pastor, followed by a relocation to a former job working for a godly boss. Shortly after returning to my old job, Ken and I moved to the small town of Powder Springs, Georgia. We soon found a local church and began to get involved. We made new friends and were active in all activities. We attended a class on spiritual gifts, and I learned that my primary gift was teaching. This new insight triggered my thoughts back to the verses Benji Clark had pointed me to in Isaiah. As I pondered the connection, I was reminded of the day I was preparing for a youth fellowship at my house and I clearly heard the Lord say, "You will teach women." I had laughed then, but now I felt like it was really going to happen. I visited a ladies' class to see what it was like, only to leave with a critical attitude regarding the teacher. I was convinced I could do a much better job, especially since I had so much experience in the field of teaching. As I write, I am amazed at the arrogance I openly flaunted. What I thought was confidence was not. It was my flesh holding up the self-promotion sign right before God's eyes and that poor teacher. I am so grateful for the mercy and patience my God extended me during that season.

When it comes to self-promotion, isn't it amazing how fast we will volunteer for ministry? That is exactly what I did. I moved fast and communicated my desire to teach a ladies' class to my minister of education. Soon afterward, he called to tell me there was a need for a teacher in the senior women's class and asked if I could teach the following Sunday. I agreed and prepared a lengthy lesson from the life of Jacob. I was prepared and stationed in the teacher's chair when the first member of the class entered and advised me that a class member had agreed to take the teaching position. She thought the minister of education knew about this, but it was apparent he didn't. She was very kind and apologized for the misunderstanding. I was not hurt. I was mad. I was supposed to teach women. As I write this, I am smiling at the glaring proof of "self" in control. It was my way or no way that Sunday. I told them I had prepared and would teach them the lesson. They all sat there and smiled, nodded appropriately, and thanked me for teaching. They probably praised God when I huffed out the door. I was so mad that I skipped the worship service and went straight home to sulk. I thought I was ready, but God knew I wasn't. As I look back, it is so clear to me that God tested me and I failed the test. I didn't understand everything, but what I did understand was that I couldn't make it happen. Over the next couple of months, God revealed the truth of that experience. A dose of humility from the measuring spoon of God is hard to swallow, but worth the benefits to the soul.

A couple of years later, Ken and I were led by the Spirit to change churches. It was at this church that God placed me in a very short and intense season of preparation. It was so difficult that I began to doubt my salvation. God's timing is always right. He had been working, and I had been paying more attention. He had planned a huge test on two of the most serious matters in my life. God used a scheduled business trip to New Jersey to administer this test. The trip was extended two days due to heavy snow, and it was during those two days that God dealt with the most important issues in my life: doubting my salvation and my wounded marriage. My spiritual struggles over the years had taken a toll on my marriage. I blamed Ken in this area by using the fact that he was the spiritual head of our family. However, God and I knew that submission was an insecurity problem with me, and Ken was not to blame. When things got difficult with us, the kids, our jobs, or church, I blamed Ken and expected him to fix it. I am so grateful Ken stayed strong throughout those hard times.

That weekend, God tested the sincerity of my heart concerning my issues. It was a verbal test that required complete openness and honest answers to all questions. Acceptance of the truth had to be in the secret place of my being. After two intense days of walking, talking, and listening to the Lord, my issues were settled. These are the three things I sensed God showing me that weekend:

> My *salvation* was sealed the day I understood and accepted Jesus as my Savior.
> My *insecurity* would decrease as I became more secure in Christ.
> My *submission* to Ken would become easier the more submissive I was to the Holy Spirit.

I returned to Georgia a different woman. On the following Sunday, my pastor approached me about starting a new class for women, and I confidently agreed with full assurance this was God's will. God calls, prepares, and places according to His will.

∽

Day 1
Classroom of Tragedy

In session 3, we looked at the huge effect jealousy can have on our lives. We learned that God wants to turn destructive jealousy into Godly jealousy. He can turn our weaknesses into strengths. In this session, we will examine the effects of tragedy on the innocent.

Earlier, I used the educational classroom to illustrate the importance of preparation and testing. In the sanctification classroom, we are given "do-overs" until we pass the test. God's testing is part of His preparation. Before I move any further, I want you to know that God does not orchestrate tragedies in our lives to test us. He uses the journey of life to teach and test us. The *American Heritage Dictionary* defines *tragedy* as the results of a very sad event that produces profound unhappiness. We will experience tragic events. God's use of a tragic event will always be for our good. The purpose of our preparation is for us to be holy in our conduct. Our acceptance and application of His teaching determines the course of our life. We must trust and obey Him—for there is no other way to be truly happy.

The death of my mother devastated me. My response was detrimental to my relationship with God and my family. Did I learn from it? Yes. Have I experienced other tragedies of that magnitude? Yes. Did I learn from them? Yes. Did God use them for good? Yes. The next two sessions will touch on the good He brought into my life with each tragedy.

Before I began this session, I sensed the Holy Spirit asking me this question: "Are you allowing what I am teaching you through this study to prepare you?" This challenging question reminded me that He is the teacher and I am the student, and that remains the same as I write this study. My answer was, "Yes, Lord." I want to ask you the same question: are you allowing the Holy Spirit to teach you through this study? If your answer is yes, write at least one thing you have learned so far in this study.

Let's look at some of Matthew Henry's introductory comments about Job. "The instructions to be learned from the patience of Job, and from his trials, are as useful now, and as much needed as ever. We live under the same Providence, we have the same chastening Father, and there is the same need for correction unto righteousness. The fortitude and patience of Job, though not small, gave way in his severe troubles; but his faith was fixed upon the coming of his Redeemer, and this gave him steadfastness and consistency, though every other dependence, particularly the pride and boast of a self-righteous spirit, was tried and consumed. Another great doctrine of the faith, particularly set forth in the book of Job, is that of Providence. It is plain, from this history that the Lord watched over his servant Job with the affection of a wise and loving father."[43]

God's providence is defined as "foresight, divine care and guardianship."[44] Our understanding of God's providence is very important in this session.

Use Matthew Henry's comments to answer these questions.

- According to Matthew Henry, who lives under the same providence Job did? _____.

- According to Matthew Henry, there is still the need for _____ unto _____.

- Because we live under the same providence Job did, the Lord watches over us with the affection of a _____ and _____ father.

The Lord knows us better than we know ourselves. We can be confident that He has a purpose for our yesterdays, today, and our tomorrows.

The book of Job covers forty-two chapters and highlights one season in Job's life. A new season begins with the ending of another, followed by highlights of the next. The transition from season to season is unavoidable and important. We will get a glimpse of Job's life before the most devastating season in his life arrives. Our journey through the past, present, and future of Job will conclude with a glimpse into the next season of Job's life. For today and tomorrow, we will examine specific portions of Scripture and glean personal application from the testing of Job.

In Job 1:1–5, we are given a brief description of Job's character and relationship with God. He was very wealthy and held in high esteem by all who knew him. He was involved in the lives of his children. He cared about the condition of their souls, instructing them in the ways of repentance and forgiveness.

Read Job 1:1–5, and answer this question.

- If Job lived next door to you, how would you describe him?

    _____

    _____

In Job 1:6–12, we are given a scene that Job never knew about this side of heaven. We see in these verses that Satan found a way to come before the Lord. When the angels came to present themselves to God, he tagged along with them. When God praised Job, Satan sarcastically challenged the depth of Job's loyalty by stating that he would surely curse God if the divine hedge of protection were removed. God took on the challenge, and Satan left the scene.

> "Afflictions must not divert us from, but quicken us to our religion. If in all our troubles we look to the Lord, He will support us" (Henry, 415).

Find the answer to this question in Job 1:6–12.

- Why do you think God gave Job's possessions over to Satan?

    _____

Job's first test:

- Read Job 1:13–22, and list possessions that were stolen and destroyed. Describe Job's response in verse 22.

    _____

    _____

Job's second test:

- Read Job 2:1–10, and fill in the blanks in verse 3. "And he still maintains his _____, though you _____ me against him to ruin him without any _____."

Satan doesn't need a reason to come against God's servants. His primary reason is to get back at God for casting him out of heaven.

Search Job 2:1–10 for the answers to these questions.

- What permission did God give Satan this time? _____

- Besides Job's health, what else hurt Job? _____

I'm sure that Job's wife was devastated by such great loss. Now that Job was physically being tortured, she may have feared that she would be next to suffer. Instead of focusing on Job's pain and discouragement, she chose to hurt him by spewing words of disrespect and contempt. This little phrase is so true: "Hurt people hurt people."

Fill in the blanks in Proverbs 31:11–12.

- "Her husband has full _____ in her and lacks nothing of value. She brings him _____, not _____, all the days of _____ life."

The last sentence of Job 2:10 caught my attention. "In all of this, Job did not sin in what he said." What a man of strength and integrity! My tongue gets me in trouble faster than anything I do. There have been times in my marriage when everything that could go wrong did, and guess who lost it? I did and often became furious at Ken because he didn't. How about you?

This will not be the end of Job's time of testing. He seemed to easily pass his first two tests, yet a harder test awaits him. Let's look at a few things we can learn from Job.

> Don't allow your pain to hurt others.
> Don't allow your mind to wander from the truth.
> Don't allow your heart to conceive lies.
> Don't allow your lips to make you look foolish.

As we end today's session, take a few minutes to reflect on a season when tragedy hit you or someone close to you. The present may be that type of season. In my season, I was so devastated that I didn't realize my own hurt was consuming me. I didn't know the things to watch for or the things to do. I could have avoided the self-inflicted wounds. My wonderful husband and children could have been spared the foolish words from my mouth. God may want you to deal with something or pray specifically for someone else right now. Take a few minutes to sit quietly before the Lord and allow Him to comfort you or direct you to comfort another.

See you tomorrow at the tent of Job!

∽

Day 2
Blessings from Suffering

Job's wounds were many and deep, yet his faith remained steadfast. Let's take a few minutes to closely review his responses to his first two tests.

Test 1—Job 1:20–22: "At this, Job got up and tore his robe and shaved his head. Then he fell to the ground in worship and said: 'Naked I came from my mother's womb, and naked I will depart. The LORD gave and the LORD has taken away; may the name of the LORD be praised.' In all this, Job did not sin by charging God with wrongdoing."

Test 2—Job 2:8–10: "Then Job took a piece of broken pottery and scraped himself with it as he sat among the ashes. His wife said to him, 'Are you still holding on to your integrity? Curse God and die!' He replied, 'You are talking like a foolish woman. Shall we accept good from God, and not trouble?' In all this, Job did not sin in what he said."

In the first test, Job's response included physical postures. Describe his physical actions as he poured out his grief and worship to God.

Grief: _____

Worship: _____

In the second test, Job's physical posture was quite different. Describe his posture and the verbal responses as he suffered physically.

Pain: _____

Words: _____

When we have a season of tragedy, we must, like Job, run to God immediately and pour out our hearts. We can tear our clothes, shave our heads, cry in the shower, or scream into our pillows. God still hears and cares. We must not walk away at this point. We must focus our attention on our God. We must bow our heads, kneel beside our beds, fall on our knees at the kitchen sink, or go facedown on the floor and worship God. We must express our gratitude for His goodness and compassion as well as our pain and need for Him to comfort us. When there seems to be no end in sight, seek His calming presence. Curl up in your favorite chair and read and meditate on His Word. Listen to a favorite praise song or hymn and sing to Him. I encourage you to do these things because I know they work. Trust His Word that tells us: "Be still and know (recognize and understand) that I am God."[45]

You and I would probably agree that Job would welcome a visit from a loyal friend about now. I love my friends and enjoy spending time with them. My journey in life has included several seasons of tragedy, and the presence of my friends has always comforted me. They listened to me, cried with me, prayed for me, and sat silently beside me.

Read Job 2:11–13, and list the actions of Job's friends.

_____

_____

For the next thirty-five chapters, Job and his three friends, Eliphaz, Bildad, and Zophar, have an ongoing dialogue about the situation. *Who's Who in the Bible* provides a great summary of their lengthy conversations.

> His three concerned friends believe that Job should not protest his innocence but rather confess his sins, for they think some wrongdoing on his part must lie behind so much personal loss. Their words of comfort begin as general admonitions but soon become harsh arguments, more typical of prosecuting attorneys than of empathetic friends. In three cycles of challenge and response, Job defends his innocence against the criticisms of his friends, while summoning God to judge his case. At the end of this debate, a young bystander named Elihu again castigates Job, interpreting human illness as a refining experience and questioning Job's verbose self-righteousness.[46]

I can imagine God observing the scene and deciding it was time to involve Elihu as His spokesman. Let's look at portions of Scripture that capture the truths God wanted Job to hear through Elihu.

In 32:1–6, the conversation ends with Job's friends and begins with Elihu.

- Why was Elihu angry with Job?

_____

In Job 32:15–18, we see two reasons Elihu was compelled to speak to Job.

- What were they?

_____

_____

_____

In Job 33, Elihu pleads with Job to listen and heed his words. Elihu addresses Job's complaint to God in verse 13.

- What is the complaint?

_____

In verses 14–22, Elihu contradicts Job's complaint.

- List the ways Elihu tells Job that God speaks.

_____

_____

_____

In Job 34, Elihu proclaims God's justice and defends His right to act sovereignly. God is always good and always right. There is never a reason to complain of injustice from God. In verses 35–37, Elihu promotes the testing of Job.

- Why?

_____

_____

In Job 35, Elihu condemns self-righteousness. Job's questioning of why God allowed the righteous to suffer demonstrated his lack of trust in the One who does no wrong. Complete trust in Him produces complete obedience to Him. In verses 9–12, Elihu addresses "why" God refuses to answer the cries of the oppressed that are wicked and offer up empty words.

- What was the single word? _____

In Job 36, Elihu proclaims God's goodness and majesty. He knew that God would eventually deal with Job, and he wanted Job to be prepared. In verses 5–12, Elihu tells Job how God deals with the wicked and the righteous.

- What awaits those who do not listen?

_____

- What awaits those who obey and serve Him?

_____

In verses 32–33, Elihu describes God holding the lightning and the purpose of thunder.

- What is the purpose of God's thunder?

_____

In Job 37, it is apparent that there is lightning and thunder. Elihu describes the power of God's voice. He tells Job to listen and consider God's wonders. In verse 24, Elihu concludes with a final instruction for Job. What is it?

_____

Elihu spoke only what was given him from the Spirit. He is a picture of Ecclesiastes 12:11: "The words of the wise are like goads, their collected sayings like firmly embedded nails—given by one Shepherd." On the contrary, Job's three friends "scorned" him (Job 16:20, NKJV).

A friend loves at all times, and a brother is born for adversity" (Proverbs 17:17).

> *Elihu fits the description of a friend better than Job's other friends.*

"A true friend, like a brother, loves 'at all times,' in joy and sorrow, sickness and health, when communication is easy and when communication requires hard work. 'At all times' means there are no times when one does not love a friend. A genuine friend multiplies the joys and divides the sorrows."[47]

I appreciate my friends who love me "at all times." I would want Elihu to be on my best friend list, wouldn't you?

We've covered a lot of material today and still have five chapters to examine. So take a break, get a cup of your favorite beverage, and stay with me. It will be well worth your time and effort, trust me. I need a refill of my favorite ... *coffee*!

I bet you are like me, you needed the break! Now let's move into the final segments of Job's story. As you fill in the blanks, meditate on the scene before moving to the next question.

God comes on the scene in chapter 38. The thunder has announced the storm in chapter 37, and now God speaks out of it to Job.

- Job 38:2: "Who is this that darkens my counsel with words without _____?"

Before Job can answer, God begins a lengthy challenge of Job's abilities and knowledge and continues through chapter 39. In chapter 40, God questions Job.

- Job 40:2: "Will the one who contends with the Almighty _____ Him? Let him who accuses God _____ him!"

Job answers in verses 4 and 5.

- "I am _____, how can I reply to you? I put my hand over my mouth. I spoke once, but I have no _____—twice, but I will say no more."

In chapter 41, God continues to challenge Job. He concludes in verse 34 by placing a holy spotlight directly on Job.

- "He looks down on all that are _____; he is king over all that are _____."

In chapter 42, Job replies to the Lord.

- "I know that you can do all things; no _____ of yours can be thwarted. You asked, 'Who is this that obscures my _____ without knowledge?' Surely I spoke of things I did not understand, things too wonderful for me to know. You said, 'Listen now, and I will speak; I will question you, and you shall answer me.' My _____ had heard of you but now my _____ have seen you. Therefore I despise myself and _____ in dust and ashes."

   "Communion with the Lord effectually convinces and humbles a saint, and makes him glad to part with his most beloved sins."[48]

Read Job 42:7–17, and answer the following questions.

- What did God require of Job's three friends?

   _____

   _____

- When did the Lord make Job prosperous again?

  _____

  _____

- Who comforted Job this time?

  _____

I am glad the season of tragedy ended for Job and the blessings God restored were many. We wouldn't have known how God blessed Job if we had not been given a glimpse of his new season. I want to close with some interesting information regarding Job's beautiful daughters and their names. I have suggested some possible reasons Job chose their names and included them in his book.

> Jemimah means "turtle dove", a name often used of a bride, describing her fine form and <u>lovely voice</u>. Keziah was the name of a fragrant plant, cassia, which was a prized variety of cinnamon. Keren-Happuch was a horn of eye paint, usually black, that was used to draw attention to a woman's eyes. It was probably the equivalent of modern day eyeliner.[49]

Could the following names Job gave to his daughters have represented his encounter with the Almighty?

- Jemimah—*lovely voice*; could it represent the voice of God when He spoke to Job out of the storm? When God speaks, He needs no introduction. His voice exposes the state of man's heart and forces him to acknowledge his folly.

  Jesus said, "I am the good shepherd; I know my sheep and my sheep know me" (John 10:14).

- Keziah—fragrant plant; could it represent the sweet aroma of Job's prayer for his friends who had scorned him? When others hurt us, it is a sacrifice of our will to sincerely pray for them. His prayer also kept God's wrath from his friends. "My servant Job will pray for you, and I will accept his prayer and not deal with you according to your folly" (Job 42:8).

  Jesus said to "pray for those who spitefully use you and persecute you" (Matthew 5:44).

- Keren-Happuch—*horn of eye paint*; using the spiritual meaning for *horn*, which is strength, could it represent the strengthening of faith and spiritual vision Job received from God? God's mercy restores the repentant and strengthens their spiritual eyes to see the beauty of His sovereignty. He uses our weakness to reveal His strength. Our obedience to His purposes will always bring blessings.

  "The LORD is my rock, fortress and deliverer; my God is my rock, in whom I take refuge. He is my shield and the horn of my salvation, my stronghold" (Psalms 18:2).

As I looked at these possibilities, I saw a wonderful picture of *grace*. God saw the lurking tentacles of self-righteousness in Job's heart and knew it was the result of worshipping the Law. The testing and suffering proved Job's captivity. His friends' efforts exposed their self-righteousness as well. Elihu was placed by God to prepare Job for his encounter with the Almighty. The power of God's presence freed Job from the blindness of his captivity. Job's obedience in praying for his friends allowed God to replace his captivity with renewed spiritual strength and blessings.

We cannot end this session without a time of personal examination. What did God reveal to you in Job's journey that you needed today? Maybe you sense that He wants you to be like Elihu in the life of a friend or family member. Let's close today talking and listening to the One who knows us better than we know ourselves.

See you tomorrow at the tent of Esther!

Day 3
Fieldtrips of Maturity

Today and tomorrow, our study of Esther will reveal a different type of testing than the type Job experienced. God's providential hand rested differently on Esther, but His purpose was the same. He rescues His people. In our study of Job, we saw how the testing of God revealed Job's captivity and brought about his rescue and abundant blessings. In our study of Esther, we will see how the testing of God brings about the rescue of a nation.

The story begins with our first snapshot of God's providential hand. Esther does not come on the scene until chapter 2. Before we jump into our first snapshot of providence, it's crucial that we catch up on Esther's life up to this point. In doing so, we will a see a test that involved Esther but was not assigned to her.

Read Esther 2:5–7, and answer the following questions.

- Who was Mordecai?

  _____

- What relation was Mordecai to Esther?

  _____

- Why did Mordecai adopt Esther?

  _____

Based on the information we have, Mordecai could have been Esther's only living relative. Maybe he wasn't, but we know he adopted her as his own daughter. His decision probably didn't come easily. Mordecai's test could have been the decision to take on such a responsibility. Would Mordecai give up his plans for God's plan?

Based on those I know personally who have adopted children, their decision to adopt did not come easily. A young couple I love dearly just recently completed the first step in adopting a young boy from Latvia. As the young woman's mentor, I am well aware of the countless struggles and personal tests she has experienced prior to knowing which child God had for them. She recently shared with me that the entire process of adoption—from waiting on God's perfect timing to completing all the necessary requirements—has been the single most difficult path on her spiritual journey. It has also been the most rewarding.

Read the first chapter of Esther, and answer the following questions.

- What do you think prompted King Xerxes' command of Queen Vashti to come before him in full royal attire?

  _____

  _____

- Why do you think Queen Vashti refused?

  _____

  _____

- What were the personal repercussions of Vashti's decision?

  _____

  _____

  _____

- Who else would suffer for her decision?

  _____

- Write the part of the royal decree that revealed the providence of God for Esther to be queen of Persia?

  _____

Timing on the calendar of God is miraculously perfect. Esther was beautiful, mature, and now old enough to marry. In Esther 2:7 (KJV), we are told that she was "fair and beautiful." The words mean she was exceptionally beautiful in her face and form, a good person, one who was pleasant, sweet, gracious, kind, and loving.[50]

When King Xerxes got over his anger, his personal servants encouraged him to move forward in the process of finding the next queen. All the young, beautiful virgins from the 127 provinces of his kingdom were brought to the king's harem and prepared for the selection process. Esther was selected, and her testing began. Let's look behind the scenes and fill in the gaps that will support Esther's recorded actions.

> Their destiny was in the hands of Jehovah-sabaoth. The Lord of Hosts, who would go before them and deliver them from harm.

The Amplified Bible states in Esther 2:11 that "Mordecai [who was an attendant in the king's court] walked every day before the court of the harem to learn how Esther was doing and what would become of her." Since Mordecai was in this position, it is possible that he knew the decree was coming before it was ever written and proclaimed across the vast province. Can't you see him sharing the obvious news with Esther? What about her dreams of marrying that handsome guy who lived just a few tents away? What about his dreams of grandchildren to spoil rotten and enjoy? We can draw a strong conclusion from the text that Mordecai knew this was probably the first of many tests. The correct response to the initial test would provide the confidence and strength to pass those that followed. Mordecai knew that their destiny was in the hands of their God, Jehovah-sabaoth, the Lord of Hosts, who would go before them and deliver them from harm. The initial test would be before they came for Esther. They must willingly walk on the path set before them with confidence that this was God's plan. As we look at Scripture and answer the following questions, we should easily recognize the fingerprints of providence.

Read Esther 2:3, 8–10, and answer the following questions.

- Who was Hegai, and what were his responsibilities?

  _____

- Why do you think Hegai showed favor to Esther?

  _____

- What does verse 10 tell us about Esther?

  _____

  _____

I believe that with each phase of the process, Mordecai encouraged Esther, and she remained steadfast. Wouldn't you like to know what Hegai told Xerxes about Esther?

Read verses 11–17, and fill in the blanks in verse 17.

"Now the king was attracted to Esther more than to any of the other women, and she won his favor and approval more than any of the other virgins. So he set a royal crown on her head and _____ ____ _____ _____ ____ _____."

Write verse 18, and circle or highlight your favorite words.

_____

_____

_____

As you read verses 17 and 18, did you imagine the scene and Esther's thoughts? I loved every word and imagined her thoughts to be something like this:

> *I, Hadessa have won the favor and approval of the king. He is going to place a royal crown on my head. He has planned a banquet in my name. He has even proclaimed this day to be remembered as a holiday forever. Thank you, my Lord of Host -Jehovah-sabaoth.*

As we end our session, I want you to place your name after "I" and say these words out loud to your Lord of Host.

> "I, _____ have won the favor and approval of King Jesus. He is going to place a royal crown on my head. He has planned a banquet in my name. He has even proclaimed this day to be remembered as a holiday forever. Thank you, my Lord of Host—Jehovah-sabaoth."

See you tomorrow in the palace of Xerxes!

❧

<blockquote>
Day 4
</blockquote>

Blessings from Courage

Yesterday's look into the life of Esther reminds me of the fictional story of Cinderella. However, the story of Esther gives us much more than a happy ending from wishes that come true. Her story is real. Her journey reveals the providence of God and lessons for living. Many of us know the pain and effects of abandonment. Most of us will never wear a crown or live in a castle while on earth. But at the appointed time, just like Esther, we will move to the palace.

Today, we will see the testing of Esther's faith and courage as she stands in opposition to evil. Esther must pass a couple of smaller tests to prepare her for the biggest test of her life. Let me review a couple of things before we move forward with Esther's testing. Mordecai has forbidden Esther to reveal her nationality and background in hopes she would be safe from the evil that continually came upon the Jewish nation. Even though Esther is married, she continues to obey her foster father. Mordecai continues to sit within the king's gate, listening and watching as a concerned father.

Read 2:21–23, and list the order of events.

_____

_____

Esther's submission to Mordecai was easy, especially since it prevented the assassination of her husband. This test of obedience was a breeze. Often, God will ask us to do something easy in preparation for a more difficult assignment. Esther trusted Mordecai so it was easy for her to continue following his instruction, even though she was no longer under his authority. I have messed up so many times in my marriage, workplace, and ministry by not being submissive to the authorities over my life. I like the following definition of *submission*.

> Submission means to put all of yourself—understandings, knowledge, opinions, feelings, energies—at the disposal of a person in authority over you. This never means subjecting yourself to abusive tyranny, nor does it suggest mindless acquiescence to the whims of another. It is the yielding of humble and intelligent obedience—without suggestion of inferiority or worthlessness. Relationships in life are merely the classroom for teaching submission to the will of God.[51]

Now let's look at what the Bible says about *submission*.

Complete 1 Peter 2:13.

- "Submit yourselves for the Lord's sake to every _____ _____
  _____ _____."

In chapter 3, we see the strength of Mordecai as he refused to bow and give honor to evil Haman. Mordecai's courage brought devastating ramifications. A decree was issued to kill every Jew in the 127 provinces under the rule of Xerxes. This action would include killing Mordecai and satisfying Haman's anger against him. Evil will hide behind good, as in the courage of Mordecai.

In every situation that brings us to a crossroad of good and evil, we must not look down the evil path.

It can be like watching a horror movie. The scary scenes consume our thoughts and shatter our courage.

Underline the words in Philippians 4:8 that describe what is good.

> "Finally, brothers, whatever is true, whatever is noble, whatever is right, whatever is pure, whatever is lovely, whatever is admirable—if anything is excellent or praiseworthy—think about such things."

The verse concludes with the instructional word *think*. The definition of this word shows us that the process of "thinking" usually moves us to some form of action.

> "The way we respond to what we think can produce good or evil" (author).

"Think—to have as a thought; to formulate in the mind; to ponder; to reason; to believe; suppose; to remember; call to mind; to visualize; imagine; to devise; invent."[52]

Let's take a quick look at some examples from our text with a fun exercise.

Read the verse associated with each response and mark it either <u>G</u> (good) or <u>E</u> (evil). Mark an <u>X</u> beside the one that exposes Esther's hesitancy to obey Mordecai.

    ____ (Esther 4:4)—Esther's maids' and eunuchs' response to evil

    ____ (Esther 4:5)—Esther's response to Mordecai's refusal

    ____ (Esther 4:7)—Mordicai's response to Hathach

    ____ (Esther 4:11)—Esther's response to Mordecai

    ____ (Esther 4:12–14)—Mordecai's response to Esther

    ____ (Esther 4:15–16)—Esther's response to Mordecai

All of the responses were good. The X would have been beside Esther 4:11.

Matthew Henry states that, "We are prone to shrink from services that are attended with peril or loss. But when the cause of Christ and His people demand it, we must take up our cross, and follow Him."[53]

Esther was no different than you or I. Sometimes, a decision is so difficult that we must seek advice or direction from someone stronger. That is what Esther required from Mordecai. The challenging words of Mordecai, "who knows whether you have come to the kingdom for such a time as this" (Esther 4:14, NJKV), presented God's call to Esther. The courageous queen proceeded, willing to die for the cause of her people. Esther had another test set before her. She must expose the evil of Haman to the king.

In this exercise, you will read a chapter and fill in two blanks. The objective is to see good and evil at work in each chapter. We know that God always works for the good of His people while Satan does the opposite. As you can see, I've shown how God worked for the good of Esther and Satan worked against Mordecai in chapter 5. You will determine either God or Satan for chapters 6–10. I've given you the answer for chapter 5, but please take time to read the chapter. It will help you understand the example and how to determine the answers for chapters 6–10.

Chapter 5	<u>God</u>	a) King accepts Esther.
	<u>Satan</u>	b) Haman plans to hang Mordecai.
Chapter 6	_____	a) Xerxes honors Mordecai.
	_____	b) Haman is humiliated by his wife.
Chapter 7	_____	a) Haman fell on the couch to plead with Esther.
	_____	b) Harbona exposed plans to hang Mordecai.
Chapter 8	_____	a) Mordecai was appointed over Haman's estate.
	_____	b) Esther saves the Jews.
Chapter 9	_____	a) The Jews destroy their enemies.
	_____	b) The Feast of Purim is established.
Chapter 10	_____	a) The Jews had a spokesperson for their welfare.
	_____	b) Mordecai was raised up and made second in rank to King Xerxes.

"And who knows but that you have come to royal position for such a time as this?" (Esther 4:14).

This is the challenging question Mordecai sent to Esther. A closer look offers us three principles we must embrace if we are to fulfill God's purpose for our life.

1. No place of privilege can ever exempt a person from the responsibility to respond to God's call.
2. Although a situation may look hopeless, God is never helpless.
3. A God-given opportunity is an individual's received privilege.
   The same divine guidance that seemingly directed Esther's thoughts, words, and actions is available for you.[54]

I encourage you to answer the following questions and then close your time today in prayer regarding each one.

- Are you presently doing something God called you to do? If you are, what is it and how has He provided what you need to do it?

  _____

  _____

- Has God called you to do something and you've put it off? If you have, what is it and why are you waiting?

  _____

  _____

- Are you in a situation that seems hopeless? If yes, what is it?

  _____

  _____

See you tomorrow for a final look at Job and Esther!

☙

Day 5
Test of Truth

Recently, I spoke at a mother-daughter tea on the importance of leaving a godly legacy. While reviewing my material, I sensed the Holy Spirit telling me, "The proof is in the power." As I meditated on His statement, I realized He had just given me the message in one sentence. My notes contained three strong points taken from the lives of three women in the Bible who were given new legacies. I added my testimony at the conclusion to validate God's power in today's world. A couple of days before I spoke, I began to wonder if my testimony would really make an impact. I reflected on previous teachers and speakers who had inspired me with their testimonies. Some of them, for unknown reasons, soon fell away from God, leaving me confused and doubting the validity of their testimony. The Holy Spirit reminded me that doubting the validity of someone else's testimony can cause me to doubt my own. I must trust Him to validate His power in my life.

After giving my testimony, I asked them to raise their hands if they believed every word in the Bible was true. Immediately, every hand went up. My challenge to them was to embrace the truth that God's power can change their lives today, just as it did those of the women in the Bible. The closing brought a final look at the proof of His power. I reminded them of the creation story in Genesis, emphasizing that the same power that created and changed lives in the Bible is still creating and changing lives today.

The test of truth is found in the proof of His power.

The fourth step is another part of the ongoing journey of walking with Jesus. Sometimes, He will take us off the smooth highway of life and put us on an unknown road that is rough and very uncomfortable.

He prepares us to be living proof of His power.

In session 1, we studied the miraculous conception and birth of the Son of God who would be called Immanuel, which means "God with us."[55] He came to us when we couldn't get to Him. His mission was to open the way to a new covenant for those who believed in Him. Jesus comforts us today with the same words He spoke to His disciples, "I am the way and the truth and the life. No one comes to the Father except through me" (John 14:6). Jesus came to us, made a new way for us, and His Spirit lives within us. Let's take a few minutes to notice the change from the penalty of death in the old covenant to the promise of life in the new covenant[56] (see chart on page 85).

In this session, we looked at two people who had completely different journeys, both of which were at the providential hand of God. We learned that Job's life changed from one of ease to one of pain. Esther's life changed from one of pain to one of ease. Job and Esther had hard tests. In this session, I shared some of the hardest tests the Lord placed in my life. By no means were these all of the tests for Nancy. Some, I didn't need to retake because I heeded their lessons and learned from them the first time.

God's purpose for this type of study is twofold. First of all, it will help my sisters in Christ see the commonality of everyone's spiritual journey. The second purpose is a personal one. Each session has caused me to evaluate a particular season of my life. There have been tears and laughter with each session. It has been amazing to see His providential hand in every season of my life. I believe it is good to be reminded that our times of testing are to purify our hearts.

Our final look into the lives of Job and Esther will be focused on seeing the proof of His power in their lives in the midst of being tested.

Day 1: The Classroom of Tragedy

The two conversations between Satan and God reveal that God had singled out Job to be a tested man of faith. We all have known or heard about people like Job, who walked obediently with God and tragedy took their possessions and family. We may have personally experienced similar pain and despair. After studying Job, we can understand how God often uses Satan to test our faithfulness.

Complete the blanks in 2 Chronicles 16:9.

- "For the _____ of the LORD _____ throughout the _____ to _____ those whose hearts are fully committed to him."

In 2 Chronicles 16:9, we are told that the eyes of the Lord *range* throughout the earth. *Range* describes the "extent of perception, knowledge, experience or ability."[57] In Job 1:7, we are told that Satan *roams* the earth. *To roam* means "to move or travel through."[58]

Complete these statements from the definitions of *roam* and *range*.

- In order for Satan to see the affairs of man, he must _____ or _____ _____ to where they are on earth.

- God has the _____, _____, _____, or _____ to see the affairs of all people and strengthens them without leaving His throne.

Nothing can come against us from the enemy without God's permission. We must remain fully committed to Him with a heart of adoration. Genuine praise must flow from our heart, even during times of sorrow, discouragement, trial, and temptation. Psalm 42:5 are the words David used to describe his feelings and source of hope.

Complete the verse.

- "Why are you so downcast, O my soul? Why are you so disturbed within me? Put your hope in God, for I will yet _____ him, my Savior and my God."

The "proof of God's power" is in His omnipresence. This means He is actively present in all places and relationships. He is always with us. Look back at 2 Chronicles 16:9, and write what He does for those who are fully committed to Him.

_____

_____

_____

Day 2: The Blessings from Suffering

In a season of suffering, the last thing we need is a spouse like Job's wife or friends like his three friends. What we really need is someone like Elihu to be placed in our life as an instrument of God to help us. It would be great if that type of friend came on the scene immediately after the storm hit to begin comforting us, but often, that isn't when God will send such a person. There is something to be said about the progress pain produces in our spiritual journey. The most important thing we can do for those in a season of suffering is to be a blessing to them. To be a blessing, we need God's blessing. How do we receive His blessings? Read Psalm 1:1–6, and complete the following statements.

Blessed in the man who does not …

- listen to the advice from the _____.

- support the ways of _____.

- stay around _____.

Blessed is the man who does …

- take pleasure in the _____ of the Lord.

- meditates on it _____ and _____.

- yields _____ in season.

- prospers in what he _____.

When a season of suffering passes, it is then we can look back and see the providential hand of God. God restored everything Job lost twofold, except for the number of his children. In Job 42:15, we are told that Job gave his daughters an inheritance along with their brothers.

> According to Israelite law, daughters were not allowed to inherit if there were no sons. Thus Job's gift of an inheritance to his daughters is a special act of grace. This inheritance would allow the daughters to remain in the midst of the family with their brothers and to continue the close affectionate relationships that existed among them. Some commentators suggest that it was a sign of gratitude for his new family. Certainly throughout his ordeal, Job had learned to go beyond the letter of the Law to the Author of the Law, who in the end did not pay Job wages deserved but rewarded Job according to His grace.[59]

Take a few minutes and compare the restrictions of the law in the old covenant to the blessings of grace in the new covenant.

The Glory of the New Covenant

Old Covenant	New Covenant
The Law was written on stone tablets (2 Cor. 3:3).	The New Covenant is written on human hearts (2 Cor. 3:3).
The letter of the Law kills (2 Cor. 3:6).	The Spirit of the Lord gives liberty and life (2 Cor.3:6, 17).
The Law brings condemnation (2 Cor. 3:11).	The New Covenant brings righteousness (2 Cor. 3:9).
The old covenant was passing away (2 Cor. 3:11).	The new covenant remains forever (2 Cor. 3:11).

The Israelites could not look on God without a veil (2 Cor. 3:13).	All can look upon the glory of the Lord (2 Cor. 3:11).
The glory of the old covenant was passing (2 Cor. 3:11).	The glory of the new covenant is ever increasing (2 Cor. 3:18).

The "proof of God's power" is in His Grace.

Grace is God's Riches at Christ's expense.

Day 3: The Field Trips of Maturity

I'm sure the expression "field trip" brings back certain memories from our school days. I will never forget my sixth-grade trip to Montgomery, the capital of my home state, Alabama. I had so much fun. Recently, I ran across a charm I purchased on that trip from a gift shop in the capital. I replayed the events of that day. It was such a sweet reminder. As a sixth-grader, I was excited and energized about my future as an adult. I came home feeling older and eager to grow up. It's amazing what can change our life in a day.

There have been other trips that weren't that pleasant. One of the most devastating I shared in the introduction of this session—the death of my mother. That trip of sorrow did just the opposite. What happened in one day held me in deep sorrow for five years. Both trips brought maturity into my life. The most difficult field trips of maturity can be either long or short, but they are usually the most significant in the process of spiritual maturity. God chooses the day, person, and circumstances to miraculously change the course of our life forever.

The proof of His power is visible in the maturity of His saints.

Has God taken you on a trip of maturity that He used to change the course of your life? If He has, write a brief description and the outcome.

_____

_____

Esther had three field trips that produced maturity in her life. The first one was a trip of sorrow. After the death of her parents, she traveled to the home of Mordecai, who trained her in the ways of God. The next was a trip of uncertainty. Esther was taken to the palace and physically prepared for a meeting with the king. Mordecai's encouragement strengthened Esther's resolve to trust God completely. Her final destination was a trip of faithfulness. When Xerxes selected Esther as his queen, she was immediately moved to a place of influence. Her new position brought the test of her maturity. Would she still walk in the ways of her God?

Our King takes us on all types of field trips. Some are to teach us, some to test us, and some to settle us. At the close of my testimony for this session, I shared three issues I settled with God: (1) salvation, (2) insecurity, and (3) submission. He has used people, circumstances, and His Word to continue to keep these things settled in my life. God used the same things in Esther's life to settle her issues.

What person, circumstance, and/or scripture has He used to help you settle some issues in your life? Take a minute and thank God for providing what you needed.

As we ended day 3, I asked you to place your name in the blank and say the same words to Jesus. Esther's thoughts were about her earthly husband. Jesus is our heavenly bridegroom, who is enthralled with our inward beauty.

Read and meditate on the words of Isaiah 62:5: "As a bridegroom rejoices over his bride, so will your God rejoice over you." Rewrite the verse and replace "your" and "you" with "my" and "me."

_____

_____

Day 4: The Blessings from Courage

Fear weakens our faith. If allowed to grow, fear will kill our courage! Esther was strong in her faith and courageous in her actions until Mordecai sent her a copy of the text with the edict to annihilate the Jews. Her fear increased when he asked her to go into the king's presence to plead for the lives of her people.

Read Esther 4:11, and complete this sentence.

- Esther's fear of _____ caused her to balk at the urgent request of Mordecai.

Just about the time I accomplish an assigned task from God, the alarming face of fear appears. Sometimes, I am like Esther in that I seem to have forgotten all the miraculous things God has done for me. God knows our deepest fears. He wants to help us deal with them, remove them, and walk confidently and courageously with Him. The Word always provides a solution for our fears.

Fill in the blanks in Deuteronomy 31:6.

- "Be strong and _____. Do not be _____ or _____ because of them, for the LORD your God goes with you; he will never _____ you nor _____ you."

The first thing we need to do is what Esther did. She acknowledged her fear. When we are open and honest with God, He delights to supply our need. Sometimes, He will provide us with a person like Mordecai who will speak revealing truth to us. Truth will always expose fear for what it really is—*false evidence appearing real.* The enemy always attempts to distract our focus onto that which we fear the most.

A few years ago, God called me to a speaking ministry. Before I ever began to minister in this capacity, I had to deal with a paralyzing onslaught of fear. The greatest fear in my spiritual journey has been the fear of failure. There have been many seasons when this particular fear raised its ugly head, and Nancy bolted to Jesus for help. He never turns me away or chastises me for falling prey to the lies of my enemy. He usually brings two verses in Isaiah to my mind, and I am comforted.

> I took you from the ends of the earth, from its farthest corners I called you. I said,
> "You are my servant"; I have chosen you and have not rejected you. So do not fear,
> for I am with you; do not be dismayed, for I am your God. I will strengthen you and
> help you; I will uphold you with my righteous right hand. (Isaiah 41:9–10)

Let's close today going before the throne of God with our fears. Don't allow the enemy to stop you from stepping into the place of His promise. We learned in our study of Job and Esther that people who seem to have it all together still go through times of painful and fearful testing. We clearly saw the proof of His power in the lives of Esther and Job. That same power lives in you. If you haven't been drawing from it, begin today, dear one.

Our time with Job and Esther was challenging and fun. Get ready for a deep dive into the lives of Jacob and Hannah!

Father,

Thank You for showing us our weaknesses and using different seasons in our lives to strengthen them. I praise You for showing us the purpose of Your tests along life's path. It is comforting to know that You love us, even when we question Your ways with us. Thank You for your mercy and grace when we allow fear and doubt to overcome us. Thank You for those in Your Word who help us learn and recognize Your ways. We choose to believe that "these trials are only to test our faith, to show that it is strong and pure. It is being tested as fire tests and purifies gold—and your faith is far more precious to God than mere gold" (1 Peter 1:7, NLT). I pray this in the name above all names, Jesus Christ, the Son of God.

Session 5

Spiritual Marker #5
"The Breaking"

As I begin this session, I am on vacation with my youngest son, Paul, and his family. Today is July 4, Independence Day. I'm proud of my country and grateful for the freedom we have as a nation. Our freedom to live in America did not come cheaply and neither did our freedom to live eternally with Christ. Both were costly liberties, worthy of our remembrance and gratitude. Yes, I love my country, but I love my Savior more.

Before I type a single word of a new session, I always review the previous one. It is during this time that I sense the Spirit beginning to prepare me for what season of my life's journey I am to share next. Originally, I thought I would begin this session after vacation, but as I packed, I felt the familiar nudge of the Spirit and I knew my laptop had to be included. When I opened my laptop today, I experienced that familiar knot in my stomach. This is the sensation I always get when I begin a new session. Revisiting the past seasons of my life stirs up memories and ignites emotions that bring tears one minute and laughter the next. As I began to review, the knot seemed to get bigger, and the selfish tug of my flesh screamed to go to the beach with my daughter-in-law, LeAnn, and my grandchildren. I told LeAnn that God had a *different* plan for me while she and the kids went to the beach. The last thing I wanted to do was disappoint them, but LeAnn was supportive and assured me that she and the kids understood. She hugged me and whispered the sweetest prayer, asking God to bless as I wrote.

In session 4, we saw how the providential hand of God took Job beyond the law into the light of God's grace. We also saw how Esther was strengthened by surrendering her fear to God. As we read their stories, we didn't know all their thoughts, so we used some imagination to connect what we did know from their actions.

In session 4, we also examined the purpose of the *testing* we encounter on our spiritual journey. The Holy Spirit knows what tests we need to take. I shared the short teaching assignment I forced upon those sweet senior ladies. That test was a spiritual x-ray, revealing immature areas that had to be dealt with by my heavenly Father. The most obvious area of immaturity was my attitude. In spite of my eagerness to use my gift of teaching, the Lord knew it wasn't the time or place. I can imagine Him shaking His majestic head as I sulked all the way home and complained to Ken about my teaching experience. God loved me too much to allow me to remain in that condition. My attitude was similar to a bone that had been broken from an injury and not set properly. I can imagine the finger that wrote the Ten Commandments pressing a huge red alarm in the heavenlies alerting the Angelic Orthopedic Association. Little did I know that major adjustments were soon to follow that would require the "breaking" and resetting of spiritual areas in my life. My first of many adjustments by the Great Physician was already scheduled on the appointment book of sanctification. He knew the area requiring the most work was not my *body*, but my *mind*. He also knew that the damage had been done by a variety of perpetrators, all of whom began their assaults on my thinking before I began school as a young child. Before I share more about my preschool days, I want to touch on the power of our thoughts. A couple of years ago, I heard a pastor describe the possible impact of negative and positive thoughts.

> A thought can lead to an attitude.
> An attitude can result in action.
> An action can lead to a behavior.
> A behavior can result in a habit.
> A habit can lead to a lifestyle.
> A lifestyle usually results in a *destiny*.

As I thought about this process, I saw the origination of so many destructive strongholds in my life. A quick trip into my past revealed a truth that sent me reeling from regrets. As a young child, I loved to play outside with my friends. As I replayed some of my early years, I saw the innocence in my life. My memories came to a screeching halt as I saw two painful times that saddened and shocked me immensely. I saw the *initiation of the enemy's plan* to plant fear, shame, and guilt in my life at an early age. The shame and guilt that caused my parents to divorce was passed on to my siblings and me. Following are two stories involving child care that prove how deviously the enemy seeks to hurt us early in life.

After my parents divorced, my mother worked multiple jobs until she remarried. This meant child care for me because I was only five at the time. It was during those difficult days that I experienced my first assault of fear and shame. The enemy used the very ones who were supposed to take care of me to strike the first blows.

The first assault came through a babysitter. She was a middle-aged woman who would come to our apartment and stay with me until my brother came home from school. For years, I didn't label my treatment by this woman as child abuse, but now I know it was. She would be sweet to me in front of my mother and then treat me with cold indifference when we were alone. She never played with me or took me outside. Often, she made me sit on the couch for hours during the day, threatening to call the police if I cried, moved, or told my mother. I was *scared to death* of her. Eventually, the *routine and fear* got the best of me, and I told my mother everything. The next day, my mother made a surprise visit and found things just as I had said. The sitter was fired, and I was taken to a large day-care center the next day. My mother never discussed these events with me, but I never forgot it.

The second assault came through the day-care workers and those I thought were my friends. My first day began with the workers assuring my mother and me that I would be *safe and happy*. I was really excited because there were so many kids my age. The workers were really nice, not at all like the mean babysitter. The excitement and fun soon faded as I began to experience embarrassment for the first time. During nap time, I began to wet the bed. At first, the workers told me it was okay, calling the incident an accident. Soon my accidents became daily occurrences. It was no longer "okay." The workers didn't say anything, but their looks and disgusted sighs spoke loudly and made me feel terrible. Soon, I began to hear them talking about me in front of the other children. I tried to stay awake, and on the days I did, the teachers were happy with me. But when I fell asleep and had an accident, they were cold and silent. I didn't understand the guilt I felt when the teachers got mad at me.

To add injury to my painful nap times, something worse happened. Just prior to my nap-time accidents, the children were allowed to bring their favorite dress-up clothes and play in them on the playground. My mother made a ballerina costume for me, and my soon-to-be stepdad bought me ballet slippers. For a while, my afternoons were glorious. I would put on my dress-up clothes and run and twirl on the playground, pretending to be a real ballerina. I felt so beautiful. The kids seemed to really like me and told me they loved to watch me dance. But all that changed when my friends were told I was a "bed wetter." The whispers, giggles, looks, and exclusion of my friends made me begin to think differently about myself. Over time, I began to realize that my childhood was not as normal as I had thought.

I shared these painful snapshots from my childhood to illustrate how my unhealthy thoughts of fear, shame, and guilt began. My childhood included only a few years of innocence and uninhibited dancing. Fear, shame, and guilt over time became strongholds in my life. I ultimately became the poster woman for the "performance-based life." I always felt driven to be perfect, obeying all the rules, while I needed attention and approval. I am so grateful that what the enemy meant for bad, my Lord used for good. When He called me to teach women, I never thought that He would use the injuries of my life to help them. In most of my mentoring relationships, I've observed the miraculous work of the Holy Spirit as He used painful seasons of my past to make a spiritual impact on someone else's present situation.

We are told in Psalm 94:11 that "the Lord knows the thoughts of man; he knows that they are futile." In Isaiah 55:8, the Lord compares Himself to man, "For my thoughts are not your thoughts, neither are your ways my ways."

Uncaring actions and damaging words can be powerful enough to cripple and shackle us for life. My childhood joy and innocence were stifled, leaving me a victim of fear, shame, and guilt. As a teacher and mentor, I have found that there is a common "heart cry" among those brave enough to honestly share their hurts, needs, and desires. Most of their injuries are the result of damaging words and actions. They desperately want to be healed from their pasts and experience the peace of God in every area of their lives.

In Isaiah 55:11–12a, *Jehovah-rapha, the Lord Who Heals*, declares His power to heal the soul of man. (See inset.)

Peace is "the absence of war or other hostilities."[60] The word *peace* in this verse means "safe, i.e., well, happy, friendly, welfare, i.e., health, prosperity."[61] *Jehovah-shalom, the Lord Is Peace*, knows how desperate we are for peace. He also knows what robs us of living in peace. He wants to break the strongholds that keep us in turmoil and fill us with joy and peace.

My Spiritual Journey—Fifth Step: Sanctification's Breaking

In session 4, I concluded my testimony with God fulfilling His words, "You will teach women." He knew exactly when and where I needed to begin teaching and exactly who needed to be in that class. He knew that teaching this class would be a significant step in breaking the strongholds in my life. I am so glad I didn't know what was ahead of me. This part of my testimony reflects some of the incidents that marked my life with the *proof of His love* for me.

The first fall came in the classroom of "position."

> "So is my word that goes out from my mouth: It will not return to me empty, but will accomplish what I desire and achieve the purpose for which I sent it. You will go out in joy and be led forth in peace" (Isaiah 55:11-12a).

The first Sunday I taught, I knew God was up to something much bigger than I could imagine. I prepared an exercise to get acquainted with the class for the first week. Sunday morning came with a shock. As soon as I stepped into the shower, I began to mentally rehearse the exercise. When I finished, a thought entered my mind that immediately brought a wave of nausea. I realized it was not my thought. I knew it was the Holy Spirit who said, "Tell them what you are." The word *what* resonated in my mind. I tried to hold back the tears and compose myself, but I couldn't. His words continued to work, exposing the "what" that I had become from years of painful injuries and personal failures. I stepped out of the shower with a different plan. I sensed a peace and confidence like never before. Later, I realized that He had exposed my pride and arrogance so that I could facilitate the lesson He had provided. I am so grateful He protected those precious ladies from my previous teaching style. The lesson plans He gave me were simple, yet powerful. I asked each lady to share a personal failure or hurt. As they shared, I wrote their responses on an easel. There were about a dozen women in the class that morning, and by the time I finished writing everyone's response, I knew why He had instructed me to tell them "what" I was. Every type of hurt except abortion and rape was listed. Their teacher felt their pain. We all had the same "what." We were victims of pain caused by multiple blows from multiple sources. The *American Heritage Dictionary* defines *victim* three ways:

- *One who is harmed or killed, as by accident or disease*
- *One who is tricked, swindled, or injured*
- *A living being offered as a sacrifice to a deity*

That day, the Lord began to heal our *what* and replace it with the truth of *who* we were in Him. The class tripled over the next two years, and to this day, I have never experienced such a group of women more bonded in love and purpose. The ladies loved me and showered me with attention and praise. I began to feel popular and loved it. Soon, my focus began to shift from Him to me. How did that happen? It began with my underlying feelings of insignificance. Popularity brings with it power, and I began to feel powerful and liked it. The ego thrives on power, and mine was no different. It soon took charge, and things began to change.

You and I know people who have fallen because their egos became mountains of power. The elevation of the mountain determines the possible damage to themselves and others. God knew my ego had become a destructive power, and it was time for me to fall from the position of *popular teacher*. It was while I was teaching that class that He allowed me to fall broken before His throne. I'll never forget climbing up, feeling so popular for the first time in my life. It seemed to erase the whispers and exclusion that haunted me. One of the most painful experiences in my life was the blessed breaking of my ego at the hand of my Lord. I am already emotional as I begin to write the details.

The last Sunday I taught I did so from the very top of my mountain of power. As I walked down the hall to my class, I stopped to talk with the director of the children's department. During our conversation, she commented on having difficulty getting a teacher for the fourth-grade class. I told her I would share the need with my class. Immediately, I took it upon myself to play God. Before beginning my lesson, I scolded the class with blistering words and a pointed finger, stating that someone among us was supposed to be teaching that class and if they didn't step up to the need immediately, they would be in direct disobedience to God. I can imagine the Lord shaking His majestic head again and this time saying, "You have gone too far, my child." That night, I dreamed I was in heaven kneeling with my face down before the throne of God. He began to talk to me, telling me I was a hypocrite. He said I had fooled many, but not Him. Because I was not walking my talk, I was to resign my class on Sunday and do what I had told my class to do, serve in the children's department. His words resonated in my mind for days. I cried and fought giving up the class, but I knew He was right and I had to obey Him. The following Sunday, I resigned and immediately took the fourth-grade class. The first "breaking of my ego" was in my *position* in the church. Since then, I have never taken lightly the places He has called me to serve in His church.

The next fall came in the classroom of "promotion."

While doing the study *Experiencing God*, the Holy Spirit clearly spoke and directed me to leave my professional career and work for Him. I was amazed, especially since retirement had become a reoccurring thought and desire. Shortly afterward, Ken's boss transferred to Alaska and asked if he would consider moving there to work for her. At first, I couldn't imagine moving and refused to even consider it. Our first grandchild, Caleb Paul, was only a couple of months old, and Andrea, my daughter, was in college. Surely God wouldn't want us to move to Anchorage, Alaska.

A couple of weeks later, I saw a job opening for a position in Anchorage, Alaska. At first, I dismissed it but then decided to talk with Ken, especially since he was the one who had been asked to transfer. He was hesitant but agreed that we should send our résumés and see what happened. We did, and a month later, Ken was advised that someone else had been selected. By that time, I had been interviewed and was awaiting a call regarding selection. Instead of withdrawing my résumé, I proceeded with the interview process. It was while attending a ladies' retreat that the call came. The position had been filled with someone who lived in Anchorage. I was filled with mixed emotions. I was relieved but disappointed I didn't get the job and ashamed that I had continued to pursue it. My ego was wounded. Even worse was the shameful realization that I had brought this wound upon myself and caused my family unnecessary pain. How could I have pursued moving when I had clearly heard the Holy Spirit tell me to leave my job and work for Him? He had tested me, and I had failed the test. This time, He chose to "break my ego" in the area of *self-promotion* in my workplace.

The next fall came in the classroom of "priorities."

Three years after the Alaska experience, AT&T offered an early retirement option, and I took it. I immediately began to work for the Lord in many different capacities in my church. Nine months later, I began caring for my favorite aunt, Sissie, who had lost an eye in a terrible car accident. Those six months were hard, yet very rewarding. Six months after her recovery, Aunt Sissie came to visit during the Christmas holidays. Upon returning from a fun shopping trip to the mall, she fell and broke her hip. This time, my flesh balked at the thought of caring for her again. I got angry at the very thought of having to leave my home and church. I had things I wanted to do in my church. My family needed me. I convinced myself that I should be honest and state my case quickly by telling Ken and my brother I just couldn't do it again. Immediately, I felt shame, guilt, and fear all at once. I felt shame for not wanting to care for a person who loved me more like a daughter than a niece. Then tremendous guilt flooded over me because I knew she would do it for me. Fear crept over me as I visualized the Lord's disappointment in me. I just knew He would punish me terribly if I didn't take care of her, yet my flesh seemed to have complete control. I knew God was aware of the state I was in. I couldn't hide my feelings from Him and wasn't about to try. All I could do was admit them to Him and pray. It was several days before I finally came to a place of partial surrender. There was no one else who could care for her unless we put her in a nursing home. I consoled myself by agreeing to care for her as long as she was in Georgia, which would probably be six to eight weeks. Halfheartedly, I visited her and encouraged her daily. She didn't get better. She got worse and pleaded for the doctors to let her go to a nursing home in her hometown of Anniston, Alabama, for the remainder of her therapy and rehabilitation. They agreed, and I drove her to the nursing home. I stayed a couple of days and then left the responsibility in the hands of the nursing home and my brother.

Instead of recovering as I had hoped, she rapidly regressed and required hospitalization. The hip replacement had failed and would have to be redone. She was so run down that it took a week to get her strong enough anesthetic. After surgery, she was placed in the intensive care unit, teetering close to death for several days. It was during those days that God revealed my problem. My priorities were definitely out of order. The things on my ministry list did not line up with those on God's list. This assignment wasn't what I wanted to do, but I knew it was His priority for me. I needed more than an attitude adjustment. I needed to be delivered from the religious pride that governed the priorities of my life's energies.

My dear aunt's recovery was much longer than expected, but I joyfully and gratefully cared for her over the next year. She and I had many wonderful days together, and I will forever be grateful. It was during those days that God began to prepare me for His next assignment. He took all my priorities and replaced them with His. I returned home in October just in time to speak to the ladies of my church at our annual fall retreat. Usually, I rode with a group of ladies, but this time, I rode alone. I will never forget the gentle reminder as my thoughts drifted to a recent devotional from *My Utmost for His Highest* by Oswald Chambers. I have included the segment that permeated my soul.

The Unheeded Secret

Jesus answered, "My kingdom is not of this world" (John 18:36).

The great enemy of the Lord Jesus Christ today is the idea of practical work that has no basis in the New Testament but comes from the systems of the world. This work insists upon endless energy and activities, but no private life with God. The emphasis is put on the wrong thing. Jesus said, 'the kingdom of God does not come with observation … indeed the kingdom of God is within you' (Luke 17:20–21). It is a hidden, obscure thing.[62]

It had hit me hard when I read it, but I knew it was affirming the purpose of my recent assignment to work for Him according to His priorities instead of mine.

Day 1
Scars of Partiality

Session 4 helped us to see how God's testing reveals the things that hinder our journey of faith. There are many things besides fear, guilt, and shame that can hinder us and eventually become painful strongholds. I like to refer to these things as weaknesses because they weaken us spiritually, emotionally, and physically. Over time, we are held captive by our own weaknesses, living our lives enslaved to things that only Christ can remove. In Galatians 5:1, we are told, "It is for freedom that Christ has set you free. Stand firm, then, and do not let yourselves be burdened again by a yoke of slavery." In this session, we will look into the lives of Jacob and Hannah to see how God turned their weaknesses into strengths and set them free.

In the introduction of this session, I shared some wounds I encountered in my early childhood. These wounds produced needless fear, guilt, and shame, which intensified over the years. Eventually, they became strongholds and I became a victim of my own weaknesses. Because of the love and healing of my precious Lord, I now understand why these incidents were so vivid in my memory. When I believed the truth, the *Truth* set me free.

God loves us and promises to redeem every area of our life, from all of our foes, including injuries from the world, Satan and his team of demons, and last but not least, our own nature. With the passing of time, our wounds become the *holding tank* for deformed thoughts, attitudes, actions, and habits. Christians are not exempt from the battlefield of continuous injuries. Over the years, I've experienced many wounds, with many being the result of my own sins and self-centeredness. It wasn't until I began to feed my soul a regular diet of the *Word* of God that I began to *see* my condition. Then my dehydrated spirit became refreshed as I embraced the *Living Water* in prayer and worship. It was during these times that He began to open my ears to hear His voice and know His direction for my life. He became my stronghold. His Word applies to all His children. Have you allowed Him to become your stronghold?

> "My soul waits in silence for God only; From Him is my salvation. He only is my rock and my salvation, my stronghold; I shall not be greatly shaken" (Psalm 62:1–2, NASB).

Before we get into the work God did in Jacob's life, let's take a quick look at his entrance into this world, his family dynamic, and what prompted Jacob to leave the tent of his parents. Jacob was the son of Isaac, who was the son of Abraham. He was the second born of twin boys. He and his brother Esau were the grandsons of Abraham and Sarah. Jacob came into this world holding the heel of Esau; the meaning of his name is "he grasps the heel." Figuratively, Jacob means, "he deceives."

Matthew Henry tells us that "Esau hunted the beasts of the field with dexterity and success, 'til he became a conqueror, ruling over his neighbors. Jacob was a plain man, one that liked the true delights of retirement, better than all pretended pleasures. He was a stranger and a pilgrim in his spirit and a shepherd all his days."[63]

Let's get started by reading Genesis 25:28 and filling in the blanks.

- "Isaac, who had a taste for wild game, _____ _____, but Rebekah
_____ _____."

Isaac and Rebekah were parents who showed partiality. Matthew Henry states that "godly parents must not show partiality. They should let their affections lead them to do what is just and equal to every child, or evils will arise."[64] It's easy to imagine the heated arguments that occurred between them over the years. Many marriages are so wounded by partiality that *separation* becomes the choice of many couples. Others choose to remain in the same house, going about their daily tasks as usual, except that they are no longer a couple unified by love and commitment to each other and God. They become divided and stand firm for their own preferences and favorites. They become unaware or unconcerned that their marriage has become unhealthy and dangerous to those they love the most. Eventually, the root of partiality produces sprouts in their own precious children, and the cycle continues. We can see this very clearly in the family of Isaac and Rebekah. Partiality soon drove the "spikes of evil" deep within the hearts of their precious sons, and *separation* occurred. As we study Jacob, we will see many evils arise.

Let's look at the first "spike of evil." Read Genesis 25:29–34, and answer the following questions.

- What was on Esau's mind?

_____

- What was on Jacob's mind?

_____

While Esau's desire at that moment would be temporary, Jacob's would be permanent. What did one have to lose and the other to gain? Matthew Henry answers the question for us.

> The bargain made between Jacob and Esau was about the birthright, which was Esau's by birth, but Jacob's by promise. It was a spiritual privilege. The inheritance of their father's worldly goods did not descend to Jacob, and was not meant in this proposal. But it includes the future possession of the land of Canaan by his children's children, and the covenant made with Abraham as to Christ the promised seed. A *believing* Jacob valued these above all things; an *unbelieving* Esau despised them.[65]

The enemy *tempts* us to focus on the physical things of this world, while the Holy Spirit *teaches* us how to focus on spiritual things, which are not of this world. The *things* of this world are *temporary,* but God's *promises* are *permanent.* The next "spike of evil" brings forth the *separation.* Here is a quick summary of Genesis 27:1–45.

> Isaac is old and decides it is time to give his blessing to his firstborn, Esau. But first, he wants to eat a "tasty" meal killed and prepared by Esau. Rebekah eavesdrops on their conversation, and as soon as Esau leaves, she shares a deceptive plot with Jacob, which would give him Esau's blessing. Together, they prepared "tasty" food for Isaac, just the way he liked it. She instructed Jacob to put on Esau's best clothes and cover his hands and neck with goatskins to make Isaac think he was Esau. But when Jacob approached Isaac with the food, Isaac expressed doubts that he was really Esau. He questioned Jacob about his identity, and Jacob lied. The "deceiver" deceived his father, the giver of blessings, and the birthright was bestowed on Jacob. When Esau

returned, the truth was exposed. In an effort to protect Jacob from the wrath of Esau, Rebekah and Isaac sent him to the home of Laban, Rebekah's brother.

It's hard to imagine the "promised son" of Abraham and Sarah in this situation. It's even harder to see the future for his descendants, yet the promise made to Abraham would include Jacob.

Complete each promise.

- Promise to Abraham: Genesis 12:3 "And all _____ on earth will be blessed through _____."

- Promise to Jacob: Genesis 28:14 "All _____ on earth will be blessed through _____ and your _____."

The promise made to Abraham covered Isaac and his family. The promise to Jacob and his family covers us. Regardless of our circumstances and failures, as children of God, we can know that our Lord can make something beautiful from the broken places in our lives.

We will conclude with the tables being turned on Jacob, the deceiver. Read Genesis 29:1–29, and answer the following questions.

- Who was Laban?

  _____

- What was his occupation?

  _____

- How did Laban welcome Jacob?

  _____

- With whom did Jacob fall in love?

  _____

- How was Jacob deceived?

  _____

- What did it cost Jacob to get Rachel?

  _____

- Do you think Jacob got what he deserved? _____ Fill in the blanks, and then answer this question.

- Genesis 29:25: "Jacob said, 'Why have you _____ ____?'"

- Genesis 27:36: "Esau said, 'Isn't he rightly named Jacob? He has _____ ____ these two times; He took my _____, and now he's taken my _____!'"

Let's see what we have learned so far:

- Just as Jacob had deceived Esau and Isaac, Laban had deceived Leah and Rachel, his own daughters.

- Just as Jacob had taken Esau's birthright, Laban deceived Jacob by using their right (or custom) to give the oldest daughter before the youngest in marriage.

- Just as Rachel helped Jacob obtain the blessing and protected him from Esau's threats, Laban made sure both daughters were blessed by marriage and their husband had a stable job working for him two consecutive seven-year terms.

Let's look at the two injuries of Jacob from within the household of Laban.

1. Jacob was deeply hurt by the hand of deceitfulness.

2. Jacob was subjected to the unfairness of partiality.

I've experienced the hurtful blows of partiality and deception from within and outside my biological family. We all have observed it in the lives of friends and others. Dear one, if the Lord has opened a hurtful memory in your life today, briefly write down the incident and begin to talk to Jesus about it.

_____

_____

_____

See you tomorrow at the tent of Jacob!

❧

Day 2
Struggle for Blessings

Yesterday, we ended our journey looking at the two injuries Jacob sustained because of the character flaws of Laban. He didn't have a mark on the outside, but you can be sure he had these two on his heart. Most people would rather have a scar on their bodies than on their hearts. We all know what a physical scar looks like, but I wonder if the definition of a physical scar would help us draw a picture of an emotional scar.

> Scarring is the natural process of the skin's healing process. Scars are areas of fibrous tissue that replace normal skin after injury. Scar tissue is not identical to the tissue that it replaces and is usually of inferior functional quality. The worse the damage the worse the scar.[66]

> "Spiritual scarring begins as sprouts of bitterness that take us down the path of resentfulness, depression, anger and revenge" (author).

A couple of old clichés came to my mind as soon as I read this definition.

"If you wear your feelings on your sleeve, you are setting yourself up for a hurt."

"Let that roll off of you like water rolling off a duck's back."

"In this day and time, you've got to be thick-skinned or you won't make it."

I think emotional scarring can be much worse than physical scarring. These clichés are meant to make us aware of the possibility of emotional injuries. Emotional scars can hinder our spiritual growth and fellowship with the Lord. Let's develop a picture from the definition of physical scarring and apply it to emotional scarring. Emotional scarring also produces layers of "thick skin" or protective walls around one's heart. With each layer, one may feel more confident and in control, but in reality, it is just the opposite. The individual's ability to receive and give love becomes blocked by depression. Left alone, each one becomes a prisoner of his own heart.

Most physical scars can be greatly reduced today with new and improved topical ointments and procedures. Emotional scars can be treated with new and improved psychotropic drugs and professional counseling. The effects of *spiritual scars* require the supernatural. We must surrender to God's procedures to remove the hardness from our hearts. His ways of healing and restoring are amazing. Today, we will look at the effects of Jacob's wounds and the amazing way God healed his deepest scar. Before we examine the circumstances that caused more scarring for Jacob, let's look at evidence that indicates Jacob is following in his mother's footsteps of partiality.

Read Genesis 29:25, and answer this question.

What hurtful action is sandwiched between the fact that Jacob has married Leah and he will work for Laban another seven years?

_____

Jacob's married life began with him showing partiality between his two wives, just as his parents did between her two sons. Because of the circumstances, we can understand why he loved Rachel more. The Scriptures tell us that he didn't love Leah at all. In verse 31, the Amplified Bible states that "the Lord saw that Leah was despised." The remainder of that verse tells us that the Lord took action by making her able to bear children. In verses 32 and 33, Leah expresses the wounds she has experienced from Jacob.

Let's look at Leah's comments. Fill in the blanks in Genesis 29:32–33.

- "Leah became pregnant and gave birth to a son. She named him Reuben, for she said, 'It is because the Lord has _____ my _____. Surely my husband will _____ me now.' She conceived again, and when she gave birth to a son she said, 'Because the Lord _____ that I am not _____, he gave me this one too.' So she named him Simeon."

Leah had two more sons, and Jacob still did not demonstrate love toward her. This is a sad cycle. Leah's father, Laban, wounded Jacob who wounded Leah. Leah had three more sons for Jacob, and then the Scriptures tell us she stopped having children.

Have you experienced a full cycle of wounds like this? If so, write out the cycle listing the names or using a symbol to represent individuals.

Cycle of Wounds

_____

_____

_____

The next scene we'll examine is Laban's wounding of Rachel and Leah. In chapter 30, Jacob tells Laban he is going to leave and go back to his homeland. Laban wants Jacob to stay because he wants to benefit from the blessing of Jacob's God. Jacob agrees to remain as the shepherd of Laban's flock for a price. He did not want money but a part of Laban's flocks. Laban agrees, and God continues to bless Jacob. In chapter 31, Jacob becomes aware of the animosity Laban and his sons have toward him. God comes on the scene in verse 3 and tells Jacob, "Go back to the land of your fathers and to your relatives, and I will be with you." Jacob shares everything with Rachel and Leah, who respond with hurt toward their father, Laban.

Read Genesis 31:14–22, and answer the following questions.

- Based on Rachel and Leah's comments, how do they feel about their father and why?

_____

_____

- What possessions did Jacob take with him?

_____

_____

- Apparently, Rachel visited her father's tent before leaving. What did she steal?

  _____

  _____

- How did Jacob deceive Laban?

  _____

- Why do you think Jacob was running away?

  _____

  _____

Let's summarize these wounds.

- The jealousy of Laban and his sons wounded Jacob.

- The greed of Laban wounded Rachel and Leah.

- The deception of Laban revealed Jacob's fear.

- The theft of Laban's gods revealed Rachel's "secret belief in old heathen superstitions. Because of her father's superstitious beliefs (Gen. 31:30), Rachel likely stole the gods to ensure a prosperous journey. Such relics from the old home would guarantee all continuance of the old good fortune."[67]

The wounding has continued and spread beyond Jacob and Leah. Laban has infected his sons with *covetousness* and Rachel with *idolatry*. Often, we don't realize that our exposure to devastating character flaws makes them become part of us. This reminded me of the suffering I experienced one summer from a serious sunburn. I was old enough to know better, but vanity won over good judgment. My quest for a sun-kissed tan was costly.

Six weeks after the birth of my first child, my parents invited me to go with them to Panama City for a long weekend over the Fourth of July. I was excited for several reasons, and I am sure you will understand. I had spent nine months pregnant during the fall and winter, and with a new baby, you know I had not been near a pool. I was lily white and in desperate need of a change in scenery. In an effort to return home with a great tan, I chose to spend my last day in Florida beside the pool. I was excited because my mom took care of my baby so that I could soak in as much sun as possible. The problem was that I did not use sunscreen. Why? Stupidity is still the only answer I can give! I knew better. I would read, doze, eat, go to the bathroom, get into the pool to cool off, and then do it all over again. You know the rest of the story. I was burned to a bright lobster red. Why do we do what we do? I allowed my own condemning thoughts about my appearance to ignite the flames of vanity. When that happens, you cannot trust yourself. You are out of control. By the way, I did not achieve the great tan, only hideous flaking and peeling of dead skin. Lesson learned.

If you are still shaking your head and laughing at my character flaw, it's okay; I am too. It seems that Jacob had a problem with vanity too. Let's look further at his story. Jacob knew Laban could not be trusted, but he made another agreement with him anyway. Jacob let his vanity (from past accomplishments) override good judgment. This resulted in a worse "burn"—from Laban this time.

It's about time for God to visit Jacob. Read Genesis 30:41–43 and 31:10–13, and answer the following questions.

- Who brought prosperity to Jacob?

  _____

- When should Jacob have stopped working for Laban?

  _____

God gives Jacob a change in address. Read Genesis 35:1–4, 9–16, and answer the following questions.

- Where did He tell Jacob to relocate?

  _____

- What was significant about it?

  _____

- Who stopped Rachel from idolatry?

  _____

- What new name was given to Jacob?

  _____

- How did God bless Jacob and Rachel?

  _____

In my research on Rachel, I ran across some interesting comments that helped me understand why she stole the idols.

> Although living in a polygamous marital state, Rachel was also guilty of religious polygamy. There was a professed relationship to the God of Israel, yet at the same time she was married to idols. Rachel had no right to carry away what was not her own. Had she known that those stolen images would become a terrible snare in Jacob's family, perhaps she would not have taken them. Images and relics have always been dangerous elements in connection with true religious worship. How prone the human heart is to forsake the spiritual for the material, the unseen for the seen and temporal.[68]

The next paragraph in my research material gives us a glimpse of Rachel as a wife and mother.

> It would seem as if Rachel had surrendered her idolatry before the death stroke fell on her. The hallowing influences of divine blessing on her husband and his seed as the result of Bethel, begot within her a sense of divine awareness. Young Joseph's great reverence for God bespeaks of Rachel's godly training in his boyhood years. Jacob's love for her and his stronger faith helped to purify her character and she lived on long after her death in the life of her noble son.[69]

Sometimes, we are set up by our parents to place our security in the seen and temporal of this generation. The outcome can be a terrible snare in our homes. We must choose, as Rachel did, to give up our secret idols and follow the Unseen God for the rest of our life. We must leave that kind of legacy to our children.

Our last glimpse of Jacob will be at a wrestling match between him and God. Before we delve into this life-changing experience for Jacob, we need to see the *stage* God built for their encounter. In chapter 31, Laban pursues Jacob. After a healthy discussion concerning their offenses toward one another, they settle their differences with a covenant of friendship and a meal. "In ancient times, covenants of friendship were ratified by the parties eating and drinking together."[70]

In chapter 32, Jacob sends a message to Esau and asks him for mercy and kindness when they meet. Esau responds with a short message that he is on his way with four hundred men. Jacob is terrified and prays for God to deliver him from the hand of his brother. Then Jacob prepares three separate gifts of animals and instructs three separate messengers to go ahead of him, one behind the other. Their instructions are to tell Esau the gifts are from Jacob, who is coming behind them. Jacob hopes that his gifts will pacify Esau's anger and he will accept him. He then sends his family and possessions across the ford of the Jabbok while he stays in the camp alone.

I can imagine the fear and nausea he must have experienced as thoughts of losing his family and possessions tortured his soul. I believe Jacob fell on his knees in prayer, pleading for protection from the hands of Esau. Have you had times when prayer began with a tearful petition and became wailing sobs for help? Only Jesus can calm the inner turmoil of our soul. This was a humbling moment for Jacob. His inner turmoil could not be removed by man. Only the touch of God could remove his problem. Just as the finger of God wrote the Ten Commandments, this same majestic finger would break the stronghold of *deceit* in Jacob's heart.

This is my favorite part of Jacob's story. Read Genesis 32:24–31, and answer the following questions.

- Who do you think the man was?

  _____

- Why do you think the man wrenched Jacob's hip and then told Jacob to let him go? _

  _____

- Why did the Lord change Jacob's name?

  _____

This is God, Himself (as Jacob eventually realizes in Genesis 32:30), in the form of an angel. Matthew Henry's description of the match gives us much insight on which to reflect.

> However tired or discouraged, we shall prevail; and prevailing with Him in prayer, we shall prevail against all enemies that strive with us. Nothing requires more vigorous and unceasing exertion than wrestling. It is an emblem of the true spirit of faith and prayer. Jacob kept his ground; though the struggle continued long, this did not shake his faith, nor silence his prayer. He will have a blessing, and had rather have all his bones put out of joint than go away without one. Those who would have the blessing of Christ must resolve to take no denial.[71]

The purpose of the Amplified Bible is "to reveal, together with the single English word equivalent to each key Hebrew and Greek word, any other clarifying meanings that may be concealed by the traditional method" (Amplified Bible Preface). This translation will help us understand the deeper purpose of the questioning between both men. I've given you the text from the Amplified Version. The English word equivalents as well as other clarifying information are in brackets. Meditate on the scene while reading each verse. Allow the Holy Spirit to expand your understanding of this awesome picture of Jacob struggling with God to bless him.

> The Man asked him, "What is your name?" And [in shock of realization, whispering] he said, "Jacob [supplanter, schemer, trickster, swindler]." And He said, "Your name shall be called no more Jacob (supplanter), but Israel (contender with God); for you have contended and have power with God and with men and have prevailed." Then Jacob asked Him, "Tell me, I pray You, what [in contrast] is Your name?" But He said, "Why is it that you ask My name?" And [the Angel of God declared] a blessing on [Jacob] there. And Jacob called the name of the place Peniel [the face of God], saying, "For I have seen God face to face, and my life is spared and not snatched away." And as he passed Peniel, the sun rose upon him, and he was limping because of his thigh. (Genesis 32:27–31)

> "When the Holy Spirit deals with us, He puts His finger in the socket of our heart, pressing on those secret sins we struggle with over and over again" (author).

Jacob was blessed after he shamefully whispered his name. "In the Bible a name change marks a turning point in a person's life—a major alteration of character, direction, or status. A name change also signifies that the one doing the naming assumes power over the one named."[72] Jacob's limp would remind him that Truth had set him free. Jacob was transformed from the inside out by the touch of his God.

Israel, the name God gave to Jacob meant, "He struggles with God." From the very beginning of life, we demand to have what we want.

When we are born again, the process of sanctification begins, usually gently and slowly. At first, it is easy to change our ways, but as the seasons pass, so does the ease with which we can change our ways. Eventually, we come to a place where the process is too painful to continue. The longer we allow our will to win over His conviction, the more miserable we become. For a while, we may think we are okay, but the truth is, we aren't. Like Jacob, we know we need to get alone with our God. I've been in this place many times, and my God has never failed to replace my dangerous flaws with a broken and contrite spirit. When we are humbled, we are healed from the inside out. Just as He knew everything about Jacob, He knows everything about us. He loves us too much to allow defeating strongholds to continue to rule our lives. He has promised us that He will complete the good work He has begun in us. The more He presses, the more we struggle until we are in a spiritual wrestling match with God. We usually begin just as Jacob did by asking God to bless us or take away whatever is making us uncomfortable. We want relief without having to answer the probing question, "What are you refusing to admit about yourself?" When we come clean, the wrestling stops, and He blesses us with peace.

Are you in a wrestling match with God? I know all about this one. It is well worth it, I promise. Take a few minutes to sit quietly before your God. Be open and honest about those areas about which you sense He is speaking to you. Confess the damage they have done and leave them with Him. List the areas you surrendered and date it. You may want to write this in a private journal. The important thing is that you record and date it. This is a spiritual marker in your life!

Lord, I surrender

_____

_____

_____

Tomorrow, we will begin our study of Hannah at the tent of Elkanah!

⚮

Day 3
Pain of a Broken Heart

The next three days will not be as long as the first two. There was a lot the Lord wanted us to see and grasp from the life of Jacob. My writing about Hannah had to be put on hold while I stepped into a brief wrestling match with my Lord. I had been here before, and I knew the number of rounds depended on me. One round of complete honesty and surrender was enough. He won, and I walked away with another grateful limp from the hand of my loving Lord. Just as He blessed Jacob, He blessed me with the peace that comes from above. I would love to know how your wrestling match went.

Let's get started on our journey with Hannah. She is the mother of Samuel, the man whom God used to establish kingship in Israel. The books 1 Samuel and 2 Samuel are named after Hannah's son. Only a small portion of her life is recorded in 1 Samuel. It begins by telling us she is the wife of Elkanah, the son of Jeroham. Elkanah was a Levite, which means he was a member of the Hebrew tribe of Levi. This tribe was named after Levi, the son of Leah and Jacob. It was also from this tribe that the Levitical priesthood was established. Even though Elkanah was "of this order, and a good man, he practiced polygamy. This was contrary to the original law, but it seems to have been prevalent among the Hebrews in those days, when there was no king in Israel, and every man did what seemed right in his own eyes."[73]

Read 1 Samuel 1:1–8, and answer the questions.

- How is Hannah like Rachel?

  _____

- How is Elkanah like Jacob?

  _____

Our first glimpse of Hannah is through the eyes of her husband. His love for Hannah is untouched by her barrenness. Regardless of the passing years, Elkanah continues to love Hannah and gives her better gifts than he does his other wife, Peninnah. It is apparent that she is a strong woman of unblemished character and unmovable faith in her God. She did not stumble from the agony of childlessness or the cruelty of Peninnah's jealousy.

Let's take a different look at Hannah through the eyes of Peninnah. The text gives us a small snapshot of Peninnah and her relationship with Hannah. We are told that "year after year," Elkanah showed outward partiality to Hannah. The wounds of his partiality birthed jealousy in her heart. Year after year, Peninnah's jealousy of Hannah intensified, while Hannah's womb remained closed. They both desired something Elkanah could not give them. Peninnah had that which Hannah desired: his son. Hannah had that which Peninnah desired: his heart.

What is that "something" that you passionately desire God to give you but He hasn't yet?

_____

_____

If He has given you the desire of your heart, write what it was and how He gave it to you.

_____

_____

"Jealousy, the 'green-eyed monster that mocks the meat it feeds on,' had taken possession of Peninnah but not of Hannah."[74] Peninnah's response to her own pain continued to be to cast it upon Hannah, hitting the hardest at Shiloh. Hannah's response had always been to take her pain to her God rather than retaliate. I can sympathize with both women, can't you? I have been the giver and receiver of pain from a root of jealousy. For years, I responded like Peninnah in both situations. Then one day, I couldn't bear the cycle anymore. I had to respond in a new way. How about you? Do you want to break this cycle?

Let's look at how Hannah chose to break her cycle of pain. It is a new year, and they have just finished dinner at Shiloh. Instead of Hannah crying on Elkanah's shoulder, she goes to the temple of God. Hannah's focus is to meet with God and plead for a miracle.

Fill in the blanks in the following verses in 1 Samuel 1.

- Verse 9: "Once when they had finished eating and drinking in Shiloh, Hannah _____ up."

- Verse 10: "In bitterness of soul, Hannah _____ _____ and _____ to the Lord."

- Verse 11: "And she _____ __ _____, saying, 'O Lord Almighty, if you will only _____ upon your servant's _____ and _____ me, and not _____ your servant but _____ her a son, then I will _____ him to the Lord for _____ the days of _____ _____.'"

Answer these questions from the verses you just completed.

- What did Hannah ask God to do?

_____

- What did Hannah promise God?

_____

Now let's look at the bold actions Hannah took. _Underline_ the words that illustrate her desperation and _circle_ the words that illustrate her boldness.

- She courageously stood up and took her broken heart to God.

- She poured her bitterness and sorrow out to Him without shame.

- She acknowledged with confidence and honor that she was His servant.

- She asked Him to look at her inability to conceive and give her a son. She made a vow to give Him to the Lord completely.

What do her actions tell us about Hannah?

_____

Hannah's story challenges us to ask ourselves this question, "Why don't I run to God with my broken heart and crumbled dreams instead of crying on someone else's shoulder?" I never took a personal hurt or desire to my own earthly father, and he didn't ask me to do so. Because of this, it was hard for me to take them to my heavenly Father. The encouragement of others helped me start sharing more personal things with Him. I am so thankful for the Word of God, which reveals the compassion of our Lord to us. The comfort of an earthly father cannot heal our broken hearts. That can only come from our heavenly Father, *Jehovah-rapha, the Lord Our Healer.*

I hope you are encouraged as you complete these verses.

- Isaiah 61:1b: "He has sent me to bind up the _____."

- Psalm 34:18: "The Lord is close to the _____."

- Psalm 147:3: "He _____ the brokenhearted and binds up their _____."

Maybe you have gone year after year thriving on the encouragement of a husband or close friends. Where are you right now? Are you sad and lonely? Are you brokenhearted over something or someone?

Jesus tells us we can: "Ask and it will be given to you; seek and you will find; knock and the door will be opened to you" (Matthew 7:7).

Here is an explanation of this verse from Jamison, Faucett, and Brown's commentary.

> We ask for what we wish; we seek for what we miss; we knock for that from which we feel ourselves shut out. Answering to this threefold representation is the triple assurance of success to our believing efforts.[75]

Complete Matthew 7:8.

- "For _____ who asks _____; he who seeks _____; and to him who knocks, the door _____ _____ _____."

Take a few minutes to pour out your sorrow to your heavenly Father. He is always waiting and willing to comfort us. He is always pleased when we come to Him for help. He understands our need for healing and restoration. He is the "Most High-ly" qualified, and satisfaction is guaranteed!

See you tomorrow at the tent of Hannah and Elkanah!

⁊

Day 4
Blessing from Brokenness

Yesterday, we saw the desperation of Hannah burst forth from deep within the prison of her broken heart. Today, we will look at the compassion that flowed from the heart of her heavenly Father. Let's begin looking closer at Hannah's condition as she entered the temple. The Amplified Bible reveals Hannah's condition: "Hannah was in distress of soul, praying to the Lord and weeping bitterly" (1 Samuel 1:10). Our efforts to conceal our misery may work for a while, but then, when we least expect it, another cruel blow of reality pushes us over the limit. I suspect that the longer Hannah sat across the table from her taunting adversary, the bigger the knot in her throat became. By the time she got to the temple, she was an emotional wreck. There was no way Eli could overlook the state of Hannah.

In my times of great distress, I have been like Hannah, running to God when I became distressed of soul and was weeping bitterly. A broken heart produces more than tears. In my case, one or two tissues are not enough. I need a whole box to handle the abundance of visible grief! My nose seems to compete with my eyes, each working at maximum capacity to outdo the other. My stomach churns with nausea while my hands cover my face. Standing still is impossible. Hard sobbing brings uncontrollable movement. My own experience framed the scene of Hannah entering the temple. I bet yours does the same thing. Do your nose and eyes compete like mine?

Read 1 Samuel 1:12–18, and answer the following question.

- What effect do you think Eli's accusations had on Hannah?

  _____

  _____

- How did Hannah respond to Eli?

  _____

  _____

- How did God use Eli to encourage Hannah?

  _____

  _____

- What were the two visible signs that Hannah was at peace?

  _____

  _____

- When *peace* absorbs our pain, we are free to be ourselves. Would you agree? What are some visible signs you see in yourself when peace overshadows your pain? I'm like Hannah, "hungry and happy"!

The next day is a new day for Hannah. It begins early with worship and then the trip home. I want to add some adjectives to verse 19, don't you? Join me in adding a few.

"Early the next morning they _____ arose and _____ worshipped before the Lord and then went back to their home at Ramah."

The trip home was nothing like those of years past. Hannah went home with hope! Peninnah could not touch, much less taint, Hannah's new heart. When God gives us hope, we know it, and no one can snatch it away. It is hope that ignites the fire of our faith. The Lord does not forget about us. He *remembered* Hannah, and in the course of time, she conceived and gave birth to a son. She named him Samuel, meaning "heard of God."

Complete verse 20.

> "Hannah's heart rejoiced, not in Samuel, but in the Lord. She looked beyond the gift, and praises the Giver" (Henry, 265).

- "She named him Samuel, saying, 'Because I _____ the Lord for him.'"

Read 1 Samuel 1:21–28, and complete Hannah's steps to fulfill her vow to God.

- Hannah _____ Samuel.

- Hannah brought Samuel to the house of the _____.

- Hannah gave Samuel to the _____ for his _____ _____.

Hannah nurtured the gift God had given her. At the appointed time, she gave her gift back to the Lord for His purpose in ministry. God had a purpose for Hannah. When we are born again, God gives us spiritual gifts. These gifts must be nurtured. At the appointed time, like Hannah, we are to give our gifts back to the Lord for His use in ministry. God has a purpose for us. There is no limit to what He can birth in and through us.

Chapter 2 begins with the beautiful prayer of Hannah. It's in Hannah's prayer of praise that we can see the healing of her broken heart. Read the entire prayer out loud and listen to the passion of her words.

Fill in the missing words from these selected verses.

- Verse 1: "In the _____ my horn (strength) is lifted high. My mouth _____ over my enemies."

- Verse 2: "There is no _____ like our God."

- Verse 3: "The Lord is a God who _____."

- Verse 4: "Those who stumble are armed with _____."

- Verse 5: "Those who are hungry _____ no more."

- Verse 6: "The Lord brings _____ and makes _____."

- Verse 7: "The Lord _____ and he _____."

- Verse 8: "He lifts the _____ from the _____ heap."

- Verse 9: "He will _____ the _____ of his saints."

- Verse 10: "Those who _____ the Lord will be _____. He will thunder against them from _____; the Lord will _____ the ends of the earth. He will give _____ to his king, and exalt the horn (strength) of his _____."

According to Jamison, Fausset, and Brown's commentary, "This is the first place in scripture where the word 'anointed,' or Messiah, occurs; and as there was no king in Israel at the time, it seems the best interpretation to refer it to Christ."[76]

Matthew Henry's commentary states that "this prophecy looks to the kingdom of Christ, that kingdom of grace, of which Hannah speaks, after having spoken largely of the kingdom of providence. The subjects of Christ's kingdom will be safe, and the enemies of it will be ruined; for the Anointed, the Lord Christ, is able to save, and to destroy."[77]

After reading Hannah's prayer and the commentaries, I experienced a fresh surge of strength and confidence. I pray you did too. Hannah is a great example of someone who had barrenness of heart. Motherhood was the cure. There are many types of barrenness. The list can go on and on. Recently, I attended a Women of Faith conference. There were many nuggets of encouragement I hid in my heart and shared with others. My favorite nugget fits perfectly in the closing of our look at Hannah. It is simply this, "God has not forgotten you."

You may not be experiencing a barrenness of some kind, but you probably know someone who is. Pray for that person specifically, asking God to show you how you can minister to him or her, and then do it soon. If a person has come to mind, write the name down right now: _____.

If you have a place of barrenness in your life, I encourage you to do as Hannah did. Get up from your heap of ashes and run to your God. The enemy has taunted you long enough. Jesus knows your heart is broken, and he wants you to turn loose of your disappointments and pain and pour them into His hands. I promise you that your *God has not forgotten you*. He wants to bless you and put a new song in your heart. Now run to the throne of His wonderful grace … He is waiting for you.

See you at our final look at Jacob and Hannah!

⌇

Day 5
The Purpose of Our Wounds

"But He was pierced for our transgressions, He was crushed for our iniquities;
the punishment that brought us peace was upon him, and by his wound we are
healed" (Isaiah 53:5).

I will never forget a physical wound I received from a fall that seriously injured my left knee. It took weeks to heal. Even though it was a painful injury, I didn't stop my daily activities. Life goes on, and I had responsibilities. When my mother died, I was devastated, and for a season, I halfheartedly performed my busy cycle of responsibilities from within a prison of grief and memories. Even though the knee injury was very painful and lengthy in healing, today, it is really insignificant. Even though my mother's death painfully affected every part of my being, the peace and power of God is reducing the size of this scar in my soul. Both of these wounds were not of my own doing. The fall left a small scar, while my mother's death produced a huge one.

Whether it's an innocent stumble or the devastation of a death, our Jehovah-rapha can and wants to heal us. Our part is to allow Him to be who He is.

What about wounds we inflict on others and wounds they inflict on us? His Word gives us the recipe for His healing … forgiveness.

- How are we told to forgive in Ephesians 4:32? _____
_____

When we wound others or they wound us, for a time, fellowship is halted. The magnitude of the wound determines the degree to which fellowship is affected in the relationship. Applying this verse and receiving it will bring healing and restoration.

Let's look at another type of wounding, which I call the "self-inflicted" scar, from *disobedience*. I don't know about you, but I don't have problems with big things like murder and stealing. It is the daily instructions from the Holy Spirit that I am tempted to ignore. I often wound myself when I disobey the small, still voice that says:

"Stop!"
"Don't go there."
"This way."
"Don't listen to that condemnation."
"Memorize this verse."
"Wait."

I think you know what I mean. This is crucial to our fellowship with the Lord. Our passion to please God can be snuffed out by small stumbles in our daily walk with the Lord. I have finally realized that when I ignore Him, I usually stop talking to Him. Why do we do this? The answer is found in His Word.

Fill in the blanks in Isaiah 53:6.

"We all, like sheep, have gone _____, each of us has _____ to his own _____; and the LORD has laid on Him the _____ of us all."

Let's look in the *American Heritage Dictionary* at the meaning of the words you put in the blanks. <u>Underline</u> the key words in each meaning.

> *Astray* means "away from the correct direction."
> *Turned* means "a change of direction."
> *Way* means "a manner of doing something."
> *Iniquities* mean "wickedness, sinfulness."

How does He "heal us" or "change us" from sheep to saints? Again, the answer is found in Scripture. I really like the Amplified Bible version for this answer. *Circle* the words that describe the steps you must take in the following verse.

> Do not be conformed to this world (this age), [fashioned after and adapted to its external, superficial customs], but be transformed (changed) by the [entire] renewal of your mind [by its new ideals and its new attitude], so that you may prove [for yourselves] what is the good and acceptable and perfect will of God, even the thing which is good and acceptable and perfect [in His sight for you]. (Romans 12:2, Amplified Bible)

Day 1: Scars of Partiality

Let's roll back the calendar to Genesis 28 where Jacob has camped for the night. His destination is the tent of Laban, his mother's brother. He has a profound dream in which God speaks to him about things to come.

Read verses 10–22, and answer the following questions:

- Who does God say He is the father of? _____ and
  _____

- What personal promises does God make to Jacob?
  _____
  _____

Jacob knew the God of his father had given him "grace" right on the heels of his deceitful and manipulative actions. He responds by saying, "How awesome is this place! This is none other than the house of God; the gate of heaven." This place, Bethel, will forever be a marker in the life of Jacob. He vows to trust God as his covenant God.

The word *gate* in this text means "an opening, i.e. door."[78] F. B. Meyer's comments beautifully describe the personal journey mankind must make in search of God.

> There is an opening way between heaven and earth for each of us. The movement of the tide and the circulation of the blood are not more regular than the intercommunication between heaven and earth. Jacob may have thought that God was local; now he found Him to be omnipresent. Every lonely spot was His house, filled with angels.[79]

God does not show partiality. He offers "all" the gateway to heaven. He intentionally showed deceitful Jacob His "offer" in a dream. Look at verses 12 and 13, and try to visualize it using this additional information. A ladder connects earth to heaven. God's angels are moving up and down it. The first part of verse 13 reads, "There above it stood the Lord." As I read this verse a second time, I pondered this question, "Where and above what was God standing?" A closer look revealed a profound snapshot into Jacob's dream. The New International Version Bible's footnotes for this part of verse 13 replace "above it" with "beside him." I also looked in the Amplified Bible, and it reads, "And behold, the Lord stood over and beside him." Based on this wording, I can easily visualize God standing beside him and even leaning over, possibly looking eye to eye with Jacob. Jacob got the message, even though it was delivered in a dream. Jacob had met the God of his father and grandfather. Now their God would be his God. This was such a life-changing experience that He anointed the stone he had placed under his head and set it up as a pillar of remembrance. Jacob would never again call this place by its original name of Luz. It would forever be his Bethel, which means "house of God."

I've experienced some very special times with God outside the walls of my own church. Each has been at a special place like Jacob's Bethel. Instead of setting up a pillar, I chose various things, such as shells, rocks, leaves, pictures, and even acorns to take home as tangible reminders of each divine encounter. I found one of my Bethels when we lived in a very small city for about two years. A beautiful park with a walking path was only two blocks from our home. I loved to walk there and talk with God. The park was completely surrounded by majestic oaks. It was in this park that I sought direction from God regarding this study. I remember the exact place He confirmed my writing the study and told me what to name it. Immediately, I picked up a handful of acorns. Those acorns are reminders of my meeting with God under the mighty branches of oak trees.

Do you have a Bethel? Do you have any tangible reminders? If so, list them and why they represent your "Bethel." If you don't, ask Him for one. He delights in drawing us close to His heart and leaving an eternal mark on our soul.

Day 2: Struggle for Blessings

Based on what we know, God first approached Jacob in a dream. Then He spoke to him while living among Laban's tents, telling him to return to his father and relatives. Then He manifested Himself to Jacob as a man, and they wrestled all night. Based on what we know, the wrestling match is the third time Jacob hears the voice of his God.

> **"God broke his walk and blessed his talk" (author).**

- How do you think Jacob knew his opponent was God?

Did Jacob see the same form that stood beside and over him in his dream? Did Jacob pin him down long enough to look into those eyes? When the man said, "Let me go, for it is daybreak," did Jacob recognize his voice? I believe the answer to all three questions is "yes."

- Describe your response if you had been Jacob and heard these words: "Your name will no longer be Jacob, but Israel, because you have struggled with God and with men and have overcome."

_____

In Genesis 32:30, Jacob named this place, Peniel. What does this name mean?

_____

I can imagine Jacob declaring this name. His life will never be the same. His encounter with the living God changed him. The wounds of God are a true blessing. Many times, the way to make us stronger spiritually is to make us weaker physically. The touch of God wounded Jacob while infusing him with Godly character. Any type of encounter with God is powerful. Sometimes, we are made weak so we can experience His power and give Him the credit.

Read 2 Corinthians 12:8–10, and answer the following questions:

- Whose power is made perfect in weakness?

_____

- Did Paul complain about his weaknesses?

_____

- When was Paul strong?

_____

The power of God makes us strong when we are weak. This same power fulfilled the promise made to Abraham and Isaac through the weakness of their offspring, Jacob.

> "The Hebrew nation is spoken of as the sons of Jacob and the children of Israel."[80]

Day 3: The Pain of a Broken Heart

At the end of our first session about Hannah, you may have written a prayer needing to be healed or restored in some way. Maybe your prayer was for a child or a husband. Today, I want to address another area, a desire to be used of God. Over my years of mentoring women of all ages, this has been a common longing among the women. I remind them that God has placed that desire in their hearts. Do you have a desire to be used of God?

Fill in the blanks in Psalm 37:4.

> "Delight yourself in the _____ and He will _____ you the _____ of your heart."

The Amplified Bible adds _"the secret petitions"_ of your heart. I like that one, don't you? The secret petitions of our heart are those things we dare not say out loud. The things we want the most desperately.

All the years Hannah suffered from barrenness, as well as the evil treatment of Peninnah, she remained faithful to God in her worship and character. Hannah walked according to Psalm 37:3.

Fill in the blanks in Psalm 37:3

> "Trust in the _____ and do _____; dwell in the _____ and enjoy safe pasture."

The New Century Version of Psalm 37:3 reads, "Trust in the Lord and do good. Live in the land and feed on the truth." Hannah did not give up on God. She continued to feed her faith with prayer and righteous living. At the appointed time, God's providential hand placed Hannah beside Eli. It was time to delight Hannah.

Maybe you are in a place I've been. The place I call "God couldn't and wouldn't use me!" Yes, He can! Yes, He will! Let me add one more statement of truth: Yes, He wants to! Now, be honest with yourself and God. Do you desire to be used by Him to minister to others? If your answer is yes, then answer this question. Do you believe He put that desire in your heart? Based on what we have examined, your answer should have been "yes."

I'm going to ask you to do something that pleases the heart of God. I believe this action is one of the most powerful steps we can take in our walk with the Lord.

- Stand and lift your face and hands toward heaven.

- Acknowledge Him as Your God who is worthy to be praised.

- Express your love and adoration for who He is.

- Thank Him for your past and present blessings.

- Lie facedown on the floor or sit at a table with your face in your hands and verbalize your secret petitions.

- Commit to the "whatever and whenever" of His will for your life.

- Close by thanking Him that you can pray this in the authority of Jesus' name.

> "God is taking those He is breaking…and miraculously making them…a divine blessing" (author).

Day 4: Blessing from Brokenness

The session on Hannah ended with a phrase that still resonates in my heart: "God has not forgotten you." The reason it means so much to me is that I have heard just the opposite from the enemy.

God proved to Hannah that He remembered her request—He blessed her with a son. Hannah was faithful to the vow she made to God.

"A faithful man will be richly blessed" (Proverbs 28:20).

God's purpose was huge. He would bring forth a holy man from the womb of Hannah, who deeply desired a son—not just any son, but a son who would be set apart for the service of God for his entire life. God did not forget Hannah. Let's look at how God continued to bless her.

Read 1 Samuel 2:18–21, and list the five blessings God gave Hannah.

_____

_____

_____

I will never forget when God birthed a desire in me to minister outside my church. It began as a thought, *I think I'll start a Bible study in my neighborhood.* Two years later, we moved into my present home, and again, I thought about it, but this time, I used the excuse of being in ministry already. Eighteen months later, He softly spoke these words, "It is time to use what you know." Immediately, He reminded me of the Bible study, and I knew what He meant. I quickly responded, "Yes, Lord, I yield to *whatever* you want me to do." The next week, I attended a morning Bible study in my subdivision and was asked to lead a Bible study at night. The next week, four ladies and I met and decided to study the book of John. Nothing has blessed me more than sitting around a kitchen table enjoying the sweet fellowship of neighbors who love God and His Word. He did not forget my blessing!

Has God birthed a specific desire in you to minister to others? If He has, don't procrastinate like I did. Do it and watch Him bless you.

I am excited about our next session, which is about the blessings of God. Our characters are Jesus of Nazareth *and Mary of* Bethany!

Father,

Thank you for the wounds you gladly bore that we might have eternal life. Thank you for healing our broken hearts and blessing us with good things. It is encouraging to know that You can and will remove the scars of our yesterdays and replace them with a future with hope. Thank you for our "Bethels." It is amazing how your untouchable presence penetrates our soul and strengthens our faith. Thank you for our "Peniels." It is amazing how Your invisible touch leaves us visibly marked forever. We choose to believe that when you put a desire in our heart, it has a holy purpose and you will fulfill it. Your Word tells us "we can be confident of this: that he who began a good work in you will carry it on to completion until the day of Christ Jesus" (Philippians 1:6).

I pray this in the name above all names, Jesus Christ, the Son of God.

Session 6

Spiritual Marker #6
"The Blessing"

The word *blessing* has many definitions. Here are the ones that fit with spiritual marker #6.

(1) The act of one who blesses. (2) The prescribed words or ceremony for such an act. (3) An expression or utterance of good wishes. (4) A special favor granted by God. (5) Something promoting or contributing to happiness, well-being, or prosperity."[81]

God has blessed me tremendously in the midst of the most challenging years of my life. Time has not diminished the impact nor lessened the purpose of this current season. I do not seek to forget, but choose to embrace each sorrow and each blessing as a gift from above.

In session 5, I shared how God used three significant places to break the strongholds of *position*, *promotion*, and *priorities* in my life. Spiritual reflection can help us understand why the Lord placed us in certain situations. He always knows what is coming into our lives. Sandwiched between the classrooms of promotion and priorities was the first of many sorrows and many blessings that would come into the lives of my family. I decided to list them in the order they arrived so that you would have a reference as I share my testimony.

- Sorrow   1999—Ken's dad diagnosed with lung cancer

- Blessing   1999—Second grandchild born, girl, McKenzie (Parents: Paul and LeAnn)

- Sorrow   2000—Ken's dad died

- Sorrow   1999–2000—My aunt Sissie lost her right eye in a car accident. Six months after recovering from this traumatic loss, she fell and broke her hip and thigh.

- Sorrow   2001—Ken's mom diagnosed with cancer

- Blessing   2001—Third grandchild born, girl, Samantha (Parents: David and Staci)

The next two entries reflect two blessings that occurred within twenty-six minutes of each other. The sorrows that followed still exist, imbedded in the beauty of both blessings.

- Blessing and Sorrow   2002—Fourth grandchild born, girl, Caroline (Parents: Andrea and Shep). Caroline experienced oxygen loss as a result of Andrea's extreme reaction to an epidural problem. Caroline experienced brain damage. The outcome was cerebral palsy, with the most affected area being her upper body.

- Blessing and Sorrow   2002—My daughter, Andrea, miraculously recovered from a near-death experience during labor with Caroline. A problem with the epidural caused her to experience massive seizures and stop breathing.

- You can imagine the state of my daughter. To make things worse, she was diagnosed with rheumatoid arthritis when Caroline was three months old.

- Sorrow   2002—Ken's mom died.

- Sorrow   2002—My aunt Sissie died.

- Blessing   2004—Hope of healing: three people declare Caroline's healing.

- Blessing   2005—Fifth grandchild born, girl, Ava (Parents: Andrea and Shep)

- Blessing   2005—Sixth grandchild born, boy, Jared (Parents: David and Staci)

  Complications required emergency delivery for Jared and a second emergency surgery for Staci. Both experienced full recovery.

- Blessing   2008—Seventh grandchild born, boy, Ezekiel (Zeke) (Parents: Andrea and Shep)

This list is not all the sorrows or blessings. These are the ones that devastated my family one moment and brought exceeding joy the next. As I was compiling the list, I noticed that as of today, the blessings outnumber the sorrows. As you can see, for a long time, it *seemed* like there were more sorrows. The hard reality remains: *blessings do not lessen the effects of sorrows*. According to the *American Heritage Dictionary*, the word *sorrow* is defined as "mental suffering because of loss or injury; something that causes sadness or grief."[82] Sorrow affects people in different ways. For me, I would reach a point of overwhelming despair and drop to the floor, wailing uncontrollably.

Have you questioned why some have sorrows and others seem to escape them? The appearance of escaping sorrow is false. Sorrow does not exclude anyone.

> Everyone has experienced sorrow. *It is a fact of life*. The Bible has numerous accounts of people who experienced sorrow at some point in their lives. The psalmists experienced sorrow during oppression and times of trouble. Perhaps the ultimate sorrow for a woman was endured by Mary, the mother of the Lord, as she watched the cruel torture and execution of her Son.[83]

In Ecclesiastes 3, we are told there is a season for everything. Verse 4 of that chapter tells us that there is "a time to weep and a time to laugh, a time to mourn and a time to dance." My family has experienced this verse over and over again. Without the blessings that encourage and refresh us, our sorrows would consume us. Looking back, I also saw how God provided the strength and courage we needed during every time of sorrow. He blessed us *in* our sorrows as well as *before and after* them. Ken and I are extremely grateful for every sorrow and every blessing God has placed in our lives. Many times, Ken would remind me that God was in control and our role was to walk in faithfulness to God before our family, our church, and our neighbors. He has said this simple truth to me and many others over the years, "God blesses our faithfulness." He is a loving husband, father, and grandfather, who seeks to model the love of his heavenly Father.

"Blessings: Gifts from a Loving Father"

> The blessings of God are abundantly bestowed on all those who follow Him. God's blessings are not simply a reward for godly living but *a gift from a loving Father.*

Life's blessings are not a measure of who we are but of "who" God is. God promises personal blessings to those who follow Him in obedience and exhorts His people to be a blessing to others (Genesis 12:2, 3).

Christians need only to reflect back over their own lives to discover blessings from God. The goodness of God is also apparent when Christians look around at present blessings. Christians can also look ahead to future blessings. God promises continual blessings on earth and eternal blessings in heaven.

> The wonderful blessings of God should be remembered, not forgotten. The same gracious God who forgives sin, heals diseases, redeems lives, and bestows mercy, also promises abundant blessings.[84]

There are blessings, which I choose to call "delights" that my sweet Lord gave me during this next season I will be sharing with you. He delighted me because He loves me. He knew I was weaker than I realized. He knew it was time for me to follow Him more closely. He knew it was time for me to fellowship with Him in sufferings and blessings. He knew it was time for me to sit before Him and allow His Spirit to teach me. He knew a greater sorrow was close and that it would wound me deeply. He knew the encounters with Him would keep me from blaming Him. He knew the delights from Him would strengthen my faith in His goodness. He knew the *next step* I would take.

My Spiritual Journey—Sixth Step: Sanctification's Blessing

My testimony in session 5 concluded with me driving to a ladies' retreat with a different perspective. My selfish priorities had been exposed, and I knew my involvement in church activities had taken precedence over my private life with Jesus. Much had happened in our family: the death of Ken's dad, the birth of Kenzie, and the second injury to my aunt Sissie. I missed my family and my friends at church and was eager to get involved again.

Over the next year, I facilitated several Bible studies back-to-back. As soon as I finished one, I was ready to start another. I thought this was God's way of making my private life with Jesus better. As I charged into more study of God's word through Bible studies, I seemed to move farther away from Him. The entire year was a roller-coaster ride bringing out oppressive thoughts of unworthiness and condemnation, as well as compulsive efforts to gain more knowledge and understanding. Then God got my attention.

Priority of Followship

On September 11, 2001, while terrorists were attacking my country, I was meeting with a new group of ladies to begin a new study, *Jesus the One and Only* by Beth Moore. Ken was out of town on business, and this particular morning, he was in a meeting five blocks from the Pentagon. Within minutes, the news reached our group, and the Bible study video was replaced with the news channel. My efforts to reach Ken failed, but his efforts to reach me were miraculously successful. Minutes later, my daughter-in-law, LeAnn, called to relay a message from Ken that he was okay and would try to call me later. My priorities immediately changed, and prayer became number one. When I finally got to talk with Ken, he told me an amazing story of God's providential hand. Early that morning, he and his colleagues had been advised that the meeting would be held at the Pentagon on September 12. I was jolted by the impact of truth that gripped my heart. If the attack had come twenty-four hours later, Ken could have been killed. Immediately, my priorities were addressed. Ken was not where God wanted him to be in my life, and it was time to focus on this area of my marriage. Little did I know that it would lead me to follow Jesus much more closely.

The Proof of His Presence

When I completed the Bible study, *Jesus the One and Only* by Beth Moore, something inside wasn't satisfied. I needed something more from the Word concerning Jesus. I decided to read a chapter a day from John's perspective since the study had been written from the gospel of Luke. I began the first chapter asking the Lord to speak specifically to me through a verse. Fourteen days later, John 14:21 (KJV) was the verse He chose for me. To this day, it is still clearly fixed in my memory.

> "He that hath my commandments, and keepeth them, he it is that loveth me;
> and he that loveth me shall be loved of my Father, and I will love him, and will
> *manifest* myself to him." (Emphasis added)

The word *manifest* captured my attention. I immediately looked up the word in a dictionary. *Manifest* means "clearly apparent to the sight or understanding; obvious."[85] If I believed every word of the Bible was true, then I knew He could do it. But in my heart, I questioned if He would do it for me. That question greatly challenged me to believe this verse. I spent several days pondering the words, "will manifest myself to him." A godly friend encouraged me to pray and ask God to do this for me. My understanding of the definition meant that He would appear to me visibly and I would know it was Him. I had taken His words literally, and He knew it. Fear kept me from asking Him for several days. Then one morning, as I began my daily walk, I asked Him. Immediately, condemnation gripped me, and I took back my request and quickly asked forgiveness for asking such a thing for myself. As I was completing my walk, a black SUV pulled up beside me and stopped. An African-American man, who looked to be in his early thirties, asked me for directions to Interstate 20. I asked him where he was going, and he replied, "Alabama, that's my home." I told him Alabama was my home also and then gave him directions. I wished him well and turned to continue toward my house when he said, "Miss." I turned and looked at him. His eyes and smile reached beyond my senses, deep into my soul. He said, "Thanks for the directions. I really appreciate it." Time seemed to stop as his lingering eyes and sincere smile warmed my soul again.

I didn't understand my own emotions, so I quickly answered, "You're welcome," and turned away to walk toward my house. Immediately, I blurted the words, "Bless him, Lord."

Then a voice I will never forget said, "Could that have been me ... Nancy?"

Immediately, His voice penetrated my spirit, and I knew who was speaking. I jumped straight up and began shouting, "Yes! Yes! Yes!" as tears of pure joy poured down my cheeks. Then I started shouting again from the realization that He had spoken my name. I had seen far beyond the eyes of my flesh. I had seen Him with the eyes of my soul and heard Him with the ears of my spirit. He had answered my request in a way far beyond my imagination. That encounter immediately set my priorities in order. I still enjoyed Bible studies, but my focus was on Jesus and then my man, Ken.

The remainder of 2001 brought another sorrow and another blessing. Ken's mom was diagnosed with cancer, and our second granddaughter, Samantha Kate, arrived on December 11. January 2002 began with Ken retiring while I was busy planning the start-up of a women's mentoring ministry in May. Ken's mom seemed to be holding her own, and our fourth granddaughter was due in June. Ken decided it would be a good time for a vacation before our next grandchild arrived. When he asked me where I would like to go, I didn't waste any time telling him about a trip I wanted to take to Greece, especially since it included the filming of the videos for *The Beloved Disciple*, Beth Moore's latest Bible study. Ken was all for it, especially since he and I had just finished her study about Paul, which he really enjoyed. I was amazed we got tickets at such a late date. Later, I found out that several people had cancelled because of September 11. We were both grateful realizing this was another blessing from above.

The Seat of His Delight

Ken and I were so excited about our trip. Our first week was a whirlwind of Bible teaching and sightseeing tours of Athens. At the close of one of the sessions, Beth told a story about God delighting her with a rare opportunity to see a bear cub up close. She emphasized the point of her story stating that God wants to delight us and ended that session encouraging us to ask Him to delight us. The next morning, while Ken was gone to get bottled water, I knelt beside my bed and asked God to give me a seat up front. The reason for such a weird request did have a purpose. The men had been asked to sit in certain areas, which would ensure that only women were on the videos. I was so grateful for getting to come that I just couldn't leave Ken in the back of the room while I sat in one of the seats up front. Yet the desire of my heart was to sit up close and observe Beth's passion for God. As soon as the words left my mouth, condemnation did its work, and I took it back and pled for forgiveness.

I went down to the conference room full of guilt and shame. Immediately, I noticed a lady with beautiful honey-blond hair walking down each aisle, looking back and forth as if she was looking for someone or something. She did this again, and on the third trip down my aisle, she stopped at me and said, "Would you like a seat up front?" I was dumbfounded. I simply replied, "Why?" She told me that during her quiet time that morning, while she was thanking God for giving her seats close to the front, He had told her to give her seat away today. When she asked to whom, He told her He would show her. Each time she looked at me, a bright light was shining down on my head. She just felt sure I was the person. You can imagine my thoughts and facial expressions. I moved to the seat God had given me, which was right in front of Beth. As I sat listening and watching the face of my teacher, I knew that she had the kind of passion for God that I wanted. After the session, I told my new friend, Cheryl Seamon, my side of the story. We were blown away that God would do such an amazing thing. *As I was asking, He was providing. As she was thanking, He was affirming.* That was how we met and became sisters in Christ bonded forever by the "delights" of our Lord. Ken and I spent the rest of our trip getting to know Cheryl and her husband, Joe. They live in Aiken, South Carolina, and have continued to be our dear friends.

My Lord knew I would need the blessings of His presence and His delight exactly when He gave them. He had begun a good work in me on September 11. He began to move my attention to the most important men in my life, Himself and Ken. He refocused my thoughts from the stories of Jesus to the presence of Jesus. He delighted me with the seat of His authority and the power to increase my faith. He can and will bless anyone, anywhere, and anytime. He is in control and cares for His children. I arrived home full of faith and eager to start a mentoring ministry for the women of our church. In May of 2002, the mentoring ministry officially began, and I was excited to see so many women eager to be involved.

"Wounded for a Purpose"

One month after the mentoring ministry kicked off, "sorrow" again came upon the Dempsey family. This time would be the most devastating. On June 11, 2002, our daughter, Andrea, began her journey of labor and delivery with joy and eager anticipation to meet her first child, Caroline

Patricia. Her room was buzzing with conversation among close friends and family. The time came for the wonderful epidural that was supposed to take Andrea through the delivery without any pain. Soon, we would be taking pictures of my beautiful daughter proudly holding her beautiful little girl. What we were expecting didn't happen. Initially, the doctor placed a catheter into the epidural area and injected the first dose of anesthesia. Andrea's reaction seemed to be normal, and she felt good. A short time later, she began to feel different, not bad, just different. They told us she was probably a little apprehensive and placed her on oxygen. They asked everyone except me and her husband to leave the room. She began to feel the painful contractions. The doctor was called, but his physician's assistant came instead. I was not in the room when he administered two boluses of anesthesia. When I came back, Andrea's gown was being changed. She had experienced severe nausea and head pain while being given the additional boluses. It was obvious that Andrea was not feeling much better and was even more anxious. This was not how it was supposed to be. Soon, the pain returned, and the same procedure was used. This time, I remained in the room. As soon as the first bolus was given, Andrea began to complain about her head hurting. The physician's assistant told her to hold on while he gave the second bolus. Shep stood on the left side of her bed holding her hand, and I stood at the foot of her bed rubbing those precious feet. I attempted to project courage and confidence while sensing that something was not right. As her pain intensified, she began moaning and then screaming, pulling her hair. Then her screams ceased, and her entire body began to reel and jerk from grand mal seizures. This lasted a few seconds, and she fell backward with a loud thud that ignited a wave of fear and panic throughout my body. She was silent and motionless. Immediately, Shep and I were asked to step back away from the bed. As they began to work with Andrea, we fell on our knees crying out to God to stop what we couldn't even say out loud. I ran back to her bed and looked at her chest to see if she was breathing, and she wasn't. I looked at her hands; her nails were turning dark. We were ushered out into the hall as technicians, nurses, and doctors ran into her room. Waiting outside Andrea's room was not like we had anticipated days before. It was the beginning of a nightmare beyond anything I had ever dreamed. When her doctor finally came out, he told Shep, Ken, and me that as soon as they could get Andrea stabilized, they would deliver the baby by C-section.

What had happened? We were told later that the catheter that was placed in Andrea's back, which was the tubing for medication to enter the epidural space, moved into the wall of a blood vessel. The result was seepage of the medication into Andrea's bloodstream causing the critical effects to both mother and baby. Twenty-six minutes passed from the time Andrea flatlined until Caroline was lifted out of her mother's womb. During those twenty-six minutes, Caroline experienced brain damage from full and partial loss of oxygen. She was taken to the neonatal intensive care unit (NICU) while Andrea was being put in a drug-induced coma for twenty-four hours so extensive tests could be done. We were told that in cases such as this, the mother either came out perfectly okay or remained in a permanent vegetative state. While we waited on the results of Andrea's tests, we would visit her and assure her everything was fine and that she had a beautiful baby. This was extremely hard, especially since she was unconscious and intubated. I could not hold back the tears the first time I saw her after the delivery. Her beautiful face was tremendously swollen. She did not look like my daughter. Caroline spent her first hours having sporadic seizures and transfusions as doctors worked to stabilize her condition. She looked perfectly normal and was every mother's dream as far as outward appearance went. She had a head full of black hair, beautiful features, and her mother's light-olive complexion.

Her next ten weeks were spent at the NICU as doctors determined the extent of Caroline's brain damage. It was also the place for parents and close family to adjust to the reality of such wounds. Nothing prior to this had hit us with such magnitude of pain and sorrow. Tears still come quickly even though six years have brought much healing. I will never forget the day we took her home. It was such sorrow mixed with such joy. I will never forget looking at her as she lay sleeping in her Moses basket. Our hearts were full of pride and joy. She was such a beautiful baby. For a few moments, we refused to allow the prognosis of her future to replace our joy with despair. Caroline was diagnosed with damage to the basil ganglia, the area of the brain that controls motor skills. In simple terms, she had cerebral palsy. The most critical areas affected were her upper body. She could not suck, swallow normally, grasp a rattle, or hold her head up. She had to be fed through a G-tube, which was surgically inserted into her stomach before we took her home. To make things even worse, Andrea developed extremely painful rheumatoid arthritis when Caroline was two and a half months old. Those days were so hard, yet the strong man in our family, Ken, never wavered. He held fast to the encouraging scripture God had given him two days after Caroline was born.

> "Every good and perfect gift is from above, coming down from the Father of the heavenly lights, who does not change like shifting shadows" (James 1:17, NIV).

In the most difficult days of our lives, the Lord called two very important people in our family home to be with Him. That year ended with the death of Ken's mom in October and my Aunt Sissie in December. Try to imagine the impact. Even though we were numb with grief, God was with us. Our church ministered to us in amazing ways. I will never forget the love and kindness God poured over us during those hard days and nights. In 2003, we moved forward thankful for a year without the loss of loved ones.

"Utterances of Hope"

In the fall of 2003, while attending a retreat, I met Dana Godfrey. At the close of the retreat, she came up to me and asked if we could talk sometime soon. I agreed and gave her my number. We talked a couple of times about me mentoring her. In January, I officially met with Dana as her mentor. I had Caroline with me so Andrea could attend a morning Bible study, *Believing God*. Dana was excited to meet Caroline, especially since I had told her about Caroline's situation and that we were praying for God to heal her. We moved to the food court, and Dana stayed with Caroline while I got my food. When I returned, she was in tears. She told me she had felt compelled to pray for Caroline, and when she did, she had a vision of her in a white dress, maybe elementary age, perfectly well, standing beside Andrea on a stage. She believed, and still does, that God showed her a picture of Caroline completely healed. Dana has become a dear friend of our family. She still believes God is going to heal Caroline and that she and Andrea will stand on a stage and testify of the blessings of God.

In February, Andrea, my sister-in-law Sharon, my daughter-in-law Staci, and I attended a Living Proof event in Mobile, Alabama. On the second day of the event, while waiting for the doors to open, the four of us were talking about different Bible studies. A lady behind me, whom I didn't know, asked if I had done *Believing God*. I told her I was presently doing it. She asked what I was "believing God for," and I replied with these words, "I'm '*believing God*' to heal Caroline."

Immediately, a lady standing beside her, who had overheard our conversation began to shake and rub her hands up and down over her arms as if she were having chills. Then she emotionally declared, "That child will be healed!" That lady was Joann Skelton, who lives in Pensacola, Florida. She has become a very dear friend of our family and also believes Caroline will be healed during her lifetime.

In March, Andrea's husband, Shep, who is a lawyer by profession, met a lady named Melissa Phillips during the settlement of her father's will. While waiting on the judge to probate the will, a brief conversation about children led to Shep describing the situation with Caroline and Andrea. Melissa asked for permission to pray for them, and Shep gratefully agreed. Afterward, Melissa approached Shep again, telling him she had prayed for Caroline and Andrea and had specifically asked the Lord if there was any encouragement she could give them. He told her to tell Shep that Caroline would be made whole sometime around the age of five and so would Andrea. Melissa has remained close friends with the family and continues to pray with them, believing God does what He says.

Our family was greatly encouraged by these declarations of Caroline's healing. We had been praying from the moment we knew her condition that God would heal her. We could write a book on all the dreams, visions, and strong impressions people beyond our family have experienced regarding Caroline's healing. We are confident that her healing will touch many lives for the glory of God. We believe this generation is desperate to see a miracle of God.

> "And the prayer offered in faith will make the sick person well; the Lord will raise
> him up" (James 5:15).

In March of 2004, God also used Melissa Phillips to push me to take the next step according to God's purpose for my life. I would move from facilitating Bible studies to a ministry of communicating the transforming work of Jesus to women outside my church. I had ministered to ladies in my church and felt comfortable, especially since I knew everyone. The thought of going outside my church immediately brought out my self-consciousness and fear of rejection. Six months after my conversation with Melissa, I was asked to speak at a retreat in Tampa, Florida. Since then, I have had many experiences ministering to women outside my church. I will gladly go *wherever* He calls and say *whatever* He wants.

In 2005, God blessed us with two more grandchildren. Ava Ruth Helton was born on Saint Patrick's Day and named after her grandmother, Nancy Ruth. Jared Blake Dempsey was born a month premature in early May. Ava is like her mommy in more ways than one, and Jared is just like his daddy. They also have a little of their grandmother's *strong will*! Sandwiched between the birth of Ava and Jared, God blessed Ken and me with a wonderful thirtieth wedding anniversary. I will share more details later, but for now, I must fast forward to 2007.

In the summer of 2007, I began writing this study. God used my pastor to challenge me to share my "story" of how Jesus transformed my life into a passionate walk with Him. A couple of years prior to the nudge of my pastor, Ken had already suggested that I write a book about my life. God used these two men to plant the seed in my heart. I will forever be grateful for the confidence and unwavering support of these mighty men of God. In the fall of 2007, I began a divine journey as a part-time employee of the LifeWay Christian Store in Kennesaw, Georgia. I had never worked in retail, so the challenge was massive for this retiree. My husband and family could not believe I was going back to work, but God was not surprised because He had orchestrated the entire process. It was truly one of the most rewarding seasons in my life. The work was hard, but the atmosphere made it easy. I told the Lord that if this was where He wanted me to work, then my response was "Yes." I told Him my efforts would be as if I were working for Him. I would be an example and commit to pray for my peers. Shortly after I went to work, my daughter found out she was once again with child. I immediately knew my tenure would probably not be long since she would need help after the delivery. I also knew that He had a purpose for me being there, and it would be fulfilled. What was His purpose? *To bless me.* How? Through the experience of working with people who willingly showered me with patience, support, encouragement, faith, commitment, sacrifice, and love. For nine precious months, their friendships replenished my soul. I went there much needier than I realized and left there a stronger

Nancy. I am honored to have been a part of the dedicated associates of LifeWay in Kennesaw, Georgia! I will never forget those days. I love each one of my co-workers dearly.

In May of 2008, Ezekiel Shepherd Helton came into this family. He was the third grandson and the seventh and last grandchild. In the first trimester, the enemy tried to wound this little fellow. During a sonogram, an indicator of Down syndrome was noted. We were fearful of the worst. Immediately, people began to pray. The remainder of Andrea's sonograms failed to reveal any additional indicators. Zeke was born perfectly healthy and without Down syndrome.

On June 5, 2008, Caroline was given an injection of stem cells from the cord blood of full-term babies. We have seen tremendous improvement in several areas such as stamina, desire, arm movements, and attempts to speak and eat by mouth. Her therapists are excited with her improvements. The best is that she knows she is able to do more and shows great excitement and cooperation. This year has been full of suspense, excitement, and blessings.

Day 1
Priority of Follow-ship

In session 5, we looked at the breaking of Jacob's deceitful nature and the healing of Hannah's broken heart. Both of our characters were blessed after they experienced their own personal brokenness. In this last session, we will look at a few sorrows that brought blessings in the lives of Jesus of Nazareth and Mary of Bethany. I chose Jesus because He is the one who has ordained my steps. I chose Mary of Bethany because she personifies the type of commitment to Jesus I want to model.

We will not be looking at the entire life of Christ, but rather selected snapshots of those who chose to closely follow and intimately fellowship with the Lamb of God. The challenge of this study is not just for you but for me as well. The question for us is simple, "Will we remain committed followers of Jesus regardless of life's unexpected road rage and valleys of sorrow?" I have learned that followship and fellowship must be priorities in my relationship with Jesus. Revealing each season of my life has been painful, yet healing. The more I know Him, the more I love Him. The more I love Him, the more I realize I need Him.

Jesus' relationship with His Father was one of intimate fellowship and obedient followship. His role as the Son was to follow the leadership of His Father, especially during His tenure on earth. Let's look at the first recorded directive Jesus received from His Father.

The First Miracle: A Wedding in Cana

Read John 2:1–11, and answer the questions.

- Who brought up the need for wine?

  _____

- Based on the text, who can we assume told Jesus to choose the ceremonial jars and have the servants fill them with water? _

  _____

- When do you think the water turned into wine?

  _____

- The Amplified Bible reads, "And when the manager tasted the water just now turned into wine, not knowing where it came from – though the servants who had drawn the water knew – he called the bridegroom." Can't you see the servants' eyes as they hear the master's comments in verse 10? I can just hear the accounts of those servants, the first witnesses to the first miracle of Jesus. It is apparent the Father wanted the "servants" to be a major part in serving the best wine to the guests of the bridegroom.

- Who was praised for saving the best wine for last?

  _____

- Who knew the truth?

  _____

- How did Christ set the example of servanthood?

  _____

- I can see Mary's face as she watched Jesus and the unfolding of His first miracle. Until then, Mary's priority had been to nurture and teach Jesus in the ways of God. This day changed her priority. Mary would now follow Jesus as *His* servant and a supporter of *His* ministry.

Reread verse 11, and answer these questions about His disciples.

- Describe the different expressions that may have been visible on the faces of His disciples.

  _____

- What do you think had hindered the disciples' faith in Christ?

  _____

They were no different than you and I. They wanted and needed to see "proof" that He was who John the Baptist said He was.

> The word glory is used to describe the "nature and acts of God in self-manifestation. It was exhibited in the character and acts of Christ in the days of his flesh, Jn. 1:14; Jn. 2:11; at Cana both His grace and His power were manifested, and these constituted His glory.[86]

The turning of water into wine met a need and provided multiple blessings. In your opinion, which had the greater affect? Circle your choice: the best wine or miraculous proof.

The disciples were convinced with their hearts ablaze to follow Jesus. They probably had no idea that following Jesus would involve such miraculous works or such devastation at the end of three short years. This was truly a blessing for Jesus' young followers. Following Christ will cause us to change our priorities. He will challenge us to follow His example in Cana. We are to be godly servants who are not self-exalting, but rather participants in the betterment of others. We should seek an opportunity to glorify God out of love and obedience. He will always honor our efforts and bless others in a faith-building way.

"Often we choose Leadership over Lordship."

Have you ever allowed a good thing in your life to take priority over the best thing? There was a time when I convinced myself that my priorities were exactly in line—with God being number one, Ken number two, and then ministry. But I was wrong. I had allowed ministry to creep right past them both. As the leader of Bible studies in my church, I poured all my energy into making Bible study a part of every woman's life. Ministry is ministry, and Lordship is Lordship. In the midst of ministry, Lordship took over. As I mentioned earlier, the events of September 11 got my attention and stirred me deeply concerning the priority of my marriage. As I yielded to the Spirit, He prompted me often to pray more for my marriage. I soon began to pray differently, asking God to make me into the woman Ken needed me to be. Almost immediately, our times together changed. We began to enjoy one another in a fresh and sweet way. My *followship* of the Spirit changed my *fellowship* with my husband. The Lord was replacing my *good* with His *best*. He did not remove me from leadership in the church. He helped me reprioritize it.

Whether you are married or single, ask yourself this question, "Are my priorities in the right order compared with God's priorities?" We must be very careful not to allow good things to consume our time at the expense of the best things. If something came to your mind as you read my testimony, write it down and pray about it.

In session 1, we looked at Mary, the young virgin who met Jesus as her firstborn son. Today, we saw her again as His ministry took off at a wedding. Mary followed her son as His servant for the rest of her life. Today, we will look at another woman who met Jesus in a very different way and would also become a close follower like His mother.

The Healing Miracle: Mary Magdalene

Since there are many women named Mary mentioned in the Bible, I felt it worth the read to include the following excerpts from Herbert Lockyer's commentary on Mary Magdalene, who was born in Magdala.

> [Magdala] was a town on the coast of Galilee. The Jewish Talmud affirms that Magdala had an unsavory reputation, and because of the harlotry practiced there was destroyed. The Bible depicts Mary as a pure, though deeply afflicted woman before she met Jesus. There is no word whatever in the writings of the Christian Fathers, whose authority stands next to the apostles, as to Mary having a foul reputation. The wide acceptance of the tradition that she was a reformed prostitute is utterly baseless. Mary was only a sinner in the sense that we all are, having been born in sin and shaped in iniquity. Saved from the terrible power of hell, she gave of her best to Him who had fully emancipated her from demonic possession. When Christ saved her, He liberated the highest virtues of sacrifice, fortitude, and courage.[87]

I can't imagine the torment of seven demons possessing a person's body and mind. I do know what it is like to experience the oppressive bombardment of condemning thoughts and feelings. They are real. They can take a toll on a person and definitely affect others, especially a spouse, children, or job. Let's spend a few minutes reading about Mary from Luke's perspective.

Read Luke 8:2–3, and answer this question.

- How was Mary labeled?

_____

Let's look at another commentary for a description of demonic possession. Allow your imagination to form a picture of the Mary Jesus would have met.

> Mary met Jesus face to face, an encounter that changed her life. Jesus casts from Mary the seven evil demonic spirits that had ruled and ruined her life. The gospel writers distinguished demon possession from other diseases. The New Testament clearly describes its symptoms, for example, speechlessness, violence, blindness, convulsions, foaming at the mouth. Mary's demonic possession may have been physical, mental,

or spiritual illness or perhaps even immorality (though there is no textual evidence for prostitution on her part).[88]

Scary, isn't it? I wonder how their paths crossed. Regardless, Jesus and Mary met face-to-face, and He cast out her tormentors. She was set free and given a *new beginning* in life. Sometimes we have demon-like sins that hold us captive. I have been there, and it took Jesus to set me free. Do you have something that keeps you from total freedom? Do you need a *new beginning* in your walk with Jesus? Tell him right now and then put a symbol representing what keeps you from freedom on this line. _

Herbert Lockyer's commentary on Mary Magdalene reveals her strong followship of Jesus. This time, allow your imagination to form a picture of Mary in her new life.

> No woman superseded Mary in utter devotion to the Master. Mary was present at the mock trial. Mary was present in Pilate's Hall. Mary was one of the sorrowing groups of holy women who stood as near as they could to comfort Jesus by their presence in the closing agonies of the crucifixion. Mary Magdalene remained "sitting over against the sepulcher" and "beholding" until Joseph had laid the Lord's body away (Matthew 27:61; Mark 15:47; Luke 23:55). Last at the cross, Mary Magdalene was also the first at the garden tomb to witness the most important event in world history and the pivotal truth of Christianity, namely the Resurrection of Jesus Christ.[89]

I can imagine the gossip that spread when the healed Mary gratefully joined other holy women who served and supported Jesus. His association with outcasts was always a strike against Him and His ministry. He was not concerned about people's opinions. He was concerned about their souls.

What are you grateful to Jesus for today?

_____

Read John 20:1–18, and answer the questions.

- What was different the second time Mary looked into the tomb?

  _____

  _____

- Write the words Jesus spoke to Mary.

  _____

- Why do you think Mary didn't recognize Jesus even though she saw and heard him?

  _____

- What was her response to Jesus speaking her name?

  _____

- What did Jesus commission Mary to do?

  _____

In Mary Magdalene, we see what Jesus is able to do for and through faithful women.

- What has Jesus commissioned you to do?

  _____

- Have you done it? If not, why?

  _____

- What do you need to happen in your life for you to follow Jesus closely?

  _____

  _____

This has been a great day! See you tomorrow on the path of Jesus!

Day 2
Proof of His Presence

What extremes we saw in the life of Jesus yesterday. We began by looking at the beginning of His ministry with the first miracle, the turning of water into wine. Then we moved from the happy occasion to a dark side of life, in which Jesus cast out seven demons from a woman. The providential presence of Jesus was and is always a blessing. Today, we are going to look at a couple of situations in which a miracle was the last thing expected. Our first situation demonstrates Jesus' compassion and power over death. Let's begin with Jesus coming upon a funeral procession. Before you read the text, I want to describe coffins in those days.

"Coffins were not generally used in biblical times. The body was placed on an open bier, or bed, before burial. Often made of wooden boards, these biers were portable."[90]

Read Luke 7:11–15, and answer the following questions.

- Who is with Jesus?

  _____

- Who is being buried?

  _____

- Who is with the widow?

  _____

- Why do you think Jesus told the widow not to weep?

  _____

- What actions did Jesus take to resurrect the young man?

  _____

  _____

- What affect did this have on the large crowd from the town?

  _____

  _____

The son of this poor widow was the *first person* Jesus raised from the dead. I can imagine some whispers of a couple of the disciples sounding like this:

> Why is Jesus stopping this funeral procession? It's all the crying and the pitiful mother that got to him. I've never seen such a compassionate person, have you? No, but He isn't a regular person. He's going to comfort her and then we can continue on. Why is He lingering? Look, He's turning toward the corpse! We've seen that look

before. He is going to do something … maybe another miracle. Is He talking to the dead? The man is opening his eyes and moving. He's talking … what did he say?

Jesus spoke to the dead, and the dead became alive. The disciples may have been way too close for comfort, but they were so privileged to have had a perfect view of His resurrection power. I can see their eyes bulging with astonishment, followed by gasps of elated wonder. They had never seen such compassion or power. We, too, are privileged to have His Word before us today. Let's take a closer look at the spoken words of Christ to the widow's dead son.

> **"What mingled majesty and grace shines in this scene! The Resurrection and the Life in human flesh, with a word of command, bringing back life to the dead body; Incarnate Compassion summoning its absolute power to dry a widow's tears"** (Jamieson, Fausset, Brown, pg. 999).

Fill in the blanks in verse 14.

- "Then he went up and touched the coffin, and those carrying it stood still. He said, 'Young man, I _____ to you, _____ _____!'"

Let's take a closer look at the words Jesus spoke. The King James Version reads, "Young man, I say unto thee, Arise!" According to Strong's online commentary, the word *say* also means to call, command, or direct. The word *arise* also means to awake, lift, raise up, arouse from the sleep of death, to recall the dead to life.

Just for fun, let's use the definitions of *say* and *arise* and fill in the blanks. You choose the words you like.

- "Young man, I _____ you to _____!"

The resurrection power of His words accomplished what He said. The boy rose up and spoke. The Words of Christ are powerful over any situation. His call comes with the desire to respond. His commands come with the power to obey.

Matthew Henry's commentary states that "whenever Christ gives us spiritual life, he opens the lips in prayer and praise."[91]

- What do you think the young man said in verse 15?

  _____

  _____

- What do you think the amazed mother did?

  _____

- Imagine the questions the disciples asked Jesus as they left the city of Nain.

- Write a question you would have asked if you had been one of the disciples?

  _____

- Do you think Jesus answered their questions? Is there a question you are hesitant to ask Him? If yes, why?

_____

At the beginning of the session, as I shared my spiritual journey, I shared a segment called "The Proof of His Presence." I want to share the awesome insight the Holy Spirit gave me as I pondered my own difficulty in asking Him a question. A quick recap of the encounter drew my spiritual eyes and ears to focus on one word in the questioning sentence of the Holy Spirit, "Could that have been me, Nancy?" As His words replayed in my mind, I wondered why He used the word *that*. I believe my encounter was divinely providential. He knew how desperate I was to settle my questioning of John 14:21. Would Jesus really manifest Himself to me in a way that I would know it was Him? That morning changed my life. When I asked, He answered. I believe the man who asked me for directions was a born-again Christian who was used as a vessel to reveal the love of Christ to me. Christ in him touched my aching and troubled soul. My mind, will, and emotions were touched by the invisible hand of Jesus. My soul was literally embraced in a way I had never experienced before. The Lord's love for me was manifested through the eyes, smile, and words of that man.

The *American Heritage Dictionary* defines that as "being the one indicated or implied."[92] When I shouted, "Yes!" I agreed that my experience was with Him. Simultaneously, He revealed the proof of His presence that had been manifested to me. To seal my encounter, He demonstrated the power of His word. He spoke my name, and I knew that it was my Lord.

We are told in John 10:3b that "He calls His own sheep by name and leads them out," and in John 10:14, "I am the good shepherd; I know my sheep and my sheep know me."

Fill in the blanks in Matthew 7:7.

- "_____ and it will be _____ to you; _____ and you will _____; _____ and the door will be _____ to you."

- Read Matthew 7:8, and write what this verse says to you.

_____

_____

I want to encourage you to ask, knock, and seek from the Lord *that* for which you spiritually hunger. We will conclude our session today looking at Jesus' "water-walking" power. I want to encourage you to be very intentional about learning and applying the great lesson Jesus taught His disciples in this snapshot of His ministry.

Read Matthew 14:22–36.

Sometimes Jesus will move us from a place of blessings to a temporary place of preparation for the next assignment. That place can be full of sorrow. In our text, we saw this happen in the lives of Jesus' disciples. Let's take another look at the text and see what we can learn. When all the leftovers are collected, Jesus tells them to leave, get in the boat, and go to the other side without Him. As they are traveling to the other side, Jesus is praying. As darkness takes over the day, the forces of nature take control and the disciples are overcome with fear. Jesus doesn't come, but He knows. When the winds and waves exhaust their strength and weariness escalates their fear, Jesus moves toward them. At just the right moment, they see Him but allow their minds to grasp the ghost of death instead of the God of life. Could their weak flesh and raw emotions have assumed such a thing? Scripture tells us they "cried out in fear." The Amplified Bible says they screamed out with fright (verse 26). Immediately, Jesus spoke to His disciples saying, "Take courage! It is I. Don't be afraid" (Matthew 14:27, NIV).

The disciples were in the place we all have to go through called "transition." Sometimes it is the place between jobs, homes, ministry opportunities, or additional family members. It can also be the place of recovery from traumatic things like the death of a close friend or relative, a divorce, a major disease, a serious accident, or the loss of financial security. There are others I'm sure, but regardless, we all will experience the place of transition. Based on verses 22–27, we can see the affect the boat, waves, winds, and darkness had on the disciples. Their courage was diminished.

- What was your most recent transition place, and how did it affect you?

  _____

Based on verses 28–31, we can see the importance of keeping our eyes on Jesus instead of on the present things that weaken our *faith*. Peter's temporary surge of faith proved to be miraculous but not strong enough to sustain him. His previous fears came back even stronger, persuading Peter of sure death. Peter's faith was weakened by *doubt*.

- Did you experience setbacks during your transition? If you did, what caused them?

  _____

Based on verses 32–34, when Jesus and Peter got into the boat, nature's wrath was halted and a worship service began. Amazing how Jesus' presence restored their focus. They left worshipping Jesus full of faith and courage and would step ashore that way again. One night out of focus taught them a very important lesson they would need to remember: *Keep your focus on Jesus and continue to praise and worship Him.*

- Have you experienced a time when keeping your focus on Jesus made a transition smooth? If you have, write your prayer right now praising Him again for providing you with courage and faith during that time.

  _____

Based on verses 35 and 36, a great healing service took place!

- What was miraculously different about this healing?

  _____

Jesus can perfectly restore us when we reach out with courageous faith and take hold of the fact that He truly is … the *Son of God*.

See you tomorrow at the home of Mary of Bethany!

✐

Day 3
The Seat of His Delight

Mary of Bethany was like Mary of Magdalene in that she loved to sit at the feet of Jesus. The Bible tells us that she lived with her sister, Martha, and brother, Lazarus. They loved Jesus, and He loved them. Their home was where Jesus stayed when He was in the area. Each served a purpose in the ministry of Jesus. Martha expressed her devotion through hospitality and domestic service for Jesus and the disciples. Lazarus was used to validate the resurrection power of God. Mary's purpose was described by Jesus, "She did what she could" (Mark 14:8).

There is so much we can learn from this amazing woman. But how can we when the Bible only provides twelve words spoken by her? We must look at her actions. As a child, my mother had a saying, which I heard on a regular basis, "Your actions speak louder than your words." Hindsight proved that I got more spankings from what I did, than what I said. Things seem to have reversed for me in my more mature years. I seem to get in trouble from my talk far more often than from my walk. Do you know what I mean? Let's go to the third gospel and take a look at Mary's walk.

Read Luke 10:38–42.

In this brief snapshot into the home of Mary, we see two people with completely different priorities.

- What was Mary's priority?

_____

I could not imagine doing what Martha did. But her interruption was the very place Jesus would teach a needed lesson in priorities. While Martha was anxiously preparing their food, she was missing the spiritual food Christ was serving. I'm sure her words lined up with her actions. Jesus began His lesson with His response to her demands.

- Reread verse 41. What was the application from Jesus' lesson for Martha?

_____

The application for me is very simple. Spiritual food must come before physical food. What was the application for you?

_____

Jesus was also saying it was okay for Martha to join them. Yes, she could come out of the kitchen and take a seat right up front like Mary. I don't know about you, but I must sit up front at my church. Ken and I usually sit in the third row. I intentionally encourage my pastor with nods and smiles. Sometimes, I even cry from the strong emotions that follow conviction or confirmation from the Holy Spirit. Ken can always be counted on to provide regular "amens." I can imagine the looks Jesus got as He taught that day. Do you think He was telling them of things to come? Let's look at another snapshot in the home of Mary of Bethany from the second gospel.

Read Mark 14:1–10. This scene occurs after Christ's visit to Mary and Martha's home. The unnamed woman in this passage is Mary of Bethany.

- Who do you think may have instigated the rebuking of Mary in verse 4?

  _____

- Who revealed Mary's purpose, and what was it?

  _____

- What is revealed in verse 10?

  _____

Now back to our text. Jesus' ministry is coming to an end, and He is telling them about His death and resurrection. Our look in Mark revealed that Mary and the disciples had been told about this already. Could it have been at the Bible study Jesus held in the family room of Mary's home?

When a loved one begins to share devastating news or a miraculous blessing he or she has received, we immediately move closer and listen intently to all the details. Our eyes automatically focus on their eyes and their expressions in an attempt to see more than what is being spoken. We want to know the magnitude of their pain or joy, so that we can respond appropriately.

Imagine Mary moving from the back of the room, past the disciples, to the front when Jesus began sharing future events about His death. Maybe Mary had been sitting in the back on a previous occasion, unable to see past the twelve disciples and her brother but was afraid to say anything or perhaps felt unworthy to sit in front of them. Maybe the last time Jesus had been with them, His Words had given her hope regarding a need or desire. Maybe she had decided that the next time He came, she would move up closer. In our text today, I wonder if Jesus went to Mary and said, "Mary, come sit at my feet today." Today, she could move closer without fear of unworthiness. There, she could hear every word while looking into the very eyes of God.

- What emotions do you think Mary felt as she positioned herself in the "seat" of honor before her Lord?

  _____

  _____

- What emotions did you experience from our look at Mary's move to the feet of Jesus?

  _____

Dear ones, Jesus draws us to sit at His feet. He wants to fellowship with us up close and personal! I love Matthew Henry's comments about this topic. This poses a very personal and probing question for every child of God, "Are you ready to sit at His feet?"

In my spiritual journey for this session, I shared my "seat of delight." Jesus knew the very moment I would need to move up front. Beth was teaching the video sessions for her study, *The Beloved Disciple*, and this particular morning she taught on our identification in Christ. As I sat right in front of her, I could see so much more. Her love for the Lord was so evident. Her love for every person sitting at her feet was just as evident. Her passion for the Word was miraculously contagious. Every word that came out of her mouth penetrated my soul, freeing me from who "I thought I was" and filling me with the truth of *who I really was in Christ*. Other truths came forth with amazing power and clarity, validating my recent encounter with His presence. The pieces began to come together, and I realized that the providential hand of my Lord had truly delighted me. What I saw up close was the love and passion of God flowing through a person. He was drawing me to His Word for a purpose. He knew the hindrances that kept me from trusting Him completely. He knew I would be like before, just strong enough to ask but still too weak to believe He would do it. He also knew what Cheryl needed. We both needed proof of His unconditional love and acceptance. He intertwined our delights so that our faith would be set ablaze and our testimony would encourage others. Jesus delighted in me and wanted me to delight in Him. For me to truly delight in Him, I needed to sit at His feet.

Strong's concordance defines the word *sit* to mean "to dwell; a fixed place to be occupied."[93] In Ephesians 1:20, we are told that God's resurrection power raised Jesus from the dead and seated him at His Father's right hand so we know where Jesus is physically seated. This same power is the Holy Spirit that comes into our spirit through salvation, to dwell in us eternally.

> "Sitting at Christ's feet, signifies readiness to receive His word, and submission to the guidance of it" (Henry, 955).

Read Ephesians 2:4–7.

- With whom are we seated?

  _____

- Where are we seated?

  _____

Jesus wants us to allow His indwelling presence to empower us to live in freedom. Based on Ephesians, we know God has seated us with Jesus. He wants our soul, which is our mind, will, and emotions, to be securely fixed on Him. Remember, we are seated in the greatest place of honor … the *Throne of Christ!*

See you tomorrow at the tomb of Lazarus!

ℐ

Day 4
Wounded for a Purpose

I hope you ended your time yesterday ready to sit at the feet of Jesus. Today, we are going to look at two of the most important events in Mary's life:

1. The resurrection of Lazarus

2. The anointing of Jesus

Before we dive into our first event, we must begin with Jesus receiving word from Martha and Mary that Lazarus, their brother, was sick. This is found in the fourth gospel.

Read John 11:1–4, 11–16, and answer the questions.

- When Jesus heard about Lazarus's sickness, He told the disciples his sickness would not end in death. What was the purpose of the sickness?

  _____

- Jesus *plainly* told them Lazarus was dead and then expressed gladness that He wasn't with Lazarus when he died. What was the purpose of Him not being there?

  _____

Before we move on to Jesus' conversation with Mary, did you notice that doubting Thomas didn't hesitate to voice his fearful opinion? He also had to have the *last word* regardless of the fact that Jesus, the miracle worker, had told them Lazarus's sickness would not end in death. Jesus never said Lazarus wouldn't die. He said, "This sickness will not end in death."

Event #1—Resurrection of Lazarus

Read John 11:17–44.

Lazarus had been in the tomb for four days when Jesus arrived. Only one sister greeted Him, and that was Martha. Mary was too devastated to move. She could not get over the great loss she felt sure Jesus could have prevented. Her Lord had not come through for her. The death of her beloved brother was devastating enough, but to be disappointed in Jesus was more than Mary could handle. While Mary

> "Death was not awaiting them…an undeniable resurrection was" (author).

sat silently in the grip of hopelessness, Martha's encounter with Jesus had brought encouragement. Why was she so despairing on this day? That day, she needed hope. Timing was of the essence, and Jesus was right on time. I can imagine Mary's sorrow rising to a deadly peak just as Martha enters the house and excitedly tells her Jesus is asking for her.

Be attentive to Mary's positions as you fill in the blanks in these verses.

- Verse 29: "When Mary heard this, she _____ _____ quickly and went to Him."

- Verse 32: "When Mary reached the place where Jesus was and saw him, she _____ at His _____ and said, 'Lord, if you had been _____, my brother would not have died.'"

Since the end of Jesus' ministry was near, I want to think Mary had heard about the miraculous resurrection of a widow's son in the town of Nain. This miracle happened while the dead man was being taken for burial. What kept Mary from believing that Jesus couldn't do the same for Lazarus? Was it because Lazarus had been dead four days? Was it Mary's belief in Jewish tradition that weakened her faith in Jesus?

> Death and burial usually took place on the same day in Jesus' time, due to the hot climate. The body was carefully, but hurriedly wrapped in strips of cloth with expensive spices and ointments. Jesus probably began His journey to Bethany the day of, or the day after Lazarus' burial. The journey took two or three days. When Jesus arrived in Bethany, Lazarus would have been in the tomb four days, which John carefully noted. Jewish tradition taught that the deceased person's soul hovered over the body for three days after death in hopes of reunion. However untrue, this superstition was widely believed. The fact that Lazarus had been dead for four days instead of three left little doubt in Jewish minds that Lazarus' restoration to life by Jesus was, in fact, an unmistakable miracle.[94]

Let's look at what this Jewish tradition had done to Mary as you fill in the blank in Colossians 2:8.

- "See to it that no one takes you _____ through hollow and deceptive philosophy which depend on human tradition."

Mary was a captive of deceptive tradition.

Jesus tells us in Matthew 5:17 that He had come to us to fulfill the law of God. He had come to Mary and Martha that day to fulfill Psalm 19:7, which says, "The law of the Lord is perfect, reviving the soul."

Jesus had come that day to fulfill the law, not this Jewish tradition.

Jesus had come to resurrect more than the dead body of Lazarus, He had come to revive Mary's faith. This same power lives within us and can restore any area of our lives.

- In John 11:32, we read the only recorded words of Mary in the Bible. What posture did Mary take this time before Christ?

_____

Mary may have even gone facedown, prostrate before her Lord. She was not the peaceful student sitting joyfully before her teacher. She was a woman of *debilitating sorrow.*

- In verse 44, Lazarus has been resurrected and comes out of the tomb. Who do you think Jesus looked at when He said, "Take off the grave clothes and let him go"?

_____

Mary's captive life was set free. Her soul had been revived and her faith restored. Her *Lord of Peace, Jehovah-shalom*, had turned her sorrow into blessings!

Event #2—Anointing of Jesus

Read John 12:1–8.

This account is also in Matthew and Mark. Mary's name is not mentioned in either, but she is in fact the woman who anointed Jesus. These two gospels address the anointing of Jesus' head, while John addresses the anointing of Christ's feet. Mary of Bethany anointed both His head and His feet. In John's gospel, we might assume the dinner is at the home of Lazarus, but in fact, it is in the home of Simon the Leper. I found some additional information about the host.

> To honor Christ for the return of Lazarus from the grave a feast was prepared for the rejoicing friends in the house of Simon—a common name at that time. He had been a leper, but had been healed and converted as the result of his contact with the wonder-working Christ.[95]

In our text, we find Mary again at the feet of Jesus and again for a different purpose.

- What was Mary doing?

  _____

- What position was she in?

  _____

The dinner to honor Jesus was not what it appeared. Simon's servant should have washed Jesus' feet upon arrival. The neglect of Jesus in this manner upset Mary. She waited until after dinner and did it herself. Any dishonor that came upon her for using her hair was of no concern to Mary. I found an interesting explanation of why Mary used her hair to wipe Jesus' feet in Strong's concordance.

> While long hair is a glory to a woman, and to wear it loose or disheveled is a dishonor, yet the woman who wiped Christ's feet with her "hair" (in place of the towel which Simon the Pharisee omitted to provide), despised the shame in her penitent devotion to the Lord (slaves were accustomed to wipe their master's feet), Luke 7:38 & 44; see also John 11:2; John 12:3.[96]

- Who was the guest of honor?

  _____

- What other unspoken reasons may have instigated such rebukes of Mary?

  _____

Mary's actions exposed the negligence and disrespect of Jesus by all in attendance.

Read Matthew 26:8–13.

Jesus was upset with them and exposed the condition of their hearts. His praise of Mary spoke volumes of their willingness to serve at a cost. "She did what she could." I think that statement became a probing question to the disciples. That same statement has reached us today in a probing question, "Have you done what you could for Jesus?"

- Is there something you sense the Holy Spirit is prompting you to do in your church or your community and you keep resisting? If so, what do you think it is?

_____

Recently, I sensed the Holy Spirit prompting me to be a table mentor for MOPS (Mothers of Preschool Children) in our church. I was resistant because I was leading and participating in Age to Age, the mentoring ministry in my church. When the Holy Spirit is persistent, I know I must obey. I joined the program, and I love it. It has been a blast, and I realize each time we meet why He wants me there.

Fill in the blanks in Philippians 4:13.

- "I _____ do _____ through Him who gives me the _____."

Here are the additional words that are provided in the Amplified Bible:

> I have strength for all things in Christ Who empowers me [I am ready for anything and equal to anything through Him who infuses inner strength into me; I am self-sufficient in Christ's sufficiency.

Jesus' final words about Mary of Bethany bring our day to a sweet close.

- Write Matthew 26:13.

_____

_____

_____

I can imagine the expressions on the faces of those around the room when they heard these beautiful words from the Word Himself, some with smiles, some without. The one I would have loved to see was Mary as she took her eyes off those precious feet and looked into the very eyes of God. Can you imagine? Ponder on this personal question, and then write your answer.

What would be your private thoughts if Jesus said those words about you in public?

_____

_____

_____

See you tomorrow at our final look at Jesus and Mary of Bethany!

॰๛॰

Day 5
Utterances of Hope

Are we really at the end of this journey? As I write this final portion, I am filled with emotions that swing from humble gratitude to tender sadness. This Bible study has been life changing for me; the examination of not only my story but those of others has helped me in the process. *Jehovah-raah, My Shepherd*, has gone before me, leading me *step by step*, as I put to paper my story and the stories of others from His Word, so that others might experience a renewed sense of hope. I believe the purpose of this Bible study has been for us to see the consistent work of God, passing from generation to generation. My prayer for you has been that you would take away something very much needed in the present generation, which is the assurance that what He did for those we studied, He will do for you.

Faith commands us to add our story and pass it on to the next generation. Webster's defines *hope* as "trust that what is wanted will happen." In the spiritual sense, it means "the eager expectation of what God is going to do." We cannot have faith without hope. Hope keeps us believing God. Just when we are about to give up, He brings hope.

Jesus has never stopped providing us with hope that Caroline would be healed while here on earth. I truly believe He is going to heal her soon. As I write, her mother, Andrea, is in the process of writing their journey of faith. She is sharing all the ways God has provided hope in their darkest hours of doubting. She decided to do this on her blog so others would know the entire story and could join them in believing God to heal our precious Caroline. If you would like to join us, her blog address is www.homeof5blogspot.com. Can you imagine the effect on the body of Christ when that little girl stands, fully healed, singing praises with her mommy to *Jehovah-rapha, Our Healer*?

> **We have looked back at those who have gone before us and grasped the "hand of hope".**

- What do you want God to heal in you or in someone else?

  _____

- Do you believe He is going to do it? If yes, briefly describe how He gave you that hope.

  _____

If you said no, maybe it is because you are where I've been. I wanted Him to do for me what other people told me He did for them. Their testimonies gave me a glimpse of hope, but I needed more. Let's look at someone close to Jesus who needed more.

Read John 20:19–29, and answer the questions.

- What did Thomas require before he would believe the disciples' report?

  _____

- What did Jesus do to "make sure" Thomas believed?

Jesus didn't deny Thomas's request, and He does not deny ours. Any time we experience doubting and unbelief, our Lord knows it. Jesus intentionally came to Thomas when unbelief had separated him from the others. I've been just like Thomas so many times. How about you? Jesus doesn't come to us like He did Thomas because He is already in us. Jesus' visible presence and personal words to Thomas immediately increased his faith. His presence in us can do the same for you and me.

He came to replace our fears and doubts with hope and faith.

Day 1: Priority of Followship

We are the "delight" of Jesus! The Amplified Bible gives us a beautiful picture of ourselves in this final snapshot. Read these verses very slowly and meditate on them. Take the time to visualize yourself in this scene.

> Let us rejoice and shout for joy (exulting and triumphant)! Let us celebrate and ascribe to Him glory and honor, for the marriage of the Lamb (at last) has come, and His bride has prepared herself. She has been permitted to dress in fine (radiant) linen, dazzling and white—for the fine linen is (signifies, represents) the righteousness (the upright, just, and godly living, deeds, and conduct, and right standing with God) of the saints (God's holy people). (Revelation 19:7–8)

> Throughout scripture the marriage union is a metaphor or picture of the relationship between God and His people. In the Old Testament, Israel is pictured as the wife of Yahweh. In the Epistles and in Revelation, the church is described as the Bride of Christ.[97]

Let's spend a few minutes with Isaiah and Paul as they speak about this event.

Fill in the blanks in Isaiah 62:5b.

- "As a bridegroom rejoices over his bride, so will your _____ rejoice over _____."

Fill in the blanks in Ephesians 5:25b–27.

- "Christ _____ the church and gave himself up for _____ to make her holy, _____her by the washing with water through the _____ and to present her to himself as a _____ church, without stain or wrinkle or any other _____, but holy and _____."

I love to see how the Old Testament is fulfilled through the New Testament. Isaiah tells us the *outcome*, and Paul tells us *how we get there*! Even though we have these beautiful portraits of truth, somehow, it is still hard to grasp. It may not be hard for you, but it was for me. I want to share one of the most wonderful blessings that made this truth finally real for me.

My Thirtieth Wedding Anniversary: Restored Bride of Christ

A couple of months before my thirtieth wedding anniversary, my friend Cheryl, whom I had met during the taping of the *Beloved Disciple*, called me with another nudge to have my wedding portrait made as a surprise for Ken. She had made the decision to do the same while talking with Beth at the taping. Ken and I had attended the celebration of her and Joe's twentieth wedding anniversary and the unveiling of a new wedding portrait of Cheryl. It had been a wonderful and very moving experience that lingered deep within my heart. Neither of my marriages included a wedding dress or portrait. I knew I was a "restored bride" according to His Word, but I secretly desired to have the experience and emotions, too. Unworthiness immediately spoiled my hopeful desires with the usual comment, "You are too old to put on a wedding dress much less have a wedding portrait made!" But following Cheryl's persistent nudge, I decided to pray for God's direction and ask my daughter her opinion. When I prayed, I felt peace and freedom to talk to her about it. I knew Andrea would be honest, especially since she forbids me to wear anything with an elastic waist or made with polyester. But to my amazement, she thought it was a wonderful idea and walked with me through the entire process, especially helping me keep it a secret from her dad. Ken and I had the most wonderful time celebrating our thirtieth wedding anniversary. He loved the wedding portrait and requested a full-length portrait be placed on our bedroom wall. I will never forget putting the dress on for the first time. I felt so self-conscious and unworthy, but on the day the pictures were taken, that changed. I felt beautiful and confident. Each time I look at the portrait, I am reminded that a day is coming when I will be dressed far more radiantly than I was in my pearls and satin.

The reason I decided to share this with you is not to elevate any beauty of my flesh but to elevate the beauty of God's faithfulness. Before a single picture was taken, I had a lengthy conversation with my Lord who gave me the blessing of peace. After all the pictures were taken, I knew it was time for me to walk down the aisle. I chose to embrace the moment with everything in me. I would make sure this memory would have special effects that would set this day apart forever. As I walked down the center aisle of Frost Chapel, I placed my arm through the invisible arm of my heavenly Bridegroom. Every step was slow and intentional as I envisioned Him in my mind. I told Him how much I loved Him and how grateful I was that He gave me the peace and courage to follow through with my restoration. When we reached the altar, I knelt and recited my personal vows to Him. I confidently verbalized my assurance in His everlasting love for me. I promised to love Him all the days of my life. I left different than I came. I left fully His.

This experience was huge for me. I have no doubt that Jesus wants our places of restoration to include tangible experiences and emotions. I also know that it is okay if we capture some of them in a picture. If you have had an event similar to mine, don't allow anything to keep you from making a beautiful, visible memory of it.

- Is there an area in your life you once thought was hopeless that now you believe God can restore? If so, what is it?

Let these words soak deep within your heart. He loves you so much!

"Jesus called Himself the Bridegroom (Mark 2:19) and likened the coming of His kingdom to a wedding feast (Rev. 19:6–10)."[98]

Day 2: The Proof of His Presence

The presence of Jesus is always powerfully effective. We saw how His presence changed a funeral into a celebration and a weather-beaten boat into a place of worship. His words moved the dead son to speak and the crying disciples to courage. He is the Prince of Peace, and where He is, there will be peace.

- Read Psalm 16:11. What was made known to the psalmist?

_____

Describe the effects of being in His presence.

_____

_____

In Matthew 7:14, Jesus describes the path of life as "the small gate and narrow road that leads to life, and only a few find it." Matthew Henry describes this _life_ only a few find as "comfort in the favour of God, which is the life of the soul; eternal bliss, the hope of which at the end of our way, should make all the difficulties of the road easier for us."[99]

The Christian life is full of daily temptations, tribulations, and exposure to corruption and danger. Therefore, we must continually deal with life and follow a course of self-denial. The following comments on the "small gate and narrow road" illustrate the believer's revolving journey in sanctification.

> In other words, the whole course is as difficult as the first step; and (so it comes to pass that) few there be that find it. Its first step involves a revolution in all our purposes and plans for life, and a surrender of all that is dear to natural inclination, while all that follows is but a repetition of the first great act of self-sacrifice.[100]

This repetitive work in my life has been enormous. You can be sure that what He says, He does. He has continued to work the meaning of this verse out in my life over and over again, each time bringing me to relinquish my will for His. I have realized why the repetition of the first step is important. Just about the time I have convinced myself I am fully surrendered, the Holy Spirit reveals an area of deceit in my heart and takes me back to step one. It is there that I must allow Him to do His job of sanctifying my will for His will. Without Him, I am prone to choose a new gate of flesh and run down the path of my will. I am so thankful for His mercy and love that brings me back to the small gate and places my feet back on the path of life.

One of the most important lessons I've learned is that the voice of our flesh shouts, "I want my way!" Loud shouting gets and holds our attention! We cannot allow this distraction to keep us from following the call of our Lord. We must tune it out and listen with our spirit for the small, still voice that whispers, "Come follow me."

- Is there an area in your life shouting, "I want my way"? If so, what is it?

_____

- Have you followed the demanding shouts? If so, what was the outcome?

_____

Demanding shouts of my flesh got my attention.

I had just spent a sweet season of refreshing from the Holy Spirit. I had heard Him softly speak a new direction for me, and I had quickly obeyed. Shortly afterward, I was made aware of a new community Bible study being started for ladies who were not connected or involved in a local church. Denomination was not an issue, and child care would be provided. This endeavor had the potential to minister to a great number of women across several counties. This information came from a dear friend, who had attended an initial planning meeting for those interested in being prayer warriors. She was very excited and thought I might want to attend the study with her. I dismissed the thought of attending, especially since I had just begun leading a new Bible study in my subdivision. A couple of weeks later, my friend called me with more exciting information about the new endeavor. Immediately, I began to embrace the idea of just attending and not having to do anything but listen and allow the Spirit to feed *me* for a change. This focus brought the purchase of a ticket. The night before I was to attend the kickoff dinner, I met with the small Bible study group. They wanted to study the book of John verse by verse, and I wondered how the Spirit would lead me in this type of study. In preparation, I experienced His leadership and equipping like never before. He prompted me to prepare a handout for the ladies to note their answers and gave me insight I had never seen before. When we met, the Word Himself taught us, and we knew it! His presence was so obvious.

The next night, I attended the kickoff dinner. There was tremendous excitement and great participation. I enjoyed it, but on the way home, I knew I was not supposed to be a part of it. Nothing was wrong with the community study, but He had told me to go somewhere else. My flesh had said in a loud, yet deceitful way, "I want my way. I want to be with my friend. I want to sit back and receive for a change."

As I drove home, I asked, "Lord, what was this all about?"

I strongly sensed Him say, "This has been for you." At that moment, I didn't understand. The next day, I shared my experience and thoughts with Ken, who lovingly, but firmly, told me I didn't need to attend the community study to be fed. He reminded me that the Spirit would feed me much more as I yielded to be used to feed others. Yes, this had been for me. I immediately surrendered my natural inclinations and set my focus on the new gate to which He had called me. I continue to lead the Bible study in my subdivision just as He had called me to do. Every Monday night with those five ladies is refreshing. We all leave the study with hearts full of joy and eager to come together again to be fed by the Word Himself.

God always has our best interest in mind. He delights to bless us!

Day 3: The Seat of His Delight

On this day, we became acquainted with Mary of Bethany. Her consuming desire to be discipled by Jesus continues to inspire women today. I am so grateful for the women who helped me learn how to sit at the feet of Jesus. What have I learned about that position? It is a place like no other. It has been a seat of provision for my deepest needs. It has been a seat of mercy for my vilest sins. It has been a seat of opportunity to minister to others. It is a seat of blessings, because I am His child. If you want to learn more about Mary of Bethany, I highly recommend two wonderful books by Joanne Weaver, *Having a Mary Heart in a Martha World* and *Having a Mary Spirit*.

Mary began her spiritual journey with Jesus confidently sitting in the *seat of discipleship*. We can be sure that she had no idea of the magnitude of sorrow soon to hit her heart and home. She was probably the happiest she had ever been in her life. I can see her now, gazing into His majestic eyes as He fed her spiritual food that would sustain her then and in the crucial days soon to come.

A steady diet of spiritual food can make the difference.

One of the blessings I listed was the birth of my sixth grandchild, Jared. His delivery came about prematurely because of complications his mother experienced in her eighth month of pregnancy.

An emergency C-section was necessary to save both their lives. Immediately following the delivery, new complications began to take a toll on Staci, my daughter-in-law. The doctors were doing all they could, but things continued to spiral out of control. I began to experience the same panic and fear I had felt in the situation with Andrea and Caroline. I quickly left the ICU waiting room in search of a place to calm myself down. I felt like I was going to scream and faint at the same time. I practically ran to the other end of the hospital and into the ladies' restroom. I was relieved to be alone. I fell down and prayed, begging God to stop this awful situation. I thought I was calm enough to go get a cup of coffee, but as soon as I got to the coffee shop in the hospital lobby, I started to cry. A lady there immediately sensed my need and began to pray out loud and with great passion for God to intervene. As I began to walk back to the intensive care unit, I ran into a member of my church who worked there, and she immediately began to pray for God to intervene. I felt the calming presence of the Holy Spirit fall over me like a gossamer veil.

When I got back to the ICU waiting room, the phone rang. It was my pastor. I told him the situation, and he prayed the same way the others had. A sense of strength began to fill my being. A few minutes later, Ken called to tell me he had just landed at the airport and would be on his way to the hospital soon. I went out into the hall, and there stood my son, David, crying on the shoulder of his best friend. Immediately, I felt strength like never before. I took him with me to see Staci and get an update from the doctor. The news was not good. They told us a complete hysterectomy would have to be done in order to save her life. A stronger power in me gently, yet confidently, took David aside and told him we had to pray like never before. We walked back to the ICU waiting area, and David's pastor and a group of friends from his church were waiting there. We had a prayer meeting that permeated the entire ICU waiting area. He heard, answered, and blessed. The surgery was successful, and within days, Staci was strong enough to go home. Little Jared remained in the NICU for a couple of weeks and was released to go home strong and healthy.

Three years earlier, I had not handled the situation with Andrea and Caroline the way I did this one. I had run to God immediately, but I had also gotten mad and lashed out at the devil. I sought comfort from *people* before going to God. What was different this time? When I felt panic and fear, I immediately ran to God, and then *He* brought people to strengthen me past the emotions and shock. As I allowed them to minister to me, I became stronger, and the Word in me increased and sustained my strength. I was capable of ministering strength to my son and daughter-in-law. For three years, I had consumed His Word, and it made a difference this time.

Fill in the blanks in Psalm 1:2–3.

- "But his _____ is in the _____ of the Lord, and on His law he _____ day and night. He is like a tree planted by streams of water, which _____ _____ fruit in season and whose leaf does not _____. Whatever he does _____."

The word *prospers* in this verse means to come to maturity. The work of the Holy Spirit is to mature us spiritually so that we will be a blessing to others, especially those who are withered in their hearts from sorrow. Maturity begins in the *seat of discipleship*. As we mature spiritually, we move to the *seat of opportunity*. This is the place God uses us to bless others. As we bless others, God delights to place us in the *seat of blessings*. This is the desire of His heart.

- What has God taught you in the "seat of discipleship"?

  _____

- Where has God placed you in the "seat of opportunity"?

  _____

- How has God blessed you in the "seat of blessings"?

  _____

Write Psalm 37:3–4 in the form of a prayer.

_____

_____

_____

Day 4: Wounded for a Purpose

Lazarus was wounded for a purpose. Jesus said, "This sickness will not end in death. No it is for God's glory so that God's Son may be glorified through it" (John 11:4). As we looked at the amazing resurrection of Lazarus, we saw the power of Jesus' spoken words. The sickness brought death, but it did not end there. Just as Jesus said, the sickness ended in life. When Jesus, the Word made flesh, spoke, power accompanied and completed God's purpose. The resurrection of Lazarus validated Jesus as the Son of God.

Mary was different after the resurrection. She had a new surge of faith and devotion to her Lord. She was strong and confident in the actions of her heart. She gave Him all she had and did all she could to honor Him. Why? Because of what He would soon do for her!

Jesus was wounded with every sickness. Like Lazarus, He died and was buried, and after three days, the Holy Spirit's resurrection power raised Him to life and completed God's purpose—redemption and healing for His children.

> Surely He has borne our griefs and carried our sorrows; yet we esteemed Him stricken, smitten by God, and afflicted. But He was wounded for our transgressions, He was bruised for our iniquities; the chastisement for our peace was upon Him, and by his stripes we are healed. All we like sheep have gone astray; we have turned, every one, to his own way; and the Lord has laid on Him the iniquity of us all. (Isaiah 53:4–6, NKJV)

The word _delight_ means to _please greatly_. You please Him greatly! He did all that He could do for you. He gave you Himself. Have you done all you can do for Him? Have you given Him all of yourself? Spend some time thinking about these questions. Close by writing a short prayer expressing your _delight in Him._

_____

_____

_____

We have this promise from Jesus: "And I will ask the Father, and He will give you another Comforter (Counselor, Helper, Intercessor, Advocate, Strengthener, and Standby) that He may remain with you forever—The Spirit of Truth" (John 14:16–17a, Amplified Bible).

What a gift to us because He delights in us! We can be assured that the Spirit of Truth will use our wounds to complete God's purpose in our life.

I love the account in Luke 24:36–51 of Jesus appearing to the disciples before He ascends up into heaven. We are told in verse 45 that He opened their minds so they could understand the Scriptures.

His last words are our hope: "I am going to send you what my Father has promised; but stay in the city until you have been clothed with power from on high."

As we come to the end of this journey together, I want to leave you with this challenge: Give the Holy Spirit complete control of your life, so that His power will be exposed in your spiritual journey. Allow your heart to burn with passion for the things of God. Pour your energy into a new spiritual legacy for those coming behind you. Seek to leave His mark, one life at a time.

The day is coming, my sister, when we will see His face, the nod of His approval, and His smile of delight as we come before Him as His bride.

> *~ "And we will live happily ever after." … What a thought for us to know will truly become a reality! ~*

Father,

Thank you for the many blessings you bestow on our life. Thank you for the sorrows that become blessings in our life. It is so encouraging to know that what you did for those in your Word, you will do for us. We are strengthened as we see you as our Immanuel, "God with Us," in all our circumstances. To know that you delight in us brings us joy and confidence as we walk in fellowship with you. We are so grateful for the freedom to sit at your feet and become your disciples in our generation. Thank you for the hope and courage you supply as we yield to your call in ministry. It is wonderful to know that we can follow your spiritual footsteps. There is no greater honor than to be called the Bride of Christ. We choose to walk in obedience to your Word that says, "Since we live by the Spirit, let us keep in step with the Spirit" (Galatians 5:26). May Deity ordain every step we take for the rest of our days.

I pray this in the name above all names, Jesus Christ, the Son of God.

Afterword

As we take our next step with God …

I just got up from praying facedown in my office, the place my Lord and I met on a regular basis as I wrote *The Next Step*. Today is different. The purpose is to share what God did in my life after I walked through it with the women who diligently prayed for me during my season of study and writing. There were many times when I wanted to quit, but the Lord's strong grasp kept me on task. The greatest thing I experienced during the process was the provision of God. He proved over and over again that He knows me better than I know myself as He revealed things I had forgotten or didn't understand until this season. He never stopped providing and guiding me as we crossed the finish line of His call to this endeavor, and today, He is still guiding and providing for me.

As I wrote the last word and placed the last period of session 6, I immediately began to experience the stirring of mixed emotions. I leaned back in my chair and stared at my closing words as the emotions began to surface. Physically, I was tired; emotionally, I was producing tears faster than I could soak them up in a handful of tissues. Spiritually, I was stronger than I had ever been. I spontaneously began to express gratitude and acknowledge that my Lord had accomplished something through me far beyond my natural abilities. It was finished, and I knew without a doubt He had ordained it on the calendar of my life. I shut off my computer and fell into bed praising Him until sleep silenced me. The next morning, as I sat in bed sipping coffee, I could not withhold the tears of gratitude to my Lord, especially after so many years of personal failures.

Within a couple of days, I began to experience melancholy feelings similar to having to leave someone dear and return home. It reminded me of visits with my sister who lives in another state. As soon as we see each other, sweet fellowship begins with hugging and immediate conversation, the "catching up" kind, with both of us talking as fast as we can. Over the course of my visit, we move from laughing to crying, reminiscing about days gone by, discussing the ups and downs in the lives of our children and grandchildren, and sharing what God is doing in our church and our lives. As the visit comes to an end, we talk about the "next time" and share a sister hug. I always leave with melancholy feelings that last far too long.

I realized that the days and hours spent with my Lord had been quite similar to my times with my sweet sister. Each time was the intimate beginning of a new session with my Shepherd. The writing of my testimony was always difficult, causing me to talk to Him constantly. As I moved to each session with a new text and new characters, He talked the most as I listened and wrote. There were times in every session that I laughed and cried, and I even saw that the ups and downs in the lives of the characters were also common in my life. He showed me over and over again that He was not a God of partiality and that He had always worked in my life for a purpose. I realized that as I had journeyed through my own testimony, the Scriptures, and the stories of the characters, He had revealed the wonder of His person. And I had become more intimately acquainted with Him than ever before (Philippians 3:10). This was His purpose for me. I was melancholy because I missed Him.

Today brings closure to an adventure with the Most High God, who led me step by step through the lives of twelve real people, just like you and me. I am delighted to share my afterthoughts from each session with you.

Session 1: Encounter—Zechariah and Mary

I saw my own times of gripping fear and overwhelming unbelief in the life of Zechariah. Some of you may be like me—in the autumn season of your life—realizing you have spent too many years controlled by fear and unbelief. Maybe you are a younger woman who has recognized these emotions as a hindrance to your walk with Jesus.

Is there a next step we can take to move beyond these controlling emotions? I found my answer in the actions of Mary. I can walk in the footsteps of Mary. I can step out of my fears and doubts and into the amazing things God has planned for me. All He requires is my sincere "yes" of obedience and a heart of gratitude. I pray that you will do the same. Let's walk in the ways of Mary and leave our own footprints for those coming behind us.

Session 2: Wandering—Moses and Hagar

I saw my own season of wandering as I imagined the emotions of Moses and Hagar as they ran from unbearable circumstances. Both stopped at a place of refreshing and redirection for their lives. Moses would become a family man and Hagar a mother. Maybe you have been like me and run away from many places only to end up exhausted and in need of a safe place and someone to set your feet on the right path.

Do you wonder what makes you wander? I've realized that sometimes uncontrollable circumstances upset me, and I quickly wander off to keep from having to work things out or deal with it. Other times, I am upset because I can't have my way. What did I learn from Moses and Hagar that I can apply in my present season of life? The Lord never tires of refreshing and refocusing those who submit to Him in sincere humility. Join me in putting an end to the destructive seasons of wandering. Let's take off our boots of bondage and put on the sandals of submission. By the way, these sandals have a lifetime guarantee!

Session 3: Preparation—Joseph and Abigail

When do we realize that God has begun to prepare us to become who He created us to be? Even though my path differed from Joseph's and Abigail's, I experienced similar injustices that imprisoned me emotionally. I could relate, so that made it easy for me to imagine their thoughts and emotions. As I saw the invisible hand of God move in their lives, I began to recall personal times of hardship that I could now clearly see were ordained by God. I realized it was from those dark and sad places that God had begun my own preparation. He was working to fulfill His purpose for my life. It's a wonderful feeling, and it fans our faith to see proof of God working in our lives.

Whether I was forced or chose of my own accord, every place I found myself was used for my preparation. I was delighted to see the blessings of God on Joseph and Abigail. I imagined them bowing in gratitude as God positioned them in a place of great honor. It occurred to me that I too had been ordained and given a position of honor by God. We are of royal descent. Let's start today practicing the art of graceful bowing. Are you wondering why I want us to practice bowing? We will be wearing our crowns, and we wouldn't want them to fall off, would we?

Session 4: Testing—Job and Esther

When I thought about God's testing, I visualized a thermometer marked with spiritual growth. I am so glad He doesn't keep a report card on the progress of my sanctification! A closer look into the lives of Job and Esther reminded me of my own pain and fear that can overtake me without notice. Their actions validated a truth I have been studying recently in my quiet times. Pain and fear will put me in my own sackcloth and put ashes on my face before God more quickly than anything. I have come to realize that the pain and fear are used to point me to a stronghold of sin.

What do we do when we know the truth? To know and not obey is not good. To know and obey is good. Therefore, "intense obedience" can be the spiritual spade that reaches to the bottom of a stronghold and uproots it. Daily application of "obedience" becomes the balm that heals and even removes most of the scarring. It is so important to me that I apply "obedience" at the same time I apply my morning and night moisturizers. I challenge you to join me in living a lifestyle of proactive obedience to the Word of God. Your satisfaction is guaranteed and at no cost to you.

Session 5: Breaking—Jacob and Hannah

Just about the time you think you have God's testing figured out, He breaks your will. We say the words, "Yes, thy will be done, Father," with great passion and superficial expressions of humility, when in reality, we really mean, "Father, I want my will to be done." Our own words wound us until we are broken and desperate to have the Word heal us. Jacob and Hannah were two people desperate for a blessing from God. They tried it their way until they realized unless God chose to bless them, they would be without the blessing they so desperately wanted.

Jacob and Hannah gave me a fresh look at approaching God. Sometimes, we need to wrestle out the desperation in us even if we walk away with a limp. We must get some things settled. God blessed Jacob's persistence. I want to be persistent like Jacob. I want to discuss my desires with God as Hannah did, even if I must give up that which I could only keep for a season. How do we move into this place with God? We must take hold of the one who has taken hold of us. When He places something in us that must be birthed, we must realize we cannot make it happen; only He can. I am ready for Him to do whatever He wants with my life. Let's put our hospital gowns on and get ready to deliver.

Session 6: Blessings—Jesus and Mary of Bethany

As I looked back over my journey through session 6, several phrases resonated in my soul and caused me to embrace them in a fresh and forever way. Embrace them again with me. Let them move you into the arms of Truth.

- Some of the greatest blessings of my life have come out of sorrow.
- Life's blessings are not a measure of who we are but of who God is.
- The wounds of God are for a purpose and declarations of hope.

- It is time for me to move beyond where I have been.

- Lord, keep me from seeking leadership over Lordship.

- Incarnate Compassion spoke, "I say to you arise," and it was so.

- The "that" of God marked my life beyond my understanding, but the Holy Spirit revealed the meaning and healed me with it.

- His call comes with desire to respond.

- His commands come with the power to obey!

- It is time for us to get up close and personal with Jesus.

- We will leave this earth different than we came.

- We must participate with Jesus.

- The Holy Spirit wants to prosper us and mature us to handle life.

- He has a seat of opportunity for us to bless others.

- We will live happily ever after!

The next step you take with Jesus can make a huge difference in your life. I pray you will continue to walk with Him into the places He has ordained for you. My desire is that the Holy Spirit has exposed the mighty hand of God at work in your own spiritual journey. May your journey continue to take you to new heights of trust and joy as you delight in the presence of *Elohim, your Creator.*

The Lord has shown me my next step, and I am delighted to share it with you. A couple of weeks after finishing the study, Ken and I took a short trip to visit my sister. While walking on the beach, I began to talk with the Lord about all sorts of things and finally sensed a great need to ask Him a very serious and personal question. Following is the simple yet profound dialogue between my Lord and me:

> Nancy: "Lord, what is my next step with you? You know I want to finish well."
>
> Holy Spirit: "The Finishing Well."
>
> Nancy: "Lord, did you say 'the finishing well' with the word *well* as a noun? Is this the title of … do you mean another study?"
>
> Holy Spirit: "The Finishing Well."
>
> Nancy: "Yes, Lord."

My friend, I am delighted to have been a part of your journey, and I will be praying for you in the days ahead. My prayer is that you will live in the mighty power of the Spirit daily and grow in confidence to take the next step He calls you to take. When it is all said and done, as true and faithful servants of our Lord Jesus Christ, we will truly desire to finish well.

I'm taking my next step … See you at the Finishing Well!

Nancy

Notes

Nancy's photograph by Paula Boyer, Paula's Portraits.

Gifts of Salvation

1 *Woman's Study Bible.*

2 Nelson Inc. 1995, 1961.

Session 1

3 Matthew Henry, *Matthew Henry's Concise Commentary on the Whole Bible* (Nashville, TN: Thomas Nelson Inc., 1997), 14.

4 The New International Version of the Holy Bible (Grand Rapids, MI: Zondervan Publishing, 1988), 1161.

5 James Strong, LLD, STD, *The New Strong's Expanded Exhaustive Concordance of the Bible* (Nashville, TN: Thomas Nelson Inc., 2001), 45.

6 ***Ibid.***

7 Ibid.

8 Ibid.

Session 2

9 *Woman's Study Bible* (NKJV)

10 *The New International Version of the Holy Bible (Grand Rapids, MI: Zondervan Publishing, 1988), 62.*

11 *Matthew Henry,* Matthew Henry's Concise Commentary on the Whole Bible *(Nashville, TN: Thomas Nelson Inc., 1997), 76–77.*

12 Ibid, 77.

13 Ibid, 76.

14 Dorothy Kelly Patterson, et al., eds., *The Woman's Study Bible, NKJV* (Nashville, TN: Thomas Nelson Inc., 1995), 93.

15 Henry, 30.

16 Ibid.

17 James Strong, LLD, STD, *The New Strong's Expanded Exhaustive Concordance of the Bible* (Nashville, TN: Thomas Nelson Inc., 2001), 357.

18 Henry, 31.

19 Strong, 3045.

20 Ibid, 4263.

21 Henry, 30.

22 Ibid, 31.

Session 3

23 *Dorothy Kelly Patterson, et al., eds.,* The Woman's Study Bible, NKJV *(Nashville, TN: Thomas Nelson Inc., 1995), 1966.*

24 James Strong, LLD, STD, *The New Strong's Expanded Exhaustive Concordance of the Bible* (Nashville, TN: Thomas Nelson Inc., 2001), 268.

25 Oswald Chambers, *Daily Thoughts for Disciples* (Grand Rapids, MI: Zondervan, 1976), August 15.

26 Patterson, 1461.

27 J. H. Sammis and D. B. Towner, "Trust and Obey," Church Hymnal (Cleveland, TN: Tennessee Music and Printing Co., 1951), 157.

28 Strong, 286.

29 Patterson, 1118.

30 Margery S. Berube, et al., eds., *The American Heritage Dictionary* (New York, NY: Dell Publishing Co. Inc., 1983), 783.

31 Strong, 84.

32 Joseph L. Gardner, et al., eds., *Who's Who in the Bible* (Pleasantville, NY: Reader's Digest Association Inc., 1994), 245.

33 Matthew Henry, *Matthew Henry's Concise Commentary on the Whole Bible* (Nashville, TN: Thomas Nelson Inc., 1997), 62–63.

34 Strong, 248.

35 Henry, 285.

36 Strong, 74.

37 F. B. Meyer, *Notes from the Amplified Bible* (Grand Rapids, MI: Zondervan, 1987), 350.

38 Berube, 541.

39 Patterson, 1119.

40 Berube, 473.

Session 4

41 Margery S. Berube, et al., eds., *The American Heritage Dictionary* (New York, NY: Dell Publishing Co. Inc., 1983), 437.

42 J. H. Sammis and D. B. Towner, "Trust and Obey," Church Hymnal (Cleveland, TN: Tennessee Music and Printing Co., 1951), 157.

43 Matthew Henry, *Matthew Henry's Concise Commentary on the Whole Bible* (Nashville, TN: Thomas Nelson Inc., 1997), 415.

44 Berube, 554.

45 James Strong, LLD, STD, *The New Strong's Expanded Exhaustive Concordance of the Bible* (Nashville, TN: Thomas Nelson Inc., 2001), 486.

46 Joseph L. Gardner, et al., eds., *Who's Who in the Bible* (Pleasantville, NY: Reader's Digest Association Inc., 1994), 229.

47 Dorothy Kelly Patterson, et al., eds., *The Woman's Study Bible, NKJV* (Nashville, TN: Thomas Nelson Inc., 1995), 1051.

48 Henry, 451.

49 Patterson, 855.

50 Strong, 248.

51 Patterson, 2069.

52 Berube, 705.

53 Henry, 409.

54 Patterson, 788.

55 Strong, 423.

56 Patterson, 1931.

57 Berube, 568.

58 Ibid., 594.

59 Patterson, 855.

Session 5

60 Margery S. Berube, et al., eds., *The American Heritage Dictionary* (New York, NY: Dell Publishing Co. Inc., 1983), 673.

61 James Strong, LLD, STD, *The New Strong's Expanded Exhaustive Concordance of the Bible* (Nashville, TN: Thomas Nelson Inc., 2001), 280.

62 Oswald Chambers, *My Utmost for His Highest* (Uhrichsville, OH: Barbour and Company, Inc., 1963), 280.

63 Matthew Henry, *Matthew Henry's Concise Commentary on the Whole Bible* (Nashville, TN: Thomas Nelson Inc., 1997), 43.

64 Ibid.

65 Ibid.

66 *Wikipedia*, s.v. "Scar," accessed August 2008 http://en.wikipedia.org/wiki/Scar.

67 Herbert Lockyer, *All the Women of the Bible* (Grand Rapids, MI: Zondervan Publishing House, 1958), 129.

68 Ibid.

69 Ibid., 130.

70 Henry, 51.

71 Ibid., 52.

72 John A. Pope, Jr., et al., eds., *Who's Who in the Bible* (Pleasantville, NY: The Reader's Digest Association, Inc., 1994), 178.

73 Jamieson, Fausset & Brown, *Jamieson, Fausset & Brown Commentary* (Grand Rapids, MI: Zondervan Publishing House, 1961), 205.

74 Lockyer, 65.

75 Jamieson, Fausset & Brown, 206.

76 Ibid.

77 Henry, 265.

78 Strong, 287.

79 F. B. Meyer, *Through the Bible Day by Day* (Grand Rapids, MI: Zondervan Publishing House, 1941), 123.

80 Herbert Lockyer, *All the Men of the Bible* (Grand Rapids, MI: Zondervan Publishing House, 1958), 167.

Session 6

81 Margery S. Berube, et al., eds., *The American Heritage Dictionary* (New York, NY: Dell Publishing Co. Inc., 1983), 74.

82 Ibid., 652.

83 Dorothy Kelley Patterson, et al., eds., *The Woman's Study Bible, NKJV* (Nashville, TN: Thomas Nelson Inc., 1995), 2132.

84 Ibid., 28.

85 Berube, 415.

86 James Strong, LLD, STD, *The New Strong's Expanded Exhaustive Concordance of the Bible* (Nashville, TN: Thomas Nelson Inc., 2001), 71.

87 Herbert Lockyer, *All the Women of the Bible* (Grand Rapids, MI: Zondervan Publishing House, 1958), 99–101.

88 Patterson, 1797.

89 Lockyer, 100–102.

90 Patterson, 1704.

91 Henry, 950.

92 Berube, 703.

93 Strong, 125.

94 Patterson, 1777.

95 Lockyer, 105.

96 Strong, 117.

97 Patterson, 1461.

98 Ibid., 2130.

99 Henry, 870.

100 Jamieson, 911.